What do you think will happen when you die?

AYN RAND ANSWERS . . .

I assume I'll be buried. I don't believe in mysticism or life after death. This doesn't mean I believe man's mind is necessarily materialistic; but neither is it mystical. We know that we have a mind and a body, and that neither can exist without the other. Therefore, when I die, that will be the end of me.

I don't think it will be the end of my philosophy.

AYN RAND
ANSWERS

The Best of Her Q & A

EDITED BY ROBERT MAYHEW

 NEW AMERICAN LIBRARY

NEW AMERICAN LIBRARY
Published by New American Library, a division of
Penguin Group (USA) Inc., 375 Hudson Street,
New York, New York 10014, USA
Penguin Group (Canada), 90 Eglinton Avenue East, Suite 700, Toronto,
Ontario M4P 2Y3, Canada (a division of Pearson Penguin Canada Inc.)
Penguin Books Ltd., 80 Strand, London WC2R 0RL, England
Penguin Ireland, 25 St. Stephen's Green, Dublin 2,
Ireland (a division of Penguin Books Ltd.)
Penguin Group (Australia), 250 Camberwell Road, Camberwell, Victoria 3124,
Australia (a division of Pearson Australia Group Pty. Ltd.)
Penguin Books India Pvt. Ltd., 11 Community Centre, Panchsheel Park,
New Delhi - 110 017, India
Penguin Group (NZ), cnr Airborne and Rosedale Roads, Albany,
Auckland 1310, New Zealand (a division of Pearson New Zealand Ltd.)
Penguin Books (South Africa) (Pty.) Ltd., 24 Sturdee Avenue,
Rosebank, Johannesburg 2196, South Africa

Penguin Books Ltd., Registered Offices:
80 Strand, London WC2R 0RL, England

First published by New American Library,
a division of Penguin Group (USA) Inc.

First Printing, November 2005
10 9 8 7 6 5 4 3 2 1

NEW AMERICAN LIBRARY and logo are trademarks of Penguin Group (USA) Inc.

LIBRARY OF CONGRESS CATALOGING-IN-PUBLICATION DATA:

Rand, Ayn.
    Ayn Rand answers/edited by Robert Mayhew.
        p. cm.
    Includes index.
    ISBN 0-451-21665-2
1. Philosophy—Miscellanea.   I. Mayhew, Robert.   II. Title.
    B68.R36 2005
    191—dc22   2005010438

Set in New Baskerville

Printed in the United States of America

ACKNOWLEDGMENTS

I wish to thank Leonard Peikoff for encouraging me to undertake this project. Although Dr. Peikoff did not check the transcription of the Q&A and has not read through the manuscript, he did answer a constant stream of queries related to issues both editorial and philosophical. Many thanks are also due Tara Smith and Tore Boeckmann, for their excellent comments on a draft of the entire manuscript.

Finally, and for all the usual reasons, many thanks to Estelle, my sine qua non.

CONTENTS

INTRODUCTION

After the publication of *Atlas Shrugged* in 1957, Ayn Rand turned to nonfiction writing and (to a lesser extent) lecturing. Her aim in giving lectures was to make her philosophy, Objectivism, more widely known, and to apply it to current cultural and political issues.

Most of her lectures were followed by question-and-answer periods, many of which were taped. This volume is a collection of the best of that material.

Ayn Rand was always a firsthand thinker. She did not take with her into a lecture hall a set of pat, standard answers to questions—for example, about the immorality of altruism or her opposition to Ronald Reagan. Her answers always grew not only out of her general philosophy but also out of the context, which included the topic of her lecture, the nature of her audience, the attitude of the questioner, and even the era in which she was speaking (for example, the early sixties or late seventies). So, different answers to roughly the same questions about altruism or Ronald Reagan might take different, complementary approaches, which together provide us with a richer understanding of her outlook. (I have not described the full context for each Q&A, but I have added in brackets at the end of every answer the year and nature of the question-and-answer period from which it was taken.)

Many, though certainly not all, of these Q&A present Ayn Rand's views on issues that she does not discuss elsewhere. Roughly half deal with political philosophy and contemporary politics; the rest deal with ethics, epistemology, metaphysics, and esthetics. The topics, as a result, are enormously wide-ranging: humor, Ernest Hemingway, modern art, Jane Fonda, the war in Vietnam, Libertarians, religious conservatives, Hollywood communists, Dagny Taggart, the correspondence theory of truth, atheism, *Don Quixote,* Terence Rattigan, abortion, gun control, love and sex, drugs, Ronald Reagan, and much more. These Q&A, in short, offer anyone interested in Ayn Rand's work something eloquent, insightful, and new.

Given the extemporaneous nature of the material, it is not surprising that the transcripts required editing—as Ayn Rand herself suggested they would. At one point during her 1969 nonfiction-writing course, she said that she was a writer, not a speaker, and that she did not speak well extemporaneously. Someone replied that she should listen to her answers to questions. She responded:

> That depends on whether the question is interesting. If it's a proper question, so that I know the context from which it's asked and I know it's worth answering, that is very inspiring. Sometimes, I may give an answer that's *almost* publishable— but not quite. It might be good for a first draft, but it would still need editing.

Most of the editing I did consisted of cutting and line-editing to bring the material closer to the level of conciseness, clarity, and smoothness appropriate to a written work. Very little had to be cut owing to repetition. I should mention, however, that some (but not much) of my editing aimed to clarify wording that, if left unaltered, might be taken to imply a viewpoint that she explicitly rejected in her written works. (The original transcripts of all of this material are held in the Ayn Rand Archives, and are available to serious scholars.)

I believe I have done a good job in editing this material. Nevertheless, no one can guarantee that Ayn Rand would have approved of editing she herself did not see. For this reason, however fascinating and useful, these Q&A should not be considered part of Objectivism.

ABBREVIATIONS

APM 62: Radio program, *Ayn Rand on Campus*, discussion of her lecture "America's Persecuted Minority: Big Business" (1962).

APM 63: Lecture, "America's Persecuted Minority: Big Business" (Chicago, 1963).

CBS 62: TV program, *The Great Challenge* (CBS, March 1962).

FF 61: Lecture, "Faith and Force: Destroyers of the Modern World" (Purdue Young Republicans, April 1961).

FHF 66: Lecture, "Our Cultural Value-Deprivation" (Boston, Ford Hall Forum, 1966).

FHF 67: Lecture, "The Wreckage of the Consensus" (Boston, Ford Hall Forum, 1967).

FHF 68: Lecture, "Of Living Death" (Boston, Ford Hall Forum, 1968).

FHF 69: Lecture, "Apollo and Dionysus" (Boston, Ford Hall Forum, 1969).

FHF 70: Lecture, "The Anti-Industrial Revolution" (Boston, Ford Hall Forum, 1970).

FHF 71: Lecture, "The Moratorium on Brains" (Boston, Ford Hall Forum, 1971).

FHF 72: Lecture, "A Nation's Unity" (Boston, Ford Hall Forum, 1972).

FHF 73: Lecture, "Censorship: Local and Express" (Boston, Ford Hall Forum, 1973).

FHF 74: Lecture, "Egalitarianism and Inflation" (Boston, Ford Hall Forum, 1974).

FHF 76: Lecture, "The Moral Factor" (Boston, Ford Hall Forum, 1976).

FHF 77: Lecture, "Global Balkanization" (Boston, Ford Hall Forum, 1977).

FHF 78: Lecture, "Cultural Update" (Boston, Ford Hall Forum, 1978).

FHF 81: Lecture, "The Age of Mediocrity" (Boston, Ford Hall Forum, 1981).

FW 58: Outtakes from Ayn Rand's 1958 fiction-writing course (which were edited and published as *The Art of Fiction*).

IBA 62: Radio program, *Ayn Rand on Campus*, discussion of her lecture "The Intellectual Bankruptcy of Our Age" (1962).

NC 69: Radio program, "Night Call" (March 1969).

NFW 69: Outtakes from Ayn Rand's 1969 nonfiction-writing course (which were edited and published as *The Art of Nonfiction*).

OC 80: Leonard Peikoff, "Objective Communication," Lecture 1 (1980).

OE 62: Radio program, *Ayn Rand on Campus*, discussion of her essay "The Objectivist Ethics" (1962).

PO5 76: Leonard Peikoff, "Philosophy of Objectivism," Lecture 5 (1976).

PO6 76: Leonard Peikoff, "Philosophy of Objectivism," Lecture 6 (1976).

PO7 76: Leonard Peikoff, "Philosophy of Objectivism," Lecture 7 (1976).

PO8 76: Leonard Peikoff, "Philosophy of Objectivism," Lecture 8 (1976).

PO9 76: Leonard Peikoff, "Philosophy of Objectivism," Lecture 9 (1976).

PO10 76: Leonard Peikoff, "Philosophy of Objectivism," Lecture 10 (1976).

PO11 76: Leonard Peikoff, "Philosophy of Objectivism," Lecture 11 (1976).

PO12 76: Leonard Peikoff, "Philosophy of Objectivism," Lecture 12 (1976).

PVA 61: Lecture, "Political Vacuum of Our Age," presented to a group of women in journalism (Indiana, 1961).

PWNI 74: Lecture, "Philosophy: Who Needs It" (West Point Military Academy, 1974).

CHAPTER ONE

Politics and Economics

The Declaration of Independence

Which of the Founding Fathers do you most admire, and why?

If I had to choose one, I would say Thomas Jefferson—for the Declaration of Independence, which is probably the greatest document in human history, both philosophically and literarily. [FHF 76]

We started with the Declaration of Independence; today we're falling apart. Would you add to, or subtract from, the Declaration of Independence?

It doesn't follow that if someone writes the greatest political document ever, thereafter people will automatically have a good society. You say the nation's falling apart, therefore the Declaration of Independence failed. No, it hasn't failed. Observe how much this nation achieved so long as it stood by the principles of the Declaration. When you see a fundamental departure from it, don't blame the original document.

Some of the Declaration's journalistic allusions are not relevant today, but its principles still are: above all, the concept of individual rights. There is, however, one minor fault on the level of fundamentals: the idea that men are endowed with rights by their Creator rather than by Nature. This is an issue of the choice of language. Philosophically, it doesn't change the Declaration's meaning. [FHF 72]

1

Freedom and Rights

Are individual freedoms in this country eroding?

"Freedom" in a political context means the absence of coercion exercised by the government (which has a legal monopoly on the use of physical force). So "erosion" is too mild for today's trend. We are moving rapidly toward the loss of all freedom. This trend need not continue, however; it can be changed. [CBS 62]

Isn't the government responsible for millions of Americans having the leisure and economic security necessary to indulge in liberty?

To speak of an indulgence in freedom made possible through leisure is to use "freedom" metaphorically. In the political context, "freedom" means the absence of coercion. When government regulates more and more aspects of our lives, and regulates them arbitrarily—when we are departing from objective law and granting more and more arbitrary power to government agencies—how can you speak of freedom? [CBS 62]

We are not living in the seventeenth century, when the world's population was one-tenth of what it is now. Isn't it realistic to expect that the government would grow and do more?

You take it as self-evident that if a society gets more complex, then the government must acquire more functions. But today we are so advanced technologically that we are sending men into space. The more rational a society, the less it can be ruled by brute force. As a society progresses, the more urgent it is that men must be left free. [CBS 62]

This is a chicken-or-the-egg question: Is free enterprise the result of political freedom, or is it the other way around?

The political system and the economic system are corollaries; it's not politics that creates economics, or vice versa. Basic ideas create both. The political system of free enterprise and capitalist economics were one historical development. Both were the result of a philosophy of reason, freedom, and individual rights—the basis on which this country was founded. [CBS 62]

Does the state have a right to interfere with parents who abuse their children?

Yes, in a case of demonstrable physical abuse, like beating or starvation. This is an issue of protecting individual rights. Since children cannot protect themselves from physical abuse, and are dependent upon their parents, the government can interfere to protect a child's rights—just as it can to prevent an adult from beating up, locking up, or starving another adult. Since the child is dependent for his survival on the parent, the government can see to it that the child's life is safe. But this does not extend to intellectual issues. The government has no right to interfere in the upbringing of the child, which is entirely the responsibility and the right of the parent. [APM 62]

How do the rights of children differ from those of adults, particularly given a child's need for parental support?

Both the adult and the child have the right to life, liberty, and the pursuit of happiness. But these rights depend on one's reason and knowledge. An infant can't earn his own sustenance, nor can a child exercise his rights and know what the pursuit of happiness is, nor know what freedom is and how to use it. All human rights depend upon man's nature as a rational being; therefore, a child must wait until he has developed his mind and acquired enough knowledge to be capable of the full independent exercise of his rights. While he's a child, his parents must support him. This is a fact of nature. Proclaiming some kind of children's rights won't make such "rights" real. Rights are a concept based on reality; therefore, a parent doesn't have the right to starve his child, neglect him, injure him physically, or kill him. The government must protect the child, as it would any other citizen. But the child can't claim for himself the rights of an adult, because he is not competent to exercise them. He must depend on his parents. If he doesn't like them, he should leave home as early as he can earn his living by legal means. [FHF 74]

Do severely retarded individuals have rights?

Not actual rights—not the same rights possessed by normal individuals. In effect, they have the right to be protected as perennial children. Like children, retarded people are entitled to protection because, as humans, they may improve and become partly able to stand on their own. The protection of their rights is a courtesy extended to them for being human, even if not properly formed ones. But you could not extend the actual exercise of individual rights to a retarded person, because he's unable to function rationally. Since all rights rest on human nature, a being that cannot exercise his rights cannot have full human rights. [FHF 73]

If we must give up a measure of freedom—the freedom to initiate force—to avoid anarchy, why shouldn't we give up a measure of freedom to enable the government to protect us against pollution?

I never use such formulations as "we must give up a measure of freedom." That's what conservatives say, not me. Observe how imprecision leads to trouble. If we must give up a measure of freedom, we'd end up giving up everything, because excuses can be invented for any "giving up." When I say there should be no personal retaliation, this does not imply that one is giving up some freedom. We don't *have* the freedom to attack another person—to initiate force. We have the right of self-defense; but since another person is involved, and we want to deal with other people and live in a society, we must establish objective rules by which self-defense will be exercised. Establishing a proper form of government has *nothing* to do with surrendering freedom. It involves protecting yourself and everybody else from the irrational use of force.

To give up some freedom because of allegations about pollution is to give up your freedom of judgment, your freedom of production, your freedom to control your life. Those rights are morally inalienable, and must never be surrendered. Even if the ecologists had some knowledge—which is singularly, eloquently absent—it is still up to them to convince you; then you can obey them voluntarily. Their superior knowledge would not give them the right to demand that we all give up our freedom. [FHF 70]

Are there similarities between the fall of Rome and the suicidal tendencies in our society?

Yes. The parallels between the collapse of modern Western civilization and the collapse of Rome are numerous and great. The most obvious one is that Rome grew great in its period of freedom, as a republic, and collapsed after it changed into an empire, with the growth of government controls (including a welfare state, known by the slogan "bread and circuses"). The growth of taxation and government control destroyed the Roman economy and caused the collapse of Rome, which allowed the barbarians to take over. The same thing is happening today. We need not give in to the barbarians, but they are certainly waiting anxiously. [FHF 67]

Force

What do you mean by "force"?

Force is a primary—it's this. [She makes a fist.] It's what is done not by persuasion but by physical compulsion. You are forced to do something if the alternative is physical damage: you'll be seized, imprisoned, deprived of property, or killed. In its improper form, force is what is done to you not by right, not by a process of objective law, but by might. Properly, the government has a monopoly on force, in order to prevent constant gang warfare among citizens who disagree. Government *should* use force only against those who initiate its use; government must never initiate it. But today, all governments do. Law is force, because it is enforced on you under threat of penalties. If you disagree with a private individual, he can do nothing except refuse to deal with you. If the government demands something and you disagree, it can imprison you or deprive you of your property. That's legalized force. [FHF 73]

Is a policeman taking a drunk by the neck brute force?

No, a bureaucrat taking a businessman to jail is brute force. Brute force is arbitrary power—power not subject to objective laws, so that the government is absolutely unpredictable. Antitrust laws are a mess of contradictions, which no one can interpret, and which are interpreted differently by each new judge. Therefore, when you send a man to jail under such laws, it is brute force—it is not subject to any constitutional or objectively defined legal procedure. [CBS 62]

Why do you hold, in "The Nature of Government" [in **The Virtue of Selfishness***], that individuals don't have the right to retaliate against force?*

I write that men have the right to retaliate by force against an *initiation* of force. But if men wish to live together in a free society, they must delegate that right to government. Personal retaliation is improper, because in a free society the government functions under objectively defined laws—laws that state what constitutes a crime, *and above all, what constitutes proof.* Therefore, the government properly acts as the arbiter and agent of an injured party, protects him, and retaliates in his name.

If everyone wanted to exercise his "right" to retaliate by himself, project the chaos of arbitrary whims and total irrationality that would rule the country. You could not have a society, because the honest, rational men would be at the mercy of the first dishonest and irrational man who took force into his own hands. So, a person cannot use force when there is a government that protects him according to objective standards. Force is not a recourse to be used on a whim. (Incidentally, if somebody pulls a gun on you, you have the right to fight back. But this isn't the right to initiate force; it's the right of self-defense.) [FHF 70]

Pragmatists commenting on the student rebellions [of the 1960s] claim to be against force. Aren't they in fact on the side of force?

In effect, pragmatists support the initiators of force, but not in the standard sense. For example, communists are *for* the initiation of force. But a pragmatist is, in a sense, worse. He is neither for nor against it. On his view, it was peaceful on the college campuses, when suddenly there was a violent eruption, with demands from the student rebels. The college administrators didn't know what to do. The clash was unsatisfactory to everybody. Therefore, the pragmatist claimed, we must reach a livable compromise. This approach puts the pragmatist on the side of the aggressor, though they don't advocate aggression. As a criticism of pragmatism, you can say that it is totally amoral, and every amoral system is on the side of the immoral. But the pragmatist is impersonal about force. Someone wants to bash your skull in, reach a livable compromise: tell him to break one leg. [NFW 69]

The Scope of Government

Taxation

Do you consider the government a thief?

In one sense, yes. To the question, "Should the government have the power to tax?," I'd answer, "No, all taxation should be voluntary." (See "Government Financing in a Free Society," in *The Virtue of Selfishness*.) In the sense in which we call a private individual a thief, however, you can't say the government is a thief. Too often, in a mixed economy, it seizes property it's not entitled to. But this must be settled constitutionally; it doesn't give individuals the right to rob the government. [NC 69]

Does a person have the right to refuse to pay taxes?

The moral right, yes. Unfortunately, this political right is not recognized, and he would be penalized too heavily for not paying. [NC 69]

Should the federal government be compelled to pay property taxes to local municipalities in which the federal government owns land?

I've never heard of this proposal; I'm not sure it will work. As an eloquent joke, I approve. But you'd be better off cutting taxes. [FHF 71]

Do you pay income taxes, and if so, why?

Yes, because they are taken from me at gunpoint. [FHF 76]

How can you advocate increased defense spending given your opposition to taxes?

In general, I oppose taxes. You can read my alternative to taxation in *Capitalism: The Unknown Ideal.* But so long as we have a system of taxation to finance the government, those who don't want to pay for defense—if they're honest and have integrity—should leave the country immediately. By what right do you live in this country if you aren't willing to spend money for a primary necessity: protection against military conquest. And anyone who denies that we need defense today is a candidate for the asylum. [FHF 81]

Pollution and preventive law

Should the government control air and water pollution for the sake of public health?

No. The government's only proper role is protecting individual rights. That means: the military, the police, the law courts. Problems like pollution can be settled by agreement among free individuals. If anyone is demonstrably hurt by pollution, he can appeal to the courts and prove his case. No special laws or government controls are required. [FHF 67]

Concerning pollution, what is the property status of air and water?

I'm against all *preventive* government controls. Let people demonstrate an actual harm, and then sue the individual polluter. For instance, you create unsanitary conditions on your property that are not merely visually offensive but create an actual health hazard that affects your neighbor's property. He can sue you if he can demonstrate that the damage comes from your property. He will then, properly, be awarded damages, and you'll be ordered to clean up the menace. These laws already exist, and involve the relationship between property owners. Beyond that, before we can even discuss pollution sensibly, we need to get all vested interests out, because there are people who make a living out of complaining about pollution. I don't believe factory owners and other capitalists want to pollute the air. If and when you can demonstrate that they are causing harm, take the appropriate action—but without forcing them to close their doors and create unemployment, for which you'll also blame them. [FHF 69]

Are some pollutants worse inside the home than they are outside, such as hair spray and floor wax?

That depends on the home. I don't think the things you mentioned are dangerous. In fact, my hairdresser didn't use enough hair spray yesterday, which has made it very uncomfortable for me. This is an issue of personal choice; people should be free to use whatever they please, so long as they don't harm others. No government planner has the right to forbid products for the consumer's own good. Let the consumer decide. [FHF 70]

What do you predict air pollution will do to cities like Los Angeles, which seems to be getting worse? What should be done?

Unlike ecologists, I make predictions only on issues about which I have knowledge, and today nobody knows enough about pollution. Ecologists themselves proclaim they can't give proofs. But if they can't, on what grounds do they ask for total power to

plan our lives? What I've read on the subject is so unscientific—
even when written by scientists—that nobody can tell the extent of
any danger from pollution, including smog. Smog is visible to the
naked eye, and can be uncomfortable. Some claim it stings their
eyes. I lived in Los Angeles for eight years, and it didn't hurt me.
But assume smog hurts people with weak lungs, which is all we can
assume about it today. What should be done? People who are hurt
by smog should move—if their doctors advise them or if they are
uncomfortable. This is a large and free country. Nobody can order
a person to live in Los Angeles or New York City. If some place is
bad for your health, you shouldn't live there. But don't forbid others to live there. [FHF 70]

Under capitalism, what force would prevent pollution?

The ecology movement is a political fraud. In actual cases of pollution, the preventive "force" is public opinion—which is not force,
but the power of persuasion: people protesting and suing for damages. If physical damage to a city or its air, or to someone's property,
can be demonstrated, there is recourse in a court of law. It's in the interest of industry to avoid pollution whenever possible. Industries
should *not* avoid pollution or save endangered species, however, at
the price of massive unemployment and the destruction of an industry. But the ecology movement won't get away with what it's doing,
even in a semi-free society, so long as men are not insane. [FHF 76]

Would you turn nuclear energy over to private industry?

The great error was that nuclear energy was originally developed by the government. Since it is, in effect, government property and the government owns the patents or rights to it, there is
nothing you can do but go from one tangle to another, each step
progressively worse. Therefore, there's no way to control nuclear
energy today. To whom would you turn it over?

In a fully free economy, all industrial development is controlled
by individuals. When men invented dynamite, or guns and gun-
powder, that was a physical danger to people. The difference here

is only in scale. Nobody used dynamite to blow up the world. And if any industrialist manufacturing explosives located his plant too close to homes or schools, and it could be demonstrated that such a factory endangered lives, then he could be ordered by law to relocate. The protection of citizens from physical danger is the proper function of the government. If it were proved that nuclear testing is a danger, then such testing would be prohibited or, more likely, moved.

I am not a nuclear scientist, but I do not believe those stories about nuclear fallout, because they all come from leftist sympathizers of Soviet Russia. When we have better scientific evidence of that danger, we can take it seriously. We are given press releases and comments, but no facts. So when you are deciding which economic system is proper, don't start with such issues as nuclear fallout.

A private industrialist does have a power controlling him: he is prohibited from blowing up his neighbors, and he cannot force people. All he has is economic power—the power of production, to offer a product that people are willing and able to buy. If he produces a bad product, the control over him is the same public, which does not have to deal with him and can go to his competitors, making him go broke. If an industrialist attempted to use force against anyone, the government could properly stop him.

But today there are atomic weapons in the hands of bureaucrats and a government. There's a race between two governments: one totally irresponsible (Russia), and one semi-responsible (the United States), with today's trends going in the direction of greater irresponsibility—that is, more centralized and totalitarian government. If you are afraid of a private businessman handling nuclear energy, or even nuclear weapons, why aren't you afraid of bureaucrats who hold total power and have no responsibility?

Further, the only protection against nuclear war is freedom—namely, a country in which nobody can use force and people are forbidden by law to force their own citizens. Then nobody could unleash an atom bomb on you, and no dictatorship would have the power to spy and steal secrets from us, which is what happened. No foreign country can be a threat to a free country. But once it's not free, then anything goes. And something could happen by sheer accident, because bureaucrats have power but no responsibility, and no checks on them. So don't worry about private capitalists who might obtain atomic energy two hundred years from now. [PVA 61]

Should the government establish building codes?

In establishing these codes, the government does not *protect* anyone; they *regulate*—that is, they arbitrarily impose certain rules or decisions on men involved in the building industry. The government enforces its view of what is proper building, and as such, that is improper government interference. Now, shouldn't government inspectors protect us from faulty housing and collapsing buildings? The answer is: (a) this "protection" doesn't protect us from anything; we have as many dangerous buildings now as we would without government housing codes; and (b) in a free society, laws against fraud protect tenants from unsafe buildings. Builders would not be ordered to obey arbitrary and often contradictory regulations. But if a builder rents a building that is unsafe, and its tenants are hurt, there would be very severe penalties: the tenants could sue the landlord for fraud—for presenting a building as safe when it was not. Of course, there would have to be objective ways to prove that the landlord or builder had been negligent. He should not be blamed for not knowing how to prevent what no one could prevent. In a free society, a builder's own self-interest would prevent him from resorting to such practices as building shoddy houses. The occurrence of building accidents would not be necessary to prevent builders from improper practices. The mere existence of laws against fraud would be sufficient protection against the rare dishonest builder, and honest builders would be left free. [APM 62]

Should the government license physicians and dentists?

The government has no right to pass judgment on the fitness of professionals. So, what would protect us from quacks in a free society? The free judgment of individual men, and the professional organizations and publications that report to its members or subscribers on the standing of various practitioners. Government licenses and medical school diplomas do not protect us from quacks. We must still exercise our judgment in selecting a physician, which is what we would do in a free society. Government licensing protects us from nothing, but could be used to keep better people out of a controlled profession. [APM 62]

Should the government require inoculations against diseases, or the quarantine of people with communicable diseases?

Requiring inoculation against disease is definitely not a job for the government. If it is medically proven that a certain inoculation is desirable, those who want it will take it. If some disagree and don't want it, they alone are endangered, since the others will be inoculated. Nobody has the right to force a person to do anything for his own good and against his own judgment.

If someone has a contagious disease, however, against which there is no inoculation, then the government has the right to quarantine him. The principle here is to prevent diseased people from passing on their illness to others. Here there is a demonstrable physical damage. In all issues of government protection against physical damage, before the government can properly act, there must be an objective demonstration of an actual physical danger. To quarantine people who are ill is not a violation of their rights; it merely prevents them from doing physical damage to others. [APM 62]

Drugs, prostitution, etc.

Should dope peddling, bootlegging, gambling, and prostitution be forbidden by law? Are antitrust laws like laws against such activities?

In answer to your first question: No, they should not be forbidden. Some of these practices are improper. Prostitution is evil by almost any standard of morality. So long as it isn't forced on anyone, however—so long as a woman chooses to engage in that kind of activity (one shouldn't call it a profession) and some men take advantage of it—that is between them and not the business of society. It is their moral degradation; but it should not be a legal crime—society has no right to forbid it. The same applies to selling drugs.

Antitrust laws are different. Business is not an immoral activity. Antitrust violations are considered a crime, and men who have not used force in any way are punished. There is a difference between the moral character of convicted bootleggers or gamblers and convicted businessmen. They are not in the same category morally. Businessmen are not only punished for a noncriminal activity, they are punished for a virtue—for success and ability. [APM 63]

What is your view on laws against cyclamates and marijuana?

I do not approve of any government controls over consumption, so all restrictions on drugs should be removed (except, of course, on the sale to minors). The government has no right to tell an adult what to do with his own health and life. That places a much greater moral responsibility on the individual; but adults should be free to kill themselves in any way they want.

It is the moral responsibility of the individual not to take substances that destroy his mind. I would fight for your legal right to use marijuana; I would fight you to the death that you morally should not do it—except that in a free society, I wouldn't have to deal with you at all. What the government *should* do is protect citizens from the criminal consequences of those who take drugs. But drugs would be much cheaper if it weren't for government, as liquor was much more expensive under Prohibition. Bootleggers didn't want the repeal of Prohibition, because they made a fortune. Similarly, the underworld is spreading drugs. It would be cheaper, easier, and morally more vicious on the part of the drug addict if drugs were legalized.

On the issue of cyclamates—which I use myself in the form of diet soft drinks—doctors claim they are not harmful. Doctors must decide this and inform their patients. It is not the role of government to pass laws on a moment's notice, on the basis of unproved experimental whim.

My hypothesis about why people are calling for the prohibition of cyclamates involves the psychology of the critique of capitalism. Critics attack any industry that helps people or gives them pleasure and profit. They're now going after TV dinners because they contain preservatives that are supposedly harmful. Of course, TV dinners are a big time-saver for busy housewives. And there is another motive: such attacks get you in the newspapers. Take Ralph Nader—that's his real motive. [FHF 69]

Is the government control of drugs and narcotics consistent with Objectivism?

Government control of medical drugs is completely improper. There can be laws against someone misrepresenting the nature of the drug he is selling—that's what laws against fraud are for. But government control does not prevent that possibility, so there should be no government control beyond a quick and efficient legal system in which one could go to court and prove one's case if one discovers that some manufacturer of drugs is dishonest.

As for narcotics, the government should not forbid them either, except in the case of minors. If adults want to hurt themselves, that's their privilege. I believe that when they tried legalizing narcotics in England, they found it minimized the use of drugs, because drug addicts lost the incentive to push drugs—to sell drugs to minors or create new addicts—out of a need to pay for illegal drugs. There were contrary reports, so I say this only for what it's worth—but it's worth investigating. Theoretically, it's likely that if you made narcotics legal, it would reduce drug addiction and crime; but this is ultimately an issue for doctors and criminologists. [FHF 68]

Suicide and euthanasia

You defend an individual's right to choice in the case of abortion and birth control. Do you have the same attitude toward suicide and euthanasia?

Birth control and abortion involve the actions of the agent alone. They do not infringe on anyone's rights. Suicide falls into the same category. So in principle, a man has the right to commit suicide—but it is very inadvisable. Further, a government can't pass laws to prevent suicide. The Soviets tried that in Russia in the 1920s, because of a wave of suicides among Party members. The penalty was death—which illustrates the problem. In general, there are many reasons why a man should not take his life. There are situations, however, in which suicide is perfectly valid, and it *is* his own life; there is nothing the law or other people can do about it.

Euthanasia is more complex, because the life of another person is involved. If a man makes arrangements stating that he does not want to feel unbearable pain, and it can be proved that this was his desire, in principle I'd say it is his right and the doctor's right to perform euthanasia. But it would be difficult to put this into law, because of the safeguards needed to prevent unscrupulous doctors in cahoots with unscrupulous relatives from killing somebody who is not dying and in pain. The danger here is legally giving to the doctor the arbitrary power of killing. I suspect, however, that there are many cases of euthanasia about which we do not know and probably shouldn't know; in such cases, it is up to the doctor involved. Only he can know if a terminally ill patient is suffering truly unbearable torture. I feel like saying I would not assume to pass judgment on him. I don't know. The situation is too horrible. I sympathize with the doctor who helps the patient die, but I would not advocate euthanasia as a law. [FHF 68]

Abortion, sex, and marriage

Would you comment on the rights of individuals, particularly with reference to abortion?

For a full presentation of my views on this subject, see "Of Living Death" [reprinted in *The Voice of Reason*]. It was a commentary on the papal encyclical on contraception (*Humanae Vitae*). I am certainly in favor of abortion. Or rather, I do not mean that everyone should have an abortion, I mean that I am in favor of a woman's perfect moral right to have one if she so decides. I think it is an issue to be decided by a woman and her doctor. I am in agreement with the Supreme Court decision on this subject. And this is one reason I am against Ronald Reagan. That so-and-so, claiming to be a defender of capitalism and Americanism, has come out against abortion. If he doesn't respect so fundamental a right, he cannot be a defender of any kind of rights. [FHF 76]

Does an unborn child have any rights with regard to abortion?

No. I'd like to express my indignation at the idea of confusing a living human being with an embryo, which is only some undeveloped cells. (Abortion at the last minute—when a baby is formed—is a different issue.) The right to abortion is the right to get rid of some cells in your body, which you can't afford to support if it grows into a child. The idea of some bitches—and I don't apologize for that—trying to prescribe to all other women what they should do with their lives is disgusting. And they call it a right to life! The basic principles here are: never sacrifice the living to the nonliving, and never confuse an actuality with a potentiality. An "unborn child," before it's formed, is not a human, it's not a living entity, it has no rights. The woman has rights. [FHF 74]

On AR's opposition to five Supreme Court decisions upholding the censorship of pornography, see "Censorship: Local and Express" (in Philosophy: Who Needs It).

How do you reconcile the Supreme Court's decision on abortion—which was pro-freedom—with its decision on censorship?

That question should properly be asked of the Supreme Court, not of me. I don't know, except to say that people who hold inconsistent premises will act inconsistently. Apparently, some better premises were in their minds on the occasion of the abortion case, but not when they were discussing obscenity.

What is your view of laws prohibiting homosexuality and bigamy?

All laws against homosexual acts should be repealed. I do not approve of such practices or regard them as necessarily moral, but it is improper for the law to interfere with a relationship between consenting adults. Laws against corrupting the morals of minors are proper, but adults should be completely free.

Bigamy is a different issue. If a man wants a *relationship* with two women, he does not need the law to sanction it. But the state should have standards about what it considers a legal *marriage*. The law should be uniform, and there are good reasons why in most civilized countries marriage is a monogamous institution. If a man wants a wife and another woman, he doesn't need the legality of bigamy if he's open about it. Bigamy laws concern cases in which a man has two legal wives in two different cities, and leads a double life. Here there are good grounds, legally and morally, to prosecute him. [FHF 68]

Should the state prescribe the obligations of a marriage, or should this be left to the contractual desires of the couple?

This is an important and difficult subject, because of two complex issues: the rights of children and property rights.

If two people are married, they may want or have children. Once a child is born, he is entitled to support until he is self-supporting.

In general, a husband and wife can make any property arrangements they want. But today, the law is a bit too much on the side of the woman. There was a time when the woman was at the economic mercy of her husband; today, she is not. There is a great deal of irrationality and contradictions in many state marriage laws, so there's room for improvement, provided the basic principles are clearly stated and not arbitrary.

The government cannot undertake to enforce any contract any two people decide to make. If your contract falls under a certain legal category, then the government can undertake to enforce it; but it cannot be asked to enforce some contradictory contract. This is one reason why there must be a uniform code of law—why individuals are not entirely free to make contracts in any manner. But proper marriage laws—and even the mixed ones of today— allow two parties to make legal contracts regarding their relationship. [FHF 68]

Gun control

What is your opinion on gun control laws?

I do not know enough about it to have an opinion, except to say that it's not of primary importance. Forbidding guns or registering them is not going to stop criminals from having them; nor is it a great threat to the private, noncriminal citizen if he has to register the fact that he has a gun. It's not an important issue, unless you're ready to begin a private uprising right now, which isn't very practical. [FHF 71]

What's your attitude toward gun control?

It's a complex, technical issue in the philosophy of law. Handguns are instruments for killing people—they are not carried for hunting animals—and you have no right to kill people. You do have the right to self-defense, however. I don't know how the issue is to be resolved to protect you without giving you the privilege to kill people at whim. [FHF 73]

Freedom of speech and of the press, and government funding of the arts

Could you comment on the Nazi march on Skokie, Illinois, considering the issue of freedom of speech versus the overt expression of genocide?

That's a very complex issue. So long as the courts interpret a march through the streets as a form of freedom of speech, so long as communists or leftists or anyone else are permitted to march, the Nazis have to be permitted to do it, too. In that respect, I agree very reluctantly with the ACLU (reluctantly, because I seldom agree with them): they do not like the Nazis, but they find they have to fight for the Nazis' "right" to march. If demonstrations are regarded as a form of speech, then anyone and everyone must be permitted.

But what I challenge (and not only because of that particular case) is the interpretation of demonstrations and of other actions as so-called symbolic speech. When you lose the distinction between action and speech, you lose, eventually, the freedom of both. The Skokie case is a good illustration of that principle. There is no such thing as "symbolic speech." You do not have the right to parade through the public streets or to obstruct public thoroughfares. You have the right of assembly, yes, on your own property, and on the property of your adherents or your friends. But nobody has the "right" to clog the streets. The streets are only for passage. The hippies, in the 1960s, should have been forbidden to lie down on city pavements. (They used to lie down across the street and cause dreadful traffic snarls, in order to display their views, to attract attention, to register a protest.) If they were permitted to do it, the Nazis should be permitted as well. Properly, both should have been forbidden. They may speak, yes. They may not take action at whim on public property.

I would like to add that the matter of "the overt expression of genocide" is irrelevant to the issue of free speech. The principle of free speech is not concerned with the *content* of a man's speech and does not protect only the expression of *good* ideas, but *all* ideas. If it were otherwise, who would determine which ideas are good and which are forbidden? The government? [FHF 78]

What do you think of libel and slander laws?

They are appropriate laws, because the freedom of ideas does not permit you to lie about a person. Under the older interpretation of the courts, truth was your defense. If you know something defamatory about someone, and it's true, then you have the right to say it. But today, you can practically say anything, so long as you're supposedly not motivated by malice. There are some standards, but they're unclear and impractical.

This type of law is strictly to protect specific individuals; it has nothing to do with ideas. It's an issue of whether or not you lied about someone, and caused him damage. [FHF 73]

In the copyright bill that was just passed by the U.S. Senate, there are several provisions for compulsory licensing—that is, removing from the author the choice of to whom he will give a license. Will you comment on that?

I think it is unspeakably evil. It's interesting that that is one of the items I was going to include in the talk tonight, the issue of this copyright bill, but I didn't have room for it. The most vicious thing about that bill is the aspect you didn't mention: it is the question *to whom* one would be forced to license one's work (this applies to writers and composers). The answer is: to the so-called public service television and radio stations. These stations are run by parasites who are on government-paid salaries. And, as a rule, these men are paid much more than they would be paid in commercial television. They are paid by the government—that is, by taxpayers. These men do not have a wide audience, just a small audience of their own cliques—and yet they claim to represent the public interest. They propose to violate—to abolish—the rights of writers and composers, and creative people in general. The bill, as it stands, proposes that the public service stations will have the right to use your work, but there will be a public board that will determine how much you will be paid for it. They do not ask your consent as to whether you want your work produced on those stations—which I would not. As far as I am concerned, I would rather destroy all copies of my books than permit it—except that I am not in a position to do it: there are too many copies in existence. The Senate has passed that copyright bill, but the House has not; both authors and publishers are fighting it. Therefore, if any of you are interested, please, for my sake, and for the sake of other valuable creators who do still exist, write to your congressmen opposing that particular section. The copyright bill otherwise is a very good law. But that section is unspeakable. And not only in regard to creative people. Just think of the precedent it is setting for expropriation. [FHF 76]

Is today's public television a valid method of arts funding?

No. It's vicious and unfair. Why is commercial television—which gives people something for free, in exchange for their consideration of some commercials, and thereby makes millions—not considered in the public interest? Because it earns what it gets, and apparently pleases the public. But some station that gets less than ten percent of the audience is *public* television, because nobody will pay for what they offer. The whole concept is collectivist and rotten. [PO10 76]

Does the military have the right to censor extramilitary publications?

I assume that by "extramilitary" you mean "edited and written by military personnel for the public." I'm open to persuasion here, but offhand, I'd say the military has the right to censor anyone in the military. An army is built on opposite premises from the civilian population. It is a legal instrument for using force. Properly, it's force used in self-defense. It's honorable force in the case of the United States military. Nevertheless, the army requires a hierarchy of command, and can't function without total obedience. Freedom of publications could undermine the morale of soldiers. (I'm speaking of a voluntary, not conscripted, army. I oppose the draft as a total violation of rights.) Commanders have the right to censor the expression of ideas by those men who have joined the army voluntarily. As long as they are in that organization, they must accept the orders of their commanders. They are free to leave, and that's what permits their commanders, while they are in the army, to give them orders and censor what they'd like to publish. [FHF 73]

Does your claim that a scientist can properly accept government grants for research apply to the artist?

No. The difference is this: Government grants to the arts are a horror. They make it *harder* for artists who lack political pull and do not share in contemporary esthetic tastes. Nevertheless, at no time, not even with the WPA under Roosevelt, was the government able to close the arts, so that artists had no choice but to apply for government grants or starve. But in the case of the scientist, the government has created a situation wherein there is little private industrial research. Private money for the research necessary in an industrial society has been drained off by taxes. Private companies cannot afford research on that scale, and therefore scientists have no choice but to apply for government grants. Also, since science is more impersonal than art, although scientists on a government endowment are not entirely free, they can at least pretend or fight to be free. But since there are no artistic standards today, the artist is at the mercy of the worst kind of whim. No whim is more ugly and revolting than the esthetic whim of some bureaucrat. All an artist can do in this context is be a spiritual bootlicker; and considering the nature of art, that is the lowest kind of bootlicker. [PO10 76]

The communications industry is probably the purest example of private enterprise in the country. It's been protected by the First Amendment. However, nearly everyone recognizes that our communications system is not adequately serving us. On the one hand, I'm reluctant to see the government take a more active role; on the other, the present state of affairs is not good enough. Could you comment?

I agree with your observation, but don't see why you even consider the possibility of government stepping in. To make the culture freer or more varied? If culture and communication are directed by the point of a gun, that is the end of free communication. What you are observing is that you cannot have a country regulated by a double standard: in material production, men are increasingly controlled, while in the intellectual realm, they expect to be free. But we are not disembodied ghosts. We live in a material world, and when we use our minds and communicate ideas, we do so by material means. Here's an example in which controlling material production hinders freedom of communication. Every major newspaper and magazine that established itself before today's high taxes is beyond competition. A beginner competing with newspaper and magazine giants does not have much of a chance, because of taxes (to name just one barrier). The problem is not big business; it's government control. [CBS 62]

Miscellaneous

Do you support busing to integrate the races?

No. The government has no right playing politics with children, or disposing of a child's education against his parents' wishes. It's a terrible infringement of rights. I am an enemy of racism (see "Racism," in *The Virtue of Selfishness*) and believe people should have quality education. But I don't think the government should run schools. Education should be private, and children should go wherever their parents decide to send them. [FHF 74]

What can be done to stop busing?

Use your influence in Washington to repeal those laws—but not through a constitutional amendment, because it's too small an issue to load the Constitution with. Above all, make yourself heard. If you make it an issue of rights, you might succeed. If you make it an issue of race, you'll defeat yourself. If you argue that the government has no right to direct the education of children, you'll have a good chance. If you object to your children going to school with black children, you'll lose for sure, because right will be on the other side—or rather, it will perish between two wrong sides. Make your opposition to busing an issue of individual rights, and take it to the Supreme Court if necessary. [FHF 74]

What is your attitude toward immigration? Doesn't open immigration have a negative effect on a country's standard of living?

You don't know my conception of self-interest. No one has the right to pursue his self-interest by law or by force, which is what you're suggesting. You want to forbid immigration on the grounds that it lowers *your* standard of living—which isn't true, though if it were true, you'd still have no right to close the borders. You're not entitled to any "self-interest" that injures others, especially when you can't prove that open immigration affects your self-interest. You can't claim that anything others may do—for example, simply through competition—is against your self-interest. But above all, aren't you dropping a personal context? How could I advocate restricting immigration when I wouldn't be alive today if our borders had been closed? [FHF 73]

What should be the relation between the government and public utilities—that is, the natural monopolies, such as electric companies and the post office?

There is no such thing as a natural monopoly, any more than there is a natural crime. There isn't a single profession or service of a productive nature that should be a monopoly, enforced by law. If any one businessman in a given field can successfully provide all the services and the best products at the best price, you could loosely call that a "natural monopoly," but it is not a monopoly in the usual sense—that is, it isn't coercive. Therefore, it will remain a "monopoly" only until someone does better. There is no undertaking that, by its nature, must be a monopoly—particularly not delivering mail. If you've ever dealt with the post office, you know why. Anyone who ran his business the way the post office is run would not last long; any businessman who raised his rates every few months would be called a greedy monopolist by the same liberals who support government monopolies.

Under laissez-faire capitalism, there would be private, competing post offices, private roads, private schools. Nothing that can be done voluntarily should be done by force. And nothing has ever been done by force properly—except the proper functions of government: the police, the military, the law courts. Those are the functions of a government; they are noncompetitive umpire functions. The government should have no economic functions. [APM 63]

Do the two islands off Massachusetts [Nantucket and Martha's Vineyard] have the right to secede?

I don't know the details of their case, or the Massachusetts Constitution. But since they merely want to change their state allegiance, I think they're sort of cute. [FHF 77]

Capitalism

Is the United States Constitution proper so far as capitalism is concerned? If not, have you drawn up your own constitution?

The Constitution has contradictions and flaws that *destroyed* capitalism. At the end of *Atlas Shrugged*, I have a judge writing amendments to a properly restored constitution. That would be the job of a lawyer and a philosopher of law, which is an important and complex specialty. I wouldn't dream of writing a constitution at home, between other jobs. [FHF 71]

You say that it's against our instincts to act altruistically. But isn't laissez-faire capitalism—Adam Smith's philosophy, which you advocate—dependent upon a businessman's just representation of his product to the consumer? Isn't there a contradiction between your opposition to altruism and a businessman not cheating his customers whenever he gets a chance?

First, I don't believe in instincts, and never speak of them in my writings against altruism. Second, I am *not* an advocate of Adam Smith's philosophy. I do not believe in invisible hands leading men to altruism through the pursuit of their private interests. I reject altruism, public service, and the public good as the moral justification of free enterprise. Altruism is what's destroying capitalism. Adam Smith was a brilliant economist; I agree with many of his economic theories. But I disagree with his attempt to justify capitalism on altruistic grounds. My defense of capitalism is based on individual rights, as was the American Founding Fathers', who were not altruists. They did not say man should exist for others; they said he should pursue his own happiness. Finally, it is not in a man's rational self-interest to cheat his customers. The abler the man, the better he is able to plan long range. An able industrialist knows he is not in business to make a quick killing and run; his aim is not to cheat his customers once and then disappear. He knows that it is in his own practical, rationally selfish, interest to do the best he can economically—to create the best product and sell it at the cheapest price possible. [APM 63]

You say capitalism requires the rejection of altruism. But doesn't capitalism leave a person free to act altruistically? Further, is every act of altruism—the voluntary giving of goods or services to one who hasn't earned them—morally wrong?

The second part of this question gives us a clue to the questioner's error. He is not talking about altruism. "Altruism" is a term originated by the philosopher Auguste Comte, and has been used ever since to mean exactly what Comte intended. "Altruism" comes from the Latin *alter*, meaning "other." It means placing the interests of others above your own—existing for the sake of others. Altruism holds that man has no right to exist for his own sake, that service to others is the only moral justification of his existence, and that self-sacrifice is his highest virtue. But the questioner confuses altruism with kindness, courtesy, and generosity. Under his definition, giving someone a Christmas present is an act of altruism. But that's foolish. This kind of package deal enables altruists to get away with the evil they are perpetrating. The essence of altruism is self-sacrifice. If you do something for another that involves harm to yourself, that is altruism. But voluntarily giving something to another who hasn't earned it is not. That's morally neutral. You may or may not have a good reason for doing it. As a principle, nobody would think of forbidding all voluntary giving. Judging what giving is proper depends on the context of the situation—on the relationship of the two persons involved. Moreover, the act of giving is the least important act in life. This is not where one begins a discussion of morality or politics.

Now to the rest of the question. The questioner ignores or evades the difference between a legal and a moral principle. Legally, under capitalism, a man's property is his own, and he may do anything he pleases with it: waste it, give it away, enjoy it rationally. Morality concerns the right principles to guide a man's action, and therefore to guide the laws of society. Before one gets to the question "What can a man do with his property?," one must answer, "What are a man's rights? Should he live for himself or for others?" If under capitalism the state does not interfere with a man's disposal of his property, it is precisely because capitalism is based on the principle that man's life and the products of his work belong to him—that man exists for his own sake. If you don't start with the morality of rational self-interest, then there's no justification for the state leaving a man's property alone. If a man doesn't have the right to exist for his own sake, others may make claims on him; and under altruism, they do. According to altruism, we should live for others, and should base society on this principle. The fully consistent result of this morality is totalitarian dictatorship, whether communist or fascist.

Further, the questioner discusses only consequences. When he talks about a man's right to dispose of his property, he is talking about distribution. He's not concerned about production—the source of property. But before one can discuss distribution, one must talk about the right to produce. Here again, the clash between altruism and capitalism enters. In order to produce, man needs the moral certainty that he exists and can act for his own sake.

First, a producer holds the judgment of his mind against the minds of others. The better the mind, the more likely he is to be an innovator, and therefore, regardless of the state of knowledge in a particular society, the better mind will be at odds with the rest of society. In a free society, nobody will stop him. People have the right to agree with him or not. But nobody will tell him, "The majority disagrees with you; who are you to hold your judgment above theirs; as a good altruist, give in."

Second, the producer must decide why he wants to produce. Before he has any wealth to distribute, he must decide why he wants to work, and what he intends to do with his wealth. He needs the right to produce what he wants, and to do what he wants with the results, regardless of the ideas, wishes, or needs of others—always granting others the same rights.

It is on these two issues—the right to use your judgment, and the right to choose your goals and act to achieve them—that altruism and capitalism clash. Capitalism cannot function according to a morality that holds that it is your duty to serve others. The moment you introduce an element of duty, you're on the road to communism. Do not be concerned with giving away or hoarding things, but with a man's right to live and produce. [IBA 62]

Why, under capitalism, would it be in a businessman's self-interest to improve his product once he has become wealthy and his company is well established?

First, economically, he would have to improve his product or go bankrupt. The free market would "force" him to continue producing better and better. (I'm using "force" metaphorically.) When I say man survives by means of his mind, I mean that man's first moral virtue is to think and to be productive. That is not the same as saying: "Get your pile of money by hook or by crook, and then sit at home and enjoy it." You assume rational self-interest is simply ensuring one's physical luxury. But what would a man do with himself once he has those millions. He would stagnate. No man who has used his mind enough to achieve a fortune is going to be happy doing nothing. His self-interest does not lie in consumption but in production—in the creative expansion of his mind.

To go deeper, observe that in order to exist, every part of an organism must function; if it doesn't, it atrophies. This applies to a man's mind more than to any other faculty. In order actually to be alive properly, a man must use his mind constantly and productively. That's why rationality is the basic virtue according to my morality. Every achievement is an incentive for the next achievement. What for? The creative happiness of achieving greater and greater control over reality, greater and more ambitious values in whatever field a man is using his mind. For a man to conclude, "I have enough, so I don't have to think," would be the same as deciding, "I am rich now and can get around in a wheelchair, so why use my legs?"

Man's survival is not about having to think in order to survive physically for this moment. To survive properly, man must think constantly. Man cannot survive automatically. The day he decides he no longer needs to be creative is the day he's dead spiritually. But truly productive men rarely do this; they continue working and die at their desks. In recent times, the ones who do stop thinking are those who give up in discouragement, because the social system destroys them. [FF 61]

Is it appropriate for massive power to be transferred by inheritance?

Yes, and the more of it the better. But the word "power" is used too loosely today. There is a difference between *economic* power and *political* power. Economic power is not the power to deal with men by force. It's the power to create, to achieve. Economic power is not taken from anyone; it's created by the man who becomes rich—if he becomes rich without government help, in a free society. Political power is the power to use force. Economically, political power is merely the power to seize wealth created by somebody else, keep a big percentage, and then redistribute the rest. The number of large fortunes that are produced and transmitted to heirs is the measure of the country's freedom. The more large fortunes and worthless heirs (let alone the rare good heirs), the better. [FHF 77]

What do you think of the idea of having welfare recipients work for their grants?

I approve, though it would be much better if the government lifted some of its controls, so that these same welfare recipients could get real jobs in private industry. [FHF 77]

Has capitalism as long a road to go as you once seemed to think?

In some respects longer, in others not. It's hard to tell. For instance, ever since the 1972 election of Nixon (which was McGovern's achievement, not Nixon's), the country has been turning to the right (in the sense of capitalism) at an amazing speed. In my most optimistic view of the American people, I didn't think they would awaken that quickly. The people who are *more* asleep than I thought—who are catatonic about capitalism—are the intellectuals. They have not discovered capitalism yet, and without intellectual leadership, the people are helpless, no matter what they sense. They are being pushed into tribes. The American people don't like it at all, but they almost have no choice. However, they have not become tribalists. The destruction of the people's individualism would probably take several generations. But God only knows what horrors will happen between now and the time when there are sufficient voices to assume intellectual—not political—leadership, and explain to the people what capitalism is, why it's good, how it works, and why we should reestablish it. [FHF 77]

Technology and Prosperity

Do you consider man's altering of nature to be natural?

Well, what do you think man is? Outside of nature? A supernatural being? Of course, man is a natural being and the essential attribute of man's *nature* is his mind, a faculty that enables him to understand nature and to use it to his own advantage, which is his only way of survival. Man does not "alter" nature—he merely re-arranges its elements to serve his own purposes. [FHF 77]

How come there were so many great minds—artistic minds—who lived full lives before the industrial revolution?

You mean as trembling prisoners of a rich political patron, when they could get one? Chopin died in his thirties of consumption. Is that a full life? Before the industrial revolution, great minds were the great exception. An unusual combination of circumstances made them possible; inherited wealth or some not-too-tyrannical protector at court might permit a man, in literature or philosophy, to function. But in the nineteenth century, there was suddenly an amazing flowering of human talent.

The two other brief periods similar in quality were ancient Greece and the Renaissance. In both cases, men were relatively free and therefore could exercise their talents openly and independently; most didn't have to beg for royal sustenance or risk being imprisoned or exiled or executed for their ideas. [FHF 70]

Why do you claim that restricting technology is a contradiction in terms?

Technology depends on creative freedom—the freedom to invent and produce. Once you put restrictions on that, you put technology under a commissar and immediately lose the best men. Truly independent men won't produce under such circumstances. The better ones who remain by chance or who are more tolerant are eventually replaced by the ruling clique's favorites. This happened in Nazi Germany and is still happening in Soviet Russia, where the best minds are subject to the orders of commissars or switches in the party line. By that means, a country produces less and less.

Further, you cannot isolate one branch of technology or of knowledge from all others. You cannot tell people to proceed freely in medicine but not in refrigerator production. All knowledge is interconnected. One invention opens incalculable avenues to other inventions in other sciences. This is how free minds operate. When a man who is free to think and produce sees a development in one branch of technology, he applies it to his own. For instance, there have been important gains in medicine from space exploration. The history of science is full of such examples. Once you begin to restrict technology, you cut off all of that. How can any person or group know what genius will be born where, and what ideas might occur to him. That's impossible by definition. You cannot restrict technology; you can only destroy it. [FHF 70]

Why must ecology mean the return of man to prehistoric times? Isn't some middle course between that and our present technological society possible?

The hippie movement and Woodstock are prehistory in our own backyard. That's the return to nature, as the ecologists publicize and approve of it. What middle could exist between that and a civilization of computers and nuclear weapons, between a self-made savage (which is worse than an innocent one) and a rational man? A pretechnological civilization? No, there is no middle—with one possible exception. All the nature lovers could move out of technological nations and start their own society in nature. There are plenty of "unpolluted" places; let them move there. If—and I'm only being polite here—they prove they're right, within a few generations the world will follow their example. It certainly followed the example of capitalism, when *it* proved its validity and value. [FHF 70]

A lady professor at Columbia University told me that you once said that since the creation of material goods occurs only under capitalism, Sputnik does not exist. Could you comment?

Tell her that's B.S. (If you want to spell this out for her, you can.) What she attributes to me is rationalism, a method I never employ. I reject the idea of proving something out of context, by syllogism, without reference to reality.

I did not say: "Production occurs only under capitalism, therefore Sputnik doesn't exist." What I said at the time was that I don't believe any *Soviet* claims about Sputnik. Shortly after *Atlas Shrugged* was published [1957], there were doubts about the authenticity of the Soviet reports about Sputnik—doubts that were never answered. I now believe Sputnik exists, because they brought it here and showed our scientists. What NASA found was that the Soviet space program is far behind ours. *That* you can conclude from the fact of dealing with a dictatorship, but not from rationalistic deductions.

About a decade ago, there was a statement to the effect that a Russian spaceship had photographed the other side of the moon. Then there were some doubts; then complete silence. Nothing is said today about this Soviet claim. The moral of all this is: You cannot believe any scientific claims that come out of Soviet Russia or any other dictatorship.

It isn't true that material production is possible only under capitalism. Material *prosperity*, however—successful production, innovation, originality—is possible only under capitalism. If no goods could be produced by imitation, then the whole world, including half the United States, would die; there's that little freedom left in the world. What this professor missed is that no matter how enslaved people are, no matter how badly they treat the innovator, there is always the possibility of *stealing*. Today, I believe the Russians are doing something in space, because they've had ample opportunity to learn from this country. Further, there can always be exceptions—talented men who somehow (though I don't know how) rise to some prominence in technological or productive fields under a dictatorship. Such men don't last long, as we've seen repeatedly under Russian, German, and all other dictatorships. We can infer from the nature of the system in reality that there can be no progress, no abundance, no prosperity. So tell this lady that rationalism is a philosophical disease, and she obviously suffers from it, but that she should not ascribe it to me. [PO12 76]

Is the population explosion a problem?

There is no population problem. If people were free to produce, they'd produce enough to feed themselves. There's enough on this earth to support much larger populations. Further, as people become more affluent and educated, they don't breed large families.

There *is* a problem when populations grow through ignorance, anti–birth control campaigns, or religion, and people can't make a living for themselves because they live in controlled economies or dictatorships. That's a problem; but the solution is freedom, not more state power.

The greatest population explosion in history was in Europe during the nineteenth century: 300 percent. At that time, intellectuals of the altruist/socialist/collectivist persuasion raised the same objection: the population explosion would cause the world to perish from hunger. This was on the eve of the greatest prosperity the world had ever known, because it was the freest century ever. Today, when people yell about population and hunger, it's because they have the same ideas and the same farsightedness as nineteenth-century socialists. They sense (or even know) that under controls, a growth in population *is* disastrous. But socialism is disastrous for a population of any size: it's only a matter of time before the birth of one more human being is too much, since there'll be nothing to feed him. [FHF 70]

Does the rapidly expanding population make it harder to convince people that Objectivism or capitalism is probably in their best interest?

No. I don't see any connection between these two issues. If Objectivism is true for one infant, it will be true for a million of them. If capitalism is the only system that enables mankind to survive, then the scarcer the resources the more freedom you need, and the more you need the ingenuity of the intelligent man to make discoveries and thus improve everybody's standard of living. But I don't believe that whole story about shrinking resources. They are shrinking because freedom is shrinking. In a free economy, if any particular resource became scarce, long before we would feel the shortage there would be several different substitutes invented to take its place. Also, in a free economy, you would not use your knowledge and technology to build oil wells for tribal savages, and then permit them to nationalize your property and hold you up for ransom. [FHF 77]

In view of the energy crisis, what prospects are there for the supply of food and energy?

I see no solution except in a return to some form of free enterprise as fast as possible, and ultimately laissez-faire capitalism. No problem will be solved by means of a mixed economy, with some controls and some freedom. We can't go on forever that way. There is no solution to problems of production—including energy and food—under a dictatorship or a mixed economy. Either we go back to capitalism, or I hope some of my works survive the next Dark Ages. [FHF 78]

How does Objectivism apply to underdeveloped regions, such as in Africa or the American South?

The South is the one part of America that has never been capitalist. It was an agrarian society, and had more in common with medieval feudalism than with industrial capitalism. That's why the South held on to slavery. Objectivism advocates capitalism, and capitalism is the only system incompatible with slavery. In fact, capitalism wiped out slavery in the nineteenth century, in part through the American Civil War and even Russia's freeing of the serfs. Capitalism cannot function with slave labor, and the moral principles implicit in capitalism do not permit slavery.

Therefore, the first thing Objectivism would advocate in regard to undeveloped nations is not to send them material help but to teach them political freedom. For any nation, no matter how undeveloped, if it establishes a political system that protects individual rights, its progress and development will be phenomenal. The best in all men work to raise that society and to contribute to the progress of all—not by self-sacrifice but by plain rational self-interest. Capitalism, as history shows, raises the general standard of living, and men on all levels of ability are rewarded and get much more than they could get under any form of statism or tribal rule. If you want to help Africa, teach them the theory of freedom. If people who have lived for centuries under violence discover that they can exercise their ingenuity and create something, and that their rulers will protect them rather than forbid production or expropriate what they produce, you'd be amazed what productive talent would suddenly arise. At the start of the Industrial Revolution, most nations of the world were pretty primitive—perhaps not as undeveloped as Africa, but they were savages in the Middle Ages compared to what we are today. After one century of freedom, under government protection of individual rights and property, you couldn't recognize the nature of the civilization, material prosperity, and undreamed-of talent that suddenly appeared among men. I predict the same would happen in Africa, if there were anyone to teach them what capitalism is. Unfortunately, that's not what we're exporting today; that's not what we're teaching them. What we're doing is arming them without giving them the right ideology to go with those arms: the ideology of freedom and human rights. We're only helping them destroy each other in civil wars, as the more civilized nations of earth are doing as well.

As for the South, freedom and rational education will solve their problems, not violence, which they're now engaging in. The real evil in the South are the state laws enforcing segregation; but the solution is not enforced integration by *federal* law, which is immoral as well, and will only create more mutual hatred and underground hypocrisy. What should be done? I'd advocate the repeal of *any* law that attempts to legislate morality or that discriminates against men on any ground whatever. If you want to solve the problem, set men free. In a free country, prejudice vanishes, and such prejudice as might remain does so only among the lunatic fringe or the kind of people who'd be afraid to admit it openly—and who cares to associate with them? Leave them to their bigotry. But when government power supports prejudice—when it enforces segregation or integration—then all you get is more racial prejudice, with each racial group growing closer together and further apart from every other (not only white against black). [FF 61]

Ecologists seek, through scientific means, to prevent people from suffering. For example, in Ireland in 1845, an ecologist argued that the potato famine must be approached scientifically. No one paid attention, and mass migration and the death of thousands resulted. Isn't there a scientific side to ecology that aims at improving human life?

Of course, science is valid. It is our only means of discovering how to survive. Technology is applied science. If someone discovered how to prevent potato blight, and could prove it, that's a scientific discovery. And he wouldn't be the first person whose knowledge was ignored or who was persecuted for it. Unfortunately, that's been the history of intellectual pioneers. But what's the relevance of this to ecology?

There would be nothing wrong with a science that studied the biological relationships of the earth as a whole: the interrelationships of species, the atmosphere, and all other physical and biological factors. It's an ambitious undertaking—and one that requires a totally different philosophy, because philosophy today objects to system building and the integration of knowledge. But when people accept a proper epistemology, this could be an important science.

Ecologists, however, predict universal doom and demand totalitarian power on the basis of arbitrary hypotheses, which sets back the possibility of such a science centuries. The ecology movement disgraces science. It is a political and publicity movement. Moreover, even if their predictions were correct, they'd have no right to impose their "wisdom" by force on the rest of mankind. Those who agreed with them would be saved; those who didn't would perish. But this is an absolute: no discovery, no concept, no fact can give any individual or group the power to enforce their conclusions on others. [FHF 70]

Economics

Did the downward trend in America's economy start with the organization of unions in the 1880s?

No. The downward trend was implicit in the beginning. The collectivist element in American society and the contradictions in the Constitution enabled the government to enlarge its power. The unions were an insignificant influence in American economic history until they received government support under the New Deal. Unions were not a threat so long as they were free. (Nor were they a great advantage to the working man.) They were merely voluntary institutions, and a worker had the right to organize or not, as each judged, individually and freely. When the government began to force men into unions, however, then unions became a threat. But that wasn't the workers' fault; they are victims too. Any institution that has force behind it—an industry supported by government, or a labor union—is a threat.

The crucial turning point in the descent of the American economy was the passing of antitrust laws. This ended the freedom of the American businessman. It is disgraceful to penalize the best industrialists under totally nonobjective laws. [PVA 61]

Should antitrust laws be applied to labor unions as well? Should unions be broken up into smaller unions under the power of antitrust?

No! Antitrust laws are so vicious and so nonobjective an injustice that one does not correct the injustice against businessmen by extending the same evil to another group of people. There are many conservatives who, instead of advocating the repeal of antitrust laws, try to solve the problem by victimizing labor unions the way businessmen are victimized, in the hope that this would equalize the bargaining position of business and labor. But nobody gains from those laws except bureaucrats and the government. The extension of antitrust to labor unions would *not* help business; it would merely help enslave a part of the population that is still relatively free. You cannot correct one injustice with another injustice.

Labor is often more philosophically alert on the issue of freedom than are businessmen—probably because labor leaders are still free to speak, whereas businessmen are not, owing to antitrust laws. Labor is a powerful force for freedom, in this sense: Labor is aware of government encroachment, as witness the opposition of George Meany to Secretary Goldberg's attempt to sacrifice both labor and management to the "public interest"—to dictate in labor negotiations what the public interest is. If you want to protect freedom, leave labor and every other group free. [APM 62]

Is gold-backed currency essential to a free-enterprise system and the preservation of freedom?

Yes. I won't give you a detailed treatise on money, but I'll indicate the essential issue. Gold has an objective material value—its value is not established by arbitrary decree. Gold was selected as the medium of exchange in most civilizations because it had an actual physical use and value; it was not a mere piece of paper. When currency is not backed by gold, then we are under the power of a government that arbitrarily sets the value of money, devaluates the currency, inflates credit, and taxes us indirectly through the manipulation of money (which is more disastrous than direct taxation). The government's power to destroy the objective value and security of currency is precisely what ultimately destroys the economy. The latest example is Kennedy's tax cut and simultaneous refusal to reduce government spending, thereby indulging in deficit spending. This will have disastrous consequences. Such a policy would be impossible if we had a gold-backed medium of exchange. [APM 63]

Why did the businessman not do more to protect himself against progressive infringements by the government?

A man's ideas and actions are not determined by his economic status, as the Marxists claim. The fact that someone is a businessman does not automatically give him the right ideas or show him what to do or where his interests lie. Being a businessman doesn't guarantee that one will do what is proper to protect business. In fact, businessmen are perhaps more guilty of self-destruction than any other group.

In a mixed economy, the greatest damage to any group is always imposed by that group itself, for the "special interests" in each group operate short range; each group contributes to granting the government more and more power. There were and are many businessmen, as there are men in every other group, who believe in pragmatic shortcuts—who run to Washington and sell out their futures for a momentary advantage.

Historically, many businessmen—though not the better ones—had an "interest" in encouraging antitrust legislation. And to this day, it is the alleged defenders of business who champion antitrust. The notion that antitrust law protects free competition is a widespread economic fallacy. Only within the past few years—and especially since the General Electric case—have businessmen begun to realize that antitrust laws do not benefit business.

Why didn't businessmen—or any other group—put up a better fight for their rights? I refer you to *Atlas Shrugged*. The enemy of capitalism is the altruist morality. So long as men are told that morality requires a person to sacrifice himself, capitalism cannot survive for long. You cannot have a happy, successful, prosperous society existing on a moral code that depends on and demands misery, self-sacrifice, self-renunciation. This conflict is destroying civilization. Businessmen, as the creators of material wealth, would necessarily be its first and greatest victims. [APM 63]

Is collective bargaining a right of labor in a free economy?

Yes, if it is *free* collective bargaining. If men want to organize into a union and bargain collectively with their employer, that is their right, provided they don't force anyone to join, or force their employer to negotiate with them. Today's labor legislation, however, is a violation of rights, because men are forced to join unions and employers are forced to negotiate with unions. [APM 63]

The economist Alan Greenspan became a friend of AR's in the mid-1950s.

What role will Alan Greenspan play in the Nixon administration?

As far as I know, Mr. Greenspan does not intend to go into politics. He is working for President Nixon as a "dollar-a-year man"—that is, as a volunteer. He has a business of his own, and is not contemplating a job in Washington. During the campaign, he was Nixon's top economic coordinator for domestic affairs. He is still acting as Nixon's economic advisor, and was recently appointed to act as Nixon's representative on the commission studying the budget that Johnson prepared. That is all I know of his plans. Of course, to have an Objectivist as economic advisor to a president, even temporarily, is a marvelous sign for the country and for President Nixon. [FHF 68]

How much do you think Alan Greenspan will be able to accomplish in his present role?

I don't know. Five years ago, he wouldn't have considered going to Washington. He's not interested in politics. He accepted the invitation because the situation is desperate, on the chance that he might persuade some honest people in Washington. Nobody can tell what any one person can do, particularly in politics. A single individual like Roark, against a board of private individuals, has a better chance of success, because if he disagrees with one board he can go to ten others or to individual clients. But in Washington today, I don't know whether intelligent and good men—and there are some, particularly in economics—can accomplish anything. The executive branch does not write the laws, Congress does. Congress is afraid of its constituents; so indirectly, it's up to public opinion. But to the extent that Greenspan might succeed in some area or in softening some disaster, he'll save us time and maybe our lives. I hope so. [FHF 74]

What do you think of the Austrian School of Economics?

I think they are a school that has a great deal of truth and proper arguments to offer about capitalism—especially von Mises—but I certainly don't agree with them in every detail, and particularly not in their alleged philosophical premises. They don't have any, actually. They attempt—von Mises particularly— to substitute economics for philosophy. That cannot be done. [FHF 77]

Have you seen Milton Friedman's program Free to Choose on public television?

I saw five minutes of it; that was enough for me, because I know Friedman's ideas. He is not for capitalism; he's a miserable eclectic. He's an enemy of Objectivism, and his objection is that I bring morality into economics, which he thinks should be amoral. I don't always like what public television puts on, but they have better programs than *Free to Choose*—the circus, for instance. [OC 80]

Certain economists predict an imminent and large-scale economic depression and possible world war. Could you comment on this prediction and their advice to move away from large cities to avoid riots and food shortages?

Anyone who makes such apocalyptic predictions is not being entirely honest. Nobody can predict such things. Before World War Two, I knew an intelligent woman who concluded that in case of a war the cities would starve. She had a house in the country, which she loved; but she thought it was too close to New York City, so she sold it and was miserable thereafter. She wasn't cowardly or ignorant; she was pessimistic. To plan your life on an unforeseeable disaster is foolish. If a nuclear war started, you might not survive no matter where you go—unless you live in a cave, and even then you can't be sure. Certain things you cannot prepare for.

It's a mistake always to project too much optimism—that is, to count on everything going well. You may be hurt that way. But it's just as bad (if not worse) always to prepare for the worst. That's when you'll bring disaster on yourself. Watch reality and act on the evidence, as far as you can predict. But don't talk about the apocalypse; it's useless. [OC 80]

Law, Crime, and Punishment

In a society with a proper government, is there a place for common law?

Common law is good in the way witchdoctors were once good: *some* of their discoveries were a primitive form of medicine, and to that extent achieved something. But once a science of medicine is established, you don't return to witchdoctors. Similarly, common law established—by tradition or inertia—some proper principles (and some dreadful ones). But once a civilization grasps the concept of law, and particularly of a constitution, common law becomes unnecessary and should not be regarded as law. In a free society, anyone can have customs; but that's not law. [FHF 72]

What is the justification of judicial decisions based on precedents?

The maintenance of a degree of continuity, and thus stability, among the country's laws. But once a bad precedent is set, or an indefensible law is introduced, it is moral—particularly for the Supreme Court—to repeal it. Judges are not omniscient. [FHF 73]

Do you have a solution to the problem of crime?

No. I am much too interested in crimes of a different kind and on a larger scale: philosophical crimes. In a sense, these crimes are behind the crimes that concern the police. They can be traced to the philosophy of a culture. But they are predominantly the choice of individuals. I am not a specialist on those crimes however—except for what I pick up from television. [FHF 67]

Patty Hearst was forced to act against her will. Should she be held criminally liable?

If she was given a loaded gun by alleged abductors, don't tell me they were coercing her. If she was coerced *and* they were insane enough to give her a loaded gun, then she could have found a way to get to a policeman. For instance, she could have pretended to faint and fallen down. She was not in an enemy camp but in a civilized society. If she had that chance to escape, don't tell me—unfortunately, you could tell the California jury—that she was compelled to act under duress. Further, if she were compelled, why did she plead the Fifth Amendment forty-two times? That alone proves what she is. [FHF 76]

If a man infringes the rights of another, what is the moral justification of incarceration as a punishment, as opposed to monetary retribution?

The moral justification for incarceration is that if a man has committed a crime and it's been proved, something of an unpleasant nature has to be done about it—something in the nature of a punishment. It is not society's duty to rehabilitate criminals—even if we knew how, which nobody knows, and I highly doubt whether it can be done. If a man permits himself to be a criminal, we treat him in the same manner that he demands. He wants to deal in force; we answer him by force, and put him in jail to protect the rest of us from the next time he feels like "expressing himself." [FHF 77]

Do you support capital punishment?

Yes and no, from two different perspectives. In principle, a man who has deliberately killed another human (that is, it's first-degree murder) should forfeit his life. Morally, he deserves it. The valid argument against capital punishment comes from the fact that humans, including juries, are fallible; mistakes can be made. It is moral to let ten guilty men go free rather than execute one inno-

cent man. That's a proper American principle—to place innocence above guilt. It's better to condemn murderers to jail for life
than risk taking the life of an innocent man through a possible
miscarriage of justice. So I'm against capital punishment on epistemological, not moral, grounds. Morally, the act of deliberately
taking another life is so monstrous that no one can atone for it. In
that sense, even death is too small a punishment. [FHF 71]

Political Activism

What political steps should be taken to achieve your goals?

I do not work for or advocate any new political party. It's much
too early for that. But since many of you are Republicans and interested in local politics, I'd say that politics must begin with an
idea. You cannot win elections with isolated slogans used once in
four years. If anything practical can be done, it is this: Work out a
consistent set of principles, and teach it to the people in your
party: precinct workers, local candidates, and perhaps national
candidates. Teach them the case for capitalism. Demand—morally,
proudly, unapologetically—a return to full capitalism.

This cannot be done overnight, so don't be crusaders in the impractical sense of demanding immediate change. But hold out that
goal to people. Instead of socialists promising people public support, hold out the promise of freedom, and proceed step-by-step
toward it. Formulate a policy of what controls should be repealed
first, and what steps could achieve a fully decontrolled economy.
But above all, base your program on a full knowledge of the history
of, and the case for, capitalism, and a full defense of capitalism
against the accusations and misconceptions preached by the left.

Begin in the high schools and colleges, because that is the
source of future politicians and men of action. You can achieve
nothing in a political election if you neglect the institutions where
ideas are formed. Make sure the educational institutions can teach
individualism and capitalism. You shouldn't aim for control of the
schools; you should support those in your schools who are good, as
the leftists support their advocates. Whereas liberals stand by any

liberal teacher or writer or columnist, conservatives do not do the same for their own. Conservatives do not show enough interest in ideas and ideological consistency. Develop that consistency. First convince yourself of the case for capitalism, then preach ideology.

Learn to defend your case so that no liberal could answer it. If you compare the state of West Germany to East Germany, you have an object lesson right there—if you know how to present and analyze it. Don't apologize for capitalism. Don't allow it to be denounced as a system of selfish greed. But you cannot do any of this so long as you simultaneously pay lip service to altruism. Learn the morality implied in the Declaration of Independence, a document that today isn't quoted enough nor sufficiently understood. The Objectivist ethics is merely the philosophically-worked-out proof of what the Founding Fathers implied in the Declaration.

If you do all of this, you could save the world without the loss of a single American life, because all the totalitarian monsters would collapse. The battle is moral and philosophical. Do not believe in Russia's power; do not believe their threats. They would run, as they twice ran in their war with Finland. Russia is winning strictly by default. The only way to stop her is with a proper anti-altruist, American morality. [PVA 61]

Is it possible to change the direction of mankind without first experiencing disaster?

Yes. England, at the time of the American Revolution, was moving in the direction of absolute monarchy. The influence of the American Revolution, and of the United States thereafter, led in England to one of the freest and greatest periods in their history—to a revival of freedom and capitalism. England was the freest country in Europe. But by the end of the nineteenth century, England was losing her traditional liberties. What destroyed her? The liberal philosophers.

So long as a country is not yet under a dictatorship, the culture can be turned around peacefully, particularly in a country like the United States, which is based on the ideas of freedom. It would be harder in Europe, where they are traditionally statist—their basic subconscious values are statist—and freedom is an exception. In America, people bear too much—too innocently and too naively—but I don't think a dictatorship could take hold. Beneath all their errors, the Americans' basic premise is freedom. That is the unspoken emotion—the sense-of-life atmosphere. Traditionally and historically, the American people can be pushed just so far, and then they stop it.

Once a country accepts censorship of the press and of speech, then nothing can be won without violence. Therefore, so long as you have free speech, protect it. This is the life-and-death issue in this country: do not give up the freedom of the press—of newspapers, books, magazines, television, radios, movies, and every other form of presenting ideas. So long as that's free, a peaceful intellectual turn is possible. [PVA 61]

Do you think a laissez-faire capitalist society is possible for America in the 1960s? If so, how could it be implemented?

The questioner doesn't make clear whether he is asking (1) Can we achieve a fully capitalist society in the 1960s? or (2) Given the present state of our culture, can we still hope to achieve capitalism? He probably meant the latter, but I'll briefly answer both, starting with the second.

To ask "Are we too far gone to return to a proper and rational society?" is like asking of a man dangerously, but not hopelessly, ill: "Should we do anything, or just let him die?" So long as men are alive, it is never too late to take the right action or adopt the right policies. And laissez-faire capitalism is the only system under which man can live properly. So long as men are not living in a dictatorship, they can advocate and begin planning for capitalism at any time. Under a dictatorship, all one can do is escape or overthrow the regime. But so long as we are in a semi-free society, it is not too late to advocate the right political system. Therefore, it is not too late for us. But whether we can establish it in the 1960s is a question nobody can answer. Nobody can establish a perfect system overnight. If we decided today to have a proper capitalist society, it would still take a long time, and nobody could predict how quickly a society would accept the idea. So such predictions are impossible, and in fact irrelevant. My *guess* is that we could establish full capitalism in the 1960s if enough people chose to think about what they are doing.

How could we achieve this? Every change in practical politics has been preceded by a cultural change—that is, a change in the philosophy dominating the culture. Therefore, as a practical matter, one must concentrate on the culture—on spreading the philosophy that makes it possible for an enlightened society to adopt laissez-faire capitalism. [APM 62]

If you were elected president of the United States tomorrow, what changes would you institute?

This is the last thing I'd attempt or advise anyone to try. But to the hypothetical question "What would I advocate if my advice were immediately put into effect?," I'd answer: Start decontrolling the economy as fast as rational economic considerations permit. I speak of "rational economic considerations" because today, every part of the population is dependent on government controls. Most professions have to function under controls, and their activities are calculated on that basis. So if anyone were to repeal all controls overnight, by legislative fiat, that would be a disastrous, arbitrary, dictatorial action. What a free country needs is to give all the people concerned sufficient notice to readjust and reorganize their economic activities. Therefore, after working out with economists the kind of program necessary to decontrol the country, and what controls should be repealed first, I would then advise passing legislation announcing that certain controls will be abolished within three years, say—the period calculated to allow people the opportunity to readjust their activities. In a free economy, no change happens out of the blue and overnight. Every economic change, every development, is gradual. Therefore, in a free society, there are no immediate and disastrous changes. But given our present situation, any sudden changes could create disastrous dislocations, and so we should decontrol gradually.

The particular legislation I'd advocate removing first would be the antitrust laws. These have contributed the most to the destruction of free enterprise. And the first antitrust laws to go—and they should go overnight—are the jail penalty provisions. Stop sending men to jail for undefined offenses that they have no way of avoiding. Once you remove the cancer of antitrust legislation, the others become easier to remove. Once you free the most essential and productive group of our society—namely, the businessmen—many of our economic problems will vanish. One would probably have to combine such decontrol with a tax-reduction law, otherwise you would be leaving society in an unbalanced condition: large companies have an advantage over competitors who never had a chance to rise because their earnings were undercut by taxes to such an extent that they could not compete with big companies who were established before today's tax rates went into effect. (I say this tentatively.) [APM 62]

Is it possible at present for the government to proceed with a program completely based on your ideas?

No—not this month, not this year, and maybe not this century. The best the government can do is stop moving toward dictatorship and collectivism, and start moving toward freedom. The way to do this is simple: decontrol. Instead of imposing new controls, try removing a few crucial ones in the areas of the economy. When the time is right, then announce that within five years, say, all government subsidies, handouts, welfare payments, and so on will be abolished. Give people enough time to make other arrangements, because today everyone's livelihood is helplessly tied to the government. But start removing those chains. [FHF 71]

Is it important to be politically involved? If so, how should we go about changing our politics and our politicians?

First, I don't think it's important to be politically active today. But it is crucially important to vote. Whenever two candidates are more or less the same, there's no obligation to vote if you can't make up your mind. But in an election like this one [Nixon vs.

McGovern], it is so clear-cut that if you want to preserve your rights, you should vote.

Next, how do I propose to change our politicians? I don't. So long as the country is even semi-free, politicians are not the determining factor. They are what public opinion makes them (or what they think public opinion wants). Therefore, before one can engage in politics, one should engage in educational work. We need an educational campaign aimed at spreading a new philosophy, to make people understand what are individual rights and why altruism is wrong. If you understand your ideas, try to spread them to as many people as possible. That is how public opinion changes, and that will change politicians. Since the cause of our problems is the universities, if you want to reform any one institution, start there, because philosophy determines a culture and thus the direction of a country, and philosophy is the specialty of the universities. If you want a crusade, start with the universities. [FHF 72]

What chance does the country have?

That depends on you, me, and the public in general. People have free will; we may have a good chance or none at all. Nobody can guess. [FHF 74]

You've argued that government spending must be curbed. What tactics should we adopt to bring this about?

There's only so much one person can do. I've given you the strategy; don't expect me to mount the barricades and lead an army on Washington. Besides, it's much too soon for that. What can you do? If everyone in this room seriously understood the problem, advocated the right measures, spoke to his neighbors, and above all, wrote to his congressman and senators, you could save the country. People in Washington take their mail seriously; they count noses. You must drown them in mail before they'll listen to you. But if you can state your case simply, briefly, and intelligently, you'll have a huge influence. That's the only action I can suggest today, because the only action I recommend is intellectual action. [FHF 74]

Is there someone in politics today about whom you are enthusiastic?

No. I wish there were. In today's cultural atmosphere, the better people—the true intellectuals—wouldn't go into politics; not yet. The battle—which is in the colleges—must first be won, and the foundation laid, outside of politics. [FHF 76]

Is it now time for an Objectivist politician?

It certainly is not. To whom would he speak? One cannot run an educational campaign and a political campaign simultaneously. In fifty years, it might be time for an Objectivist politician; but by the time it's possible, he practically wouldn't be necessary. The country's public opinion would continue in the direction of freedom and reason. Therefore, Objectivists should go to the classroom, and correct the situation there. [PO12 76]

Will the Republican Party have a role in defending capitalism?

I doubt it, but that's all we have. The alternatives to the Republican Party are totally unspeakable. If you're thinking of the Conservative Party or the Libertarian Party, I'd say join the Communist Party, you'd be cleaner intellectually. The more these parties make themselves heard, the more they disgrace capitalism. [On AR's rejection of libertarianism and the Libertarian Party, see below, pp. 72–74.]

The Conservative Party is not an American political party, but a religious party—a phenomenon forbidden by the Constitution. You're free to have any religion you wish; you're forbidden to bring it into politics—that is, to establish it by force. The one good result of the 1976 elections is that Moynihan defeated Buckley. Moynihan is not so great, but he got that conservative out of the Senate. You can trust the conservatives to raise the issue of abortion. What they've made of it is a shameful disgrace in the twentieth century. It's a move back to the Dark Ages, where the Catholic Church wants us to be, politically.

What we can do is infiltrate the Republican Party, and try to influence them in the right direction: toward capitalism and away from conservatism. Defend capitalism against religion, which is what destroyed capitalism in the first place. [PO7 76]

Is a major revolution necessary to solve our country's problems, or is the solution to be found piecemeal?

Neither. The major revolution happened in 1776. You don't stage a revolution against a country still following its basic principles. But neither is the solution to fight piecemeal. The only way to fight for a cause is intellectually—that is, philosophically, which is to say in terms of fundamental principles. When you fight in this way, it's as if you're an intellectual wholesaler rather than a retailer. You cover a whole field by means of appropriate principles, instead of fighting piecemeal, which is what activists today are trying—and they're failing. [FHF 78]

What do you recommend as political activity?

There certainly is no party you can fully support. None have consistent platforms. If you want to do something non-philosophically—more range-of-the-moment—then find a good candidate, if you can (probably a Republican, but not necessarily) and volunteer to work in his campaign. But do not go for third parties. They're all power-lusting cranks—they want to hold the balance of power and name the major party candidates. That's true of the Liberal Party and the Conservative Party in New York, and of this new horror, the Anti-Abortion Party. Don't touch those.

If you support one of the major parties, their vagueness protects you. You aren't necessarily committed to any vicious ideas; their platforms are so contradictory that you can support one part and nobody could accuse you of betraying your ideals. But if you go for one of those new third parties, you accept the most dreadful ideas, put out to delude volunteers and the public. Fortunately, these parties are not successful. The American public is very wise. Further, to work for contradictions is the worst thing you could do for the country today. We've had enough contradictions; to spread some more and confuse people more is not good. So vote Republican, if you can.

I'm not sure I'll vote for president this year. It's too early to tell. But as propaganda, let me say: *I will not vote for Ronald Reagan.* Nor will I vote for [Texas governor John] Connally or [Illinois congressman Phil] Crane. (I don't know about George Bush. Nobody quite knows what he stands for.) They're so taken over by the religionists. Reagan, the alleged champion of capitalism, had the nerve to advocate a constitutional amendment forbidding abortion. The others were not so brazen; they didn't want to destroy the Constitution. Bush said that he disapproves of abortion personally but doesn't want to monkey with the Constitution. That's to his credit.

I regard abortion as the most important issue, because the anti-abortionists have such evil motives. They have no interest in human beings, only in embryos; they want to tie down a family to animal reproduction. If you're conscientious, you cannot bring children into the world without giving them priority. This means, particularly if you're not rich, that you can't have any ambition or personal life. You are tied to the cruelest kind of drudgery. That's what a creature like Reagan—a cheap Hollywood actor who has sat on every fence—wants: the right to dictate to young people what they can do with their lives; whether they will have a chance at a career or be breeding animals. I cannot communicate how despicable that is. So, if I have any influence on you at all, think it over. But if you want to do me a favor, don't vote for Reagan. [OC 80]

In **We the Living** *and* **Atlas Shrugged,** *you give your heroes ideal solutions to the problems of socialism and communism. In* **We the Living,** *they die—either mentally, emotionally, or physically. In* **Atlas Shrugged,** *they leave society and start over, and need not face the evils of the world. How should we, who have to deal with these evils, go about creating a capitalist society?*

To follow your example, read *The Fountainhead*, in which the hero deals with society as it is today. But also question your assumptions: the heroes dying in *We the Living* is not "an ideal solution." In *We the Living*, this "ideal solution" (to use your expression) shows that the better kind of people—the people with integrity and independence—cannot survive under dictatorship, and will perish, either spiritually or physically. The characters in *We the Living* had to die, since my theme was to show the essence of a dictatorship. Anyone who escapes from a dictatorship is an exception. Given the nature of a dictatorship, the extent to which men have moral character is the extent to which they are doomed.

In *Atlas Shrugged*, I do show how to deal with collectivism. But take things literally only when they apply literally. What do I mean? In *Atlas Shrugged*, I show the men of intelligence and ability go on strike against collectivist slavery, the world left without them perishes, and the men of the mind are free to start rebuilding the world. Now, the state of collectivism we have reached today is not yet as bad as what I present in *Atlas Shrugged*. I intended *Atlas Shrugged* to present the society of about ten years "ahead," in terms of collectivism, than the time at which you read the book. It's the immediate future—the next consistent step—*if* the present collectivist trends continue. But there is no historical determinism; these trends need not continue. So long as there isn't censorship, one doesn't have to leave a society the way the characters did in *Atlas Shrugged*.

One does not yet have to break relationships with society. But what one must do is break relationships with the culture: Withdraw your sanction from those people, groups, schools, or theories that preach the ideas that are destroying you. In *Atlas Shrugged* I describe the sanction of the victim—when the good people help their own destroyers—and show in how many ways men are guilty of it, through generosity or ignorance. Anyone serious about saving the world today must first discard the dominant philosophy of the culture. Stand on your own as much as if you moved to a separate valley, like in *Atlas Shrugged*. Check your premises; define your convictions rationally. Do not take anything on faith; do not believe that your elders know what they're doing, because they don't. That's the sense in which *Atlas Shrugged* is applicable to our period. We are not yet totally collectivized; we have a chance. More than that, the enemy ideologies today—collectivism and altruism—are so bankrupt that nothing holds them up except inertia and default.

Innovators in the realm of ideas—and especially in moral philosophy—are very rare. Observe that in the history of philosophy, all ideas change in various periods, but morality is the one realm that did not change (except in superficial forms). Men have always been taught that they must live for others—that they must be sacrificial animals—and that the alternative would be some kind of dog-eat-dog existence. And in practice, dog-eat-dog *is* applicable to socialism and collectivism. In other words, morality is the one area in which men are afraid to challenge the culture, and that is what you must challenge. Break with the morality of altruism. Don't be afraid to assert your right to exist. Justify rationally why you have a right to your life, and why when men practice the morality of self-interest their interests don't clash.

America came close to this at the end of the nineteenth century. You wouldn't believe some of the popular literature from that period. They are the realistic stories of that period. I refer specifically to magazines and popular fiction, which is a good index of the sense of life of a culture. You do not know what a magnificent world America was. Now it isn't fully gone, and it's in your power to build it again. Break with altruism and with every idea based on it. At least make the effort to think about altruism carefully. You'll have to think harder than you've ever done before, because you will be on your own—relying on your own judgment and the logic of the arguments you hear or consider, rejecting all authorities and all bromides, and taking nothing on faith. If you try, you'll be surprised how close the Renaissance is. It's up to each human being to work for it. [FF 61]

You've said it would be proper to revolt if the government established censorship. Has that time come?

Fortunately, not yet, or I couldn't be giving this speech and you couldn't be listening to it. Censorship operates as it did in Nazi Germany and does in Soviet Russia. It's total government-enforced uniformity of opinion, ultimately under penalty of death. We haven't reached that point, and I don't think the government will get away with it here, at least not yet. Even in Russia (where I witnessed the process), after the Communists seized power, they didn't establish total censorship immediately. It took years of gradual steps, each one a trial balloon. They got away with it through smaller encroachments, until they established total censorship. They won't get away with it here, because the basic premises of the American people are still pro-freedom. But basic premises alone won't do any good. We must be aware of the advance of censorship. And if the government begins wholesale suppression, then it's proper to revolt. [FHF 73]

Could you comment on the ineptness of political advisors in America? Is it the result of stupidity or malice?

Stupidity, of course. You're flattering them if you think it's malice. They don't know any better, which isn't a crime. What is a crime is that they don't *want* to know any better. After all, people in politics are only the last result of the educational and cultural trends in a country. They aren't the cause of anything. They are cashing in on what they've been told, which is exclusively collectivism and statism. They see that it doesn't work, but they're unable to think of what could work. They can't return to capitalism; nobody told them to. [FHF 78]

Conservatism

Wendell Wilkie

I understand that you enthusiastically supported Wendell Wilkie when he was a presidential candidate running against Franklin Roosevelt [in 1940]. Given your present hostility to politicians, is there anyone on the horizon who commands your support?

This is an improper question. "Hostility" is a psychological term; it refers to hatred. I don't hate politicians. Unfortunately, I am forced to despise most of them. Since the impropriety may be unintentional, I'll answer the question.

I don't despise everyone in politics. Today, most politicians are mixed cases. I am opposed to mixtures, so I can't be enthusiastic about anyone in politics today. It will take some time and a different cultural trend for a proper man of stature to appear on the political scene. I have no one in mind.

The Wilkie campaign is an example of learning from one's mistakes. It wasn't a mistake to support him as he appeared; but a few months after his defeat, he announced that all his statements (the ones I liked) were mere campaign oratory. After that, one does not get enthusiastic about candidates. [FHF 69]

Barry Goldwater

What do you think about Senator Goldwater's conservatism?

Regretfully, he's mixed—just like his economics. I'm watching Senator Goldwater with great interest and great misgivings. He seems to be the most promising candidate on the right, though there are flaws in what he advocates.

I agree with him almost completely about foreign policy. Here, he's been magnificent. But I disagree with his domestic policy. He advocates a mixed economy, though he's for fewer controls than the other Republican candidates. But we can't merely go back to a stage of fewer controls. That's impossible historically and futile practically. It's like saying "I do not want to remove the cancer, I want to return to an earlier stage of it." That can't arouse any philosophical or moral enthusiasm. We either have freedom or— by gradual steps—we descend into dictatorship. I disagree with Senator Goldwater because he does not advocate a fully free economy. Perhaps a politician cannot do so today. A politician is a man of action; he cannot fight an ideological battle and thus cannot educate the country about capitalism. The job of spreading ideas belongs to the intellectuals.

But above all, I disagree with his constant references to religion or tradition as the basis of free enterprise. That will not win him converts, and should not, because religion should be a private matter. The mixture of religion and politics is very ancient and very dangerous. This is why I am worried, to say the least, about the future of Senator Goldwater. [PVA 61]

Could Senator Goldwater come to think as you do?

How could I answer that? You have to ask him. I'd never predict the convictions of another person. [PVA 61]

Is it possible that Senator Goldwater is not speaking and writing as frankly as he'd like to?

I can't discuss that. It's pure speculation. We must take a writer at his word, not guess at what he wanted to say or will think in the future. [PVA 61]

Richard Nixon

Is the economy so bad that Nixon cannot possibly avoid economic disaster?

I couldn't say. The situation is such that an economic disaster could occur at any moment, and we'll certainly have economic trouble. But nobody could say with certainty that disaster is unavoidable. Incidentally, if a recession or depression occurs during the Nixon administration, do not blame the Republicans. Each administration inherits a certain burden and must untangle the consequences of the preceding one. If economic disaster does occur, we'll be lucky Hubert Humphrey is not in Washington. [FHF 68]

What's your opinion of the Nixon administration in general, and Spiro Agnew in particular?

I didn't expect much from Nixon; I was still disappointed. I could criticize Agnew, but with reservations, because he's the victim of the most vicious smear campaign I've ever witnessed. My criticism of him is the opposite of the liberals'. I was in the same predicament in the case of Joseph McCarthy, who is still being smeared. McCarthy was not philosophical enough to undertake the battle he attempted. The same is true of Agnew. What he's doing is fine, up to a point, on the concrete level; only he has no philosophical base. Therefore, he is tragically sticking his neck out. He won't accomplish much. But for the moment, it's wonderful to hear somebody saying something that is not mealymouthed, apologetic, and middle-of-the-road. [FHF 70]

Given your displeasure with Nixon, will you support him in the 1972 election?

I endorsed Nixon in 1968, not very enthusiastically, on the premise that he was the lesser of two evils. But I no longer think I can vote for him. [Given her disgust with the 1972 Democratic candidate, George McGovern, AR did support Nixon in that election.] That would be letting him get away with being a turncoat. If a man changes his mind for some reason, rightly or wrongly, you can still have some respect for him. But study Nixon's speeches: each one plays both sides. He'll throw some slogans at those who are pro-freedom, and then throw a few to the welfare-statists. That cannot be done innocently—except that *he* thinks this is patriotism. Pragmatism taught him that. (There are two people who might be worse than Nixon: George Wallace of Alabama and New York mayor Lindsay, because Lindsay is a turncoat as well.)

Today's situation proves what I've been saying for years: a country's practical politics do not determine its fate. A president cannot reeducate a country. Today, the government is a machine without a driver. It's driven by pressure-group conflict. Salvation can come only from education—from ideas, the universities, the intellectuals. Politicians can't do it. I hope we'll never have—and it's a credit to this country that we haven't had—a Führer appear to take advantage of this chaos. Nixon is obviously not a Führer; he's a mediocrity. So are all the other prospects. Therefore, we still have time.

What can you do? *Speak*—anywhere, to anyone, in any form you can. Don't force your views on unwilling listeners—don't be evangelists out to save souls. But people are so confused today that if you clarify even one point for them, in your own circle—in a letter to an editor, a school paper, and so forth—you help make public opinion. This helps people who are less brave or more ignorant, and puts the fear of God in the politicians (who need it). [FHF 71]

What is your opinion of Nixon's present foreign policy?

What is his foreign policy? It's just as inconsistent as his domestic policy. I almost hoped that Nixon's recognition of China was his play against Soviet Russia, but it wasn't. After his disgraceful performance at the UN, I'd say an office boy from Monaco could defeat Nixon in negotiations, let alone the Chinese Communists. [FHF 71]

Since Nixon and McGovern both contradict themselves, how can one determine who is better?

In a mixed economy, you'll never get a fully consistent candidate. All one can do is consider the total of a politician's speeches, policies, and actions, determine his basic principles, and then hope for the best. Nixon is not very consistent, but at least he's never attempted to redistribute your wealth. He's not a power luster. Nixon's wage and price controls were vicious, but he wasn't asking for personal power and doesn't want to control your personal life. But look at one close-up of McGovern, and you know he's after power. He claims the right to prescribe how much money a man should make, and to keep everything else. His proposal of $12,000 a year is monstrous—it's worse than communism. (See "A Preview," in *The Ayn Rand Letter*, vol. 1, no. 22–24, July–August 1972.) [FHF 72]

Do you stand by your statement, made at your last appearance at the Forum [1972], that the Nixon administration is not the most corrupt in our country's history?

I stand by it. Moreover, even though Nixon's behavior has been contemptible—he's not the most corrupt president, but he's probably the most contemptible—I'd still vote for him over George McGovern or Ted Kennedy. [FHF 73]

Religious conservatives

We are told that religion is our best protection against communism. Why do you say we should keep religion out of politics?

For the same reasons the Founding Fathers gave. Religion is a private matter. There are many different religions. The difference between religion and philosophy is that religion is a matter of faith. You either have faith or you don't. You cannot argue about it. But when you deal with philosophy, you deal with reason and logic. That is an objective element of language common to all men. You can try to persuade others that you are right, or you are free to disagree with them. In a free country, you need not deal with them. But religion is an issue of faith. By definition, if one doesn't accept faith, or if different people believe different faiths, no common action, agreement, or persuasion is possible among them if religion is made a condition of political agreement. If religion is brought into the running of the state, or the ideology on which the state is based, then the first question is: Whose religion? Then we return to a church-and-state union, where no compromise and no agreement between men is possible, since each religion claims its own belief and its own authority, not by means of arguments and reason but by faith. That is why the Founding Fathers were very wise when they separated church and state.

Before that time, Europe was constantly torn by religious wars. Catholics and Protestants in different countries had the power of the state behind them, and men were constantly trying to force their beliefs on others. With the American separation of church and state, all religions could live together peacefully, because each man is free to hold his own beliefs but cannot force them on others.

Persuasion, reason, argument are not the province of religion. Religion rests on faith—on an acceptance of certain beliefs apart from reason. This is why it must be private. When it's a private matter, it's fine—it can even be a kind of inspiration to people. Faith is what each man may choose for himself, if he wishes. I don't. [PVA 61]

If religion is instrumental in spreading altruism, can we fight altruism in America without fighting religion?

In America, religion is relatively nonmystical. Religious teachers here are predominantly good, healthy materialists. They follow common sense. They would not stand in our way. The majority of religious people in this country do not accept on faith the idea of jumping into a cannibal's pot and giving away their last shirt to the backward people of the world. Many religious leaders preach this today, because of their own leftist politics; it's not inherent in being religious. There are many historical and philosophical connections between altruism and religion, but the function of religion in this country is not altruism. You would not find too much opposition to Objectivism among religious Americans. There are rational religious people. In fact, I was pleased and astonished to discover that some religious people support Objectivism. If you want to be a full Objectivist, you cannot reconcile that with religion; but that doesn't mean religious people cannot be individualists and fight for freedom. They can, and this country is the best proof of it.

Of course, one should not forbid religion. Today's culture is such that the moment you oppose something, people believe you want to forbid it by law. If we did that, we'd return to the Dark Ages. Leave people the right to be wrong in their own way. So long as they don't force their ideas on you, you cannot forbid religion to anyone. Further, it's not difficult to fight religion when you have a good philosophy.

In America, you would not find it difficult to divorce religion from altruism. After all, Christ said: "Love your neighbor as yourself." So you must love yourself. After that, you can argue about your neighbors. [PVA 61]

Other than atheism and religion, what differences do you have with conservatives like William Buckley?

It would be simpler to ask what similarities there are: none. Reason versus mysticism is so fundamental a difference that politics is unimportant in that context. The first issue is reason versus irrationality—and religion and mysticism are irrational. Next comes morality, and then politics. Buckley and the conservatives advocate an organized religion very interested in politics—that is, a theocracy: a society ruled by religious functionaries, as in ancient Egypt and the Middle Ages. This is one of the most primitive types of society. Religious conservatives hold that man is a low-grade helpless sinner and worm, that life on Earth is a den of iniquity or vale of tears, that man must not aspire to solve his problems by using his mind. This last is the accusation these types leveled against nineteenth-century liberals: they called it the arrogance of reason. Catholic conservatives like Buckley claim we should act on faith and bow to the Pope— the same Pope [Paul VI] who declared [in his encyclical *Populorum Progressio*—on which, see AR's "Requiem for Man," in *Capitalism: The Unknown Ideal*] that capitalism is worse than Marxism, and that the only morality is altruism. What is there in common between them and me? [FHF 72]

What is your opinion of Alexander Solzhenitsyn?

I regard him ideologically as lower than the rulers of Russia. He is the worst public caricature of a monster that has emerged in this age, which displays an awful lot of public caricatures and unappetizing characters. Before you speak of Solzhenitsyn or ask anything about him, please read the letter that he sent to the Soviet authorities shortly before he was deported. Read that letter. It has been published; it has been translated. I read it in the original Russian. In it, that man proclaims, in effect, that he is a totalitarian collectivist. He says so openly—only not in those words. He is merely against Marxism. He wants Russia to remain a dictatorship, but a dictatorship run by the Russian Church. He wants Russian religion, the Greek Orthodox Church, to be a substitute for Marxism. In other words, he wants to take Russia back to the stage before Peter the Great, to the seventeenth century or earlier. He is anti-industrial and wants to take Russia back to being an agrarian country. And that horrible, pretentious person is held as some kind of hero of liberation. He doesn't want to free the world. He is denouncing the West; he is denouncing Western civilization. He is that ancient, chauvinistic aberration: a Slavophile. He says, in that letter of his, that he wants the Russian government—the Communist Party—to keep all its economic and political power; he lists specifically the power over production, trade, and distribution, over foreign relationships, over the army. All he wants is that the government allow people to speak and write freely. Now remember, he's a writer.

And in the conclusion of this unspeakable document, he says the following (I am quoting from memory): I want nothing for myself, I am sure that you, the rulers, have never seen and cannot imagine a man who is not asking something for himself—well here I am, please look at me. Is this a "selfless" person? Or is this an example of the worst kind of conventional "selfishness" and vanity? Well, that's as much of a motive as any religious mystic-altruist would ever project. That's all that his disinterested "selflessness" means: give me freedom to write, and all the other human activities and professions can be enslaved, I'm quite willing to put up with it. With ideas of that kind, to come here and posture as a prophet of freedom is really adding insult to injury. Sure, what Solzhenitsyn wrote about the Soviet concentration camps is true. Better people have said it before. We should consider them, not a man who is philosophically the exact opposite of everything the West stands for or should stand for—a man who is a profound enemy of individualism and of reason. That's my opinion of Mr. Solzhenitsyn.

Finally, I should like to quote a remark with which I agree, but whose authorship, unfortunately, I do not know: "The enemy of our enemy is not necessarily our friend." [FHF 76]

The 1976 campaigns and elections

If elected to the U.S. Senate, Daniel Patrick Moynihan will vote for national health insurance, the federalization of welfare, national economic planning, and so on. Senator James Buckley will vote against them. Granted that Buckley's philosophical base is odious and destructive, what practical, real-world impact could his philosophy have that would justify giving practical, real-world support to liberal policies by voting for Moynihan?

The form of this question is not accidental. The questioner is obviously a Buckley supporter who believes philosophy has nothing to do with "the real world." And this is true: Buckley's philosophy has nothing to do with "the real world" or practical life. It's in another dimension, and more than any other mystical philosophy today, it's on the rampage and anxious to take over the world. But philosophy is a practical matter; it affects our lives, our future, our country's existence. The little journalistic issues the questioner names will have little or no effect. What determines the effect such issues have on the country's future is the philosophy of the voters and of the people they elect.

I'll use the questioner's method, which was to list what Buckley will vote against. Well, national health insurance, the federalization of welfare, and national economic planning are pretty bad, though the only truly dangerous one is national economic planning. But let's take a look at Buckley's record. He is against abortion, and anyone who denies the right to abortion cannot be a defender of rights. Period. Further, the gratuitous, for-no-vested-interest attitude behind this policy should lead you to ask: What do antiabortion advocates really have in mind? Obviously, what they intend is to enslave every human alive enough to have some kind of sexual life—to enslave him to procreate like the lowest farm animal, only lower, because breeders of farm animals at least take care of them. But people like Buckley want to take young people in love and make them slaves to involuntary procreation, without telling them what to do with their offspring. They tell people to create families of twelve or more children, but how are the children going to be supported? On welfare, probably, though Buckley probably wouldn't support that. He would probably agree with the Pope, who declared in his encyclical *Populorum Progressio* that we must reorganize the world so that everybody will be taken care of somehow. But who specifically will take care of those unwanted children? And what will become of the young parents—of their lives, their ambitions, their future—if they must be held down to procreation? This is so unspeakably cruel that on the abortion issue alone one should turn against Buckley.

Now, in the presidential race—just so you don't think I'm evading—I am shamefully aware that President Ford compromised on this issue. Still, we have no choice. Mr. What's-His-Name—Carter (I'm sorry, that wasn't intentional)—isn't better. He is so dangerous a power luster that one can only *hope* Ford will not carry out his mixed attitude on abortion. (It's mixed because he says he recognizes the right of states to pass laws on abortion; but he is wrong: the right to abortion is in fact a fundamental constitutional right.) But Buckley is not mixed on this issue.

Further, Buckley is pro-ecology. He wants to preserve nature. Strangely enough, the basic premise of the ecology lovers has something fundamentally in common with that of people against abortion. It's the issue of holding people down and tying them to physical labor. The ecology movement wants to eliminate industry and labor-saving devices, and if the standard of living declines, that's too bad—we must preserve nature. Anyone who is against industry is against man, against life, against reason.

Now these are merely two of Buckley's sins, and they are both worse than anything Moynihan would do. But there's a deeper issue here. Religious conservatives want to destroy the two-party system in America by destroying the Republican Party. The Republican Party, like all "defenders" of free enterprise in the world today, is busy committing suicide. They are their own worst destroyers, precisely because they don't know what to do in "the real world," since they have no philosophy to guide them. The conservatives have decided to be Trojan horses the way the communists were against the Democratic Party in the thirties and early forties. The communists didn't succeed: there are some pretty bad left-liberal Democrats, but they're far from being communist. The conservatives, however, seriously want to take over the Republican Party, as their disgraceful attempt to nominate Ronald Reagan shows. There were reports from conservative authorities openly claiming they wanted to destroy the Republican Party if Reagan wasn't nominated. Let the party collapse, and then the G.D. conservatives would take it over. Then we'd just have liberals and conservatives, which means liberals and fascists, because the religious conservatives are pure fascists. They are not for free enterprise; they want controls—spiritual, moral, and intellectual controls. They might leave you some freedom to work for a while; what they want to cut is intellectual freedom. Many of them actually advocate censorship. They want to ban dirty movies. But bad as these movies are, you better leave them free, because with the help of conservatives, you'll have serious censorship over literature and movies.

There's another consideration. Moynihan is a liberal and a Democrat. If you're pro-capitalist, the Republican Party (minus the religious conservatives) is more hopeful. Now if Moynihan votes improperly or makes a mess of things, he disgraces the opposition. If Buckley does something wrong, *he is disgracing capitalism.* Therefore, "an ally" who comes close to you, but from opposite premises, is much more dangerous than a mild enemy. I would vote for a liberal over Buckley any time.

Moynihan is good on foreign policy. He's outspoken and daring. The worst you can say about him is he's a modern liberal. Well, there's an awful lot of them, and he's not even a leftist liberal. The leftists apparently don't like him, which is in his favor. But Buckley is the Trojan horse out to destroy any hope this country ever had of a return to capitalism. Therefore, I'm not voting *for* Moynihan but *against* Buckley. We've got to get him out of Washington. Now I could not have voted for Bella Abzug. If she were running against Buckley, I wouldn't vote at all. But Moynihan is semi-decent, and so much better than Buckley that it's precisely in "the real world" where you must look long range (that is, philosophically) and get that conservative out. He got in by a fluke; get him out by the only means you have: the ballot. So please, in the name of philosophy in the real world—not the philosophy of religion and the hereafter—vote Buckley out. [PO5 76]

If the 1976 presidential election were between Carter and Reagan, would you support Carter, on the basis of Reagan's antiabortion stance?

No, I would not vote. You should vote only so long as you think a candidate has more virtues than flaws. But if you regard both candidates as evil, do not choose a lesser evil. Simply don't vote. For instance, I abstained in 1952 and 1956; I didn't vote for Eisenhower or Stevenson.

Despite everything you hear to the contrary, abstaining—particularly by people who understand the issues—is a form of voting. You're choosing "none of the above." I could not vote for either Reagan or Carter. Mr. Ford's stand on abortion is a disgrace, though he has some redeeming qualities. But my tolerance is badly strained right now. Still, you have to vote for Ford because the opposition is hopeless. [PO6 76]

Could you comment on the 1976 presidential election? Why did Ford lose? What do you expect from Carter?

Ford lost because he didn't say anything. The Ford campaign was devoid of ideological content. Carter raised the issues of trust and competence—and that's all Ford talked about: his own competence, experience, and trustworthiness. The grotesque result was that in the exit polls, a majority of voters said they trusted Ford more and believed he was better experienced and more competent. But more voters believed Carter could solve economic problems, particularly inflation and unemployment. Carter won on economic issues.

Ford, who made remarkable progress in curing the worst economic problem—inflation—never spoke about it intellectually. He never made clear why he opposed government controls and spending. He merely said, "We're on our way to lick inflation," and the like. He lost because he didn't fight on issues. I don't think it was his fault but the fault of his Republican campaign advisors. That evil seems inherent in the Republican Party: they will fight about anything but ideas.

As for Carter's victory: The next four years will probably be hell, and I dread to think in what form. I've heard people say, "I'm glad to be old," and I join them in feeling it. I'm glad I won't have to see too much of the kind of world Carter will make. But you are young enough not to want that unspeakable, cheap, small-town peanut power luster ruling your life. He's already talking about looking forward to flying in *Air Force One*. That's a man who says he has a vision for rebuilding America. The contempt for people that he shows is something totally new in American politics. He doesn't believe people can remember his statements from day to day, and so he can lie, sit on every fence, and nobody will notice. If his party holds him in check, while bowing and treating him like an emperor, they can lead him by the nose. Carter is all touchy, cheap vanity. He's the kind of man who will do something out of sheer stubbornness, if he thinks Congress has offended him. But if they flatter him, he'll probably prevent the country from collapsing.

It's hard to tell what to look for in Carter's administration; I don't think *he* knows. He's been on both sides of every key issue. He'll probably be most dangerous about spending, for example, the make-work programs. Rising inflation will result, which I hope we can survive. [PO7 76]

Could you comment on Ronald Reagan and his role in the 1976 presidential election?

Reagan is a cheap Hollywood ham. Incidentally, watch his old movies; he always played idiotic parts in grade-B movies. Of course, playing such parts is not necessarily the fault of the actor; but Reagan fit those movies. He wasn't a victim towering over his material. If you want to see the soul of that man, watch his early movies.

It is disgusting what he did in this election. The main cause of Ford's defeat is intellectual. But speaking less abstractly, of any one person responsible for it, I'd pick Reagan, because of the tone of his campaign and that ugly fight at the Republican Convention—ugly on the part of Reagan and his associates. Reagan lost the primary, and proceeded to speak of party unity and standing by Ford—and he did not. He refused to campaign in certain key states where he allegedly had a following, particularly Texas, North Carolina, and perhaps Tennessee—states that Ford lost. He obviously wanted Ford to lose; and the first squeak that comes out of him, the day after the election, is that he doesn't rule out the possibility of running in 1980.

Ladies and gentlemen, should that monster succeed in 1980—and I hope to be dead by then, because I don't want to see such a day—I damn any of you who vote for him. (I'm speaking of moral damnation.) What Reagan did should not be forgiven, because you will be the victims. [PO7 76]

Has the sense-of-life reaction of Americans changed so much since the 1972 election?

No, the sense of life has not changed. The country has gone so much toward capitalism that Carter was "me-tooing" Ford and the Republicans throughout the campaign. His goal was to prove to the country that he's not a liberal. There's a lot of evidence that he lost his thirty-point lead over Ford when people concluded he's too liberal, since he chose Mondale as a running mate, for example. He tried his best to sound "conservative," and he was often indistinguishable from Republicans. The people cannot decide an issue like that by sense of life. Many people said they are uneasy about Carter: they don't trust him; they don't know where he stands. But since there's no leadership to oppose him and a huge campaign in his favor, they voted for him. Most people voted for their party. Since the Democrats are a majority party, and since Carter seems less offensive than McGovern, Carter won.

You cannot blame the people for not seeing through Carter as they saw through McGovern. The sense of life hasn't changed—but a sense of life is not a substitute for a conscious philosophy. You cannot by means of it recognize with certainty who are your friends and who are your enemies.

It would be wonderful if the mere sense of life of the country had saved us—for at least the next four years—but we had no right to expect it. Without philosophy, nothing can be done; evil wins by default, as it did this time. [PO7 76]

Libertarianism and Anarchism

What do you think of the libertarian movement?

All kinds of people today call themselves "libertarians," especially something calling itself the New Right, which consists of hippies who are anarchists instead of leftist collectivists; but anarchists *are* collectivists. Capitalism is the one system that requires absolute objective law, yet libertarians combine capitalism and anarchism. That's worse than anything the New Left has proposed. It's a mockery of philosophy and ideology. They sling slogans and try to ride on two bandwagons. They want to be hippies, but don't want to preach collectivism because those jobs are already taken. But anarchism is a logical outgrowth of the anti-intellectual side of collectivism. I could deal with a Marxist with a greater chance of reaching some kind of understanding, and with much greater respect. Anarchists are the scum of the intellectual world of the Left, which has given them up. So the Right picks up another leftist discard. That's the libertarian movement. [FHF 71]

What do you think of the Libertarian Party?

I'd rather vote for Bob Hope, the Marx Brothers, or Jerry Lewis—they're not as funny as John Hospers and the Libertarian Party. If Hospers takes ten votes away from Nixon (which I doubt he'll do), it would be a moral crime. I don't care about Nixon, and I care even less about Hospers; but this is no time to engage in publicity seeking, which all these crank political parties are doing. (George Wallace is no great thinker—he's a demagogue, though with some courage—but even he had the sense to stay home this time.) If you want to spread your ideas, do it through education. But don't run for president—or even dogcatcher—if you're going to help McGovern. [FHF 72]

What is your position on the Libertarian Party?

I don't want to waste too much time on it. It's a cheap attempt at publicity, which libertarians won't get. Today's events, particu-

larly Watergate, should teach anyone with amateur political no-
tions that they shouldn't rush into politics in order to get publicity.
The issues are so serious today that to form a new party on some
half-baked and some borrowed—I won't say from whom—ideas, is
irresponsible, and in today's context nearly immoral. [FHF 73]

Libertarians advocate the politics you do, so why are you opposed to the Libertarian Party?

They're not defenders of capitalism. They're a group of publicity seekers who rush into politics prematurely, because they allegedly want to educate people through a political campaign,
which can't be done. Further, their leadership consists of men of
every persuasion, from religious conservatives to anarchists. Most
of them are my enemies: they spend their time denouncing me,
while plagiarizing my ideas. Now it's a bad sign for an allegedly
pro-capitalist party to start by stealing ideas. [FHF 74]

Have you heard of Libertarian presidential candidate Roger MacBride? What do you think of him?

My answer should be "I don't think of him." There's nothing to
hear. The trouble in the world today is philosophical; only the right
philosophy can save us. But this party plagiarizes some of my ideas,
mixes them with the exact opposite—with religionists, anarchists, and
every intellectual misfit and scum they can find—and they call themselves Libertarians and run for office. I dislike Reagan and Carter; I'm
not too enthusiastic about the other candidates. But the worst of them
are giants compared to anybody who would attempt something as un-
philosophical, low, and pragmatic as the Libertarian Party. It is the last
insult to ideas and philosophical consistency. [FHF 76]

Do you think Libertarians communicate the ideas of freedom and capitalism effectively?

I don't think plagiarists are effective. I've read nothing by Libertarians (when I read them, in the early years) that wasn't my

ideas badly mishandled—that is, the teeth pulled out of them—
with no credit given. I didn't know whether to be glad that no
credit was given, or disgusted. I felt both. They are perhaps the
worst political group today, because they can do the most harm to
capitalism, by making it disreputable. I'll take Jane Fonda over
them. [Earlier during this same Q&A period, AR had been asked
about Jane Fonda. For the question and her answer, see below,
p. 80.] [OC 80]

Why don't you approve of libertarians, thousands of whom are loyal readers of your works?

Because libertarians are a monstrous, disgusting bunch of people: they plagiarize my ideas when that fits their purpose, and denounce me in a more vicious manner than any communist
publication when that fits their purpose. They're lower than any
pragmatists, and what they hold against Objectivism is morality.
They want an amoral political program. [FHF 81]

Libertarians provide intermediate steps toward your goals. Why don't you support them?

Please don't tell me they're pursuing my goals. I have not asked
for, nor do I accept, the help of intellectual cranks. I want philosophically educated people: those who understand ideas, care
about ideas, and spread the right ideas. That's how my philosophy
will spread, just as philosophy has throughout history: by means of
people who understand ideas and teach them to others. Further, it
should be clear that I reject the filthy slogan "The end justifies the
means." That was originated by the Jesuits, and accepted enthusiastically by the Communists and the Nazis. The end does *not* justify
the means; you cannot achieve anything good by evil means. Finally, libertarians aren't worthy of being the means to any end, let
alone the end of spreading Objectivism. [FHF 81]

*Robert Nozick, Professor of Philosophy at Harvard University, was a
well-known libertarian.*

Could you comment on Robert Nozick's **Anarchy, State, and Utopia***?*

I don't like to read this author, because I don't like bad eclectics—not in architecture, and certainly not in politics and philosophy—particularly when I'm one of the pieces butchered. [FHF 77]

What's your view on the idea of competing governments?

It's an irresponsible piece of nonsense. That's the only answer the question deserves. [FHF 70]

Why is the lack of government in Galt's Gulch (in **Atlas Shrugged***) any different from anarchy, which you object to?*

Galt's Gulch is not a society; it's a private estate. It's owned by one man who carefully selected the people admitted. Even then, they had a judge as an arbitrator, if anything came up; only nothing came up among them, because they shared the same philosophy. But if you had a *society* in which all shared in one philosophy, but without a government, that would be dreadful. Galt's Gulch probably consisted of about, optimistically, a thousand people who represented the top geniuses of the world. They agreed on fundamentals, but they would never be in total agreement. They didn't need a government because if they had disagreements, they could resolve them rationally.

But project a society of millions, in which there is every kind of viewpoint, every kind of brain, every kind of morality—and no government. That's the Middle Ages, your no-government society. Man was left at the mercy of bandits, because without government, every criminally inclined individual resorts to force, and every morally inclined individual is helpless. Government is an absolute necessity if individual rights are to be protected, because you don't leave force at the arbitrary whim of other individuals. Libertarian anarchism is pure whim worship, because what they refuse to recognize is the need of objectivity among men—particularly men of different views. And it's good that people within a nation should have different views, provided we respect each other's rights.

No one can guard rights, except a government under objective laws. What if McGovern had his gang of policemen, and Nixon had his, and instead of campaigning they fought in the streets? This has happened throughout history. Rational men are not afraid of government. In a proper society, a rational man doesn't have to know the government exists, because the laws are clear and he never breaks them. [FHF 72]

The Left

What's the difference between welfare-statism and Democratic Socialism?

Communists advocate the violent overthrow of government. Democratic Socialists intend to use force peacefully after they've been elected to office. But by the nature of Socialism, they must use force. Democratic Socialism is one variant of modern welfare-state liberalism. Not all liberals are Democratic Socialists. Most on the Left today are not so specific in their views. Most of them are welfare-statists, which are not the same thing. Welfare-statism in theory is: assume all the advantages of capitalism are here to stay, and then undermine everything that makes capitalism possible in order to redistribute wealth. Welfare-statists want the power to hold a gun over everybody's head, *and* they want to retain those milk cows—the capitalist producers. So the welfare state is simply the last stage of, and an excuse for, a mixed economy. It's not precisely the same as Democratic Socialism, but they're all variants of one school. [NFW 69]

Do liberals believe everyone is good?

Not if you're on the Right. They don't think a Republican or the John Birch Society or anyone they call fascist is good. For example, South Africa is part fascist, and liberals don't want the United States to deal with her; in fact, they practically want to declare war.

What liberals believe is that *anyone on the Left* is good—anyone who shares their basic ideas. Welfare-state liberals, socialists, and communists are good. That is a much more damning indictment of them, because a political Pollyanna—someone who believes everybody is good—wouldn't cause much trouble in the world. It's too far from reality. But the insidiousness of their double standard, which they've been practicing since before Roosevelt, is: reason and morality apply only to their side. This is a communist technique. Anyone not on the Left (broadly speaking) doesn't exist or is outside morality. Pollyannaism is better than the violent liberal hatred for anyone not on the Left—and the sentimentality for anyone who is. That is the modern liberal idea of fairness and goodness. [NFW 69]

Why do hippies and other militant students of the New Left attack their liberal friends and protectors more than they attack the Republicans?

The large-scale disruption of public meetings started with the 1968 Democratic Convention in Chicago. They had a few people chanting outside the Republican Convention, but they didn't interfere. Then all hell broke loose at the Democratic Convention. Why? After the election, the earliest public meeting of any significance was the Peace Luncheon, in which the most left-wing members of Congress (Fulbright, McGovern, and Javits) took part. Why did the militant students attack them, and not the Republicans? Similarly, why did Foreman and the Black Council present demands to religious organizations, but not to descendants of Southern slave owners? They could easily have traced them, and presented their demands. Why didn't they? That they went after religion gives you the answer.

The New Left is cashing in—logically and with justice—on those who hold their basic premises. They have nothing in common with the Right. Fundamentally, there's no premise to appeal to—no guilt to induce. Conventional Republicans might feel a little guilty: "these are the poor, so anyone who has two shirts should feel guilty." But that's nothing compared to the guilt they can induce by confronting religious leaders and congressional liberals, who have preached every premise that the activists are now putting into practice (including the use of force, only not so crudely and openly). They are not counting on Southern guilt about past wrongs, but on guilt derived from present altruist-collectivist convictions.

For example, if religion preaches that we are all our brother's keeper, then any "brothers" who are poorer than anyone else are justified in making demands of others. The others morally owe such a person reparations. When Frank [O'Connor, her husband] and I first heard about the Foreman incident, he remarked: "Foreman is logically right in regard to religionists. The brothers asked for it." The liberals and the religionists *asked* for the appearance of some extreme leftists like Foreman and the Black Council. If liberals denounce every premise underlying capitalism, why shouldn't the Black Council stand openly against capitalism?

If I were writing an article on these incidents, I'd call it "The Power of Ideas," and dedicate it to the conservatives. There are big businessmen who still think that ideas are unimportant—that practical activity alone counts. But the black militants—consciously or not—*know* the power of ideas.

Fulbright, Javits, McGovern and the rest gave the college activists and black militants a sanction and their basic premises. The activists are simply taking these premises literally and acting on them. Observe that one of the complaints of the New Left is hypocrisy: They accept the ideas of the leftist Establishment much more profoundly than any Establishment liberal congressman. They are complete intellectual puppets of the Establishment. What they demand is that the Establishment practices what it preaches. And if the liberal altruist-collectivist premises are true, then Foreman and the student militants *are right.*

Incidentally, one of the disguises of the liberals is that they want to use force, but legally and in a gentlemanly manner, without people knowing about it. They want to be civilized elite protectors of the common man, who is helpless without them. So they are shocked to see these violent savages who want to take over; and what they'll never admit is that they created those savages. The premises now acting against them are their own. The liberals see in the New Left their own mirror image. The New Left is their Frankenstein's monster: it is the consistent exponent of every fundamental they hold, but never wanted to admit openly and consistently. That is why the liberals are so helpless. [NFW 69]

Could you comment on John Kenneth Galbraith's The Affluent Society?

Yes, with (a very unhappy) pleasure. What Galbraith advocates—in principle and spirit—is medieval feudalism. He evades the issue of rights (including property rights) altogether, as if they never existed. He asks why private individuals can spend their money as they wish, without having to give reasons, whereas every time the government wants to spend money it has to explain what the money is for. Therefore, he advocates that a percentage of everyone's income go to the government with no questions asked. The government will have the right to dispose of that money as it wishes, for the public sector. What does he think we need? Trust a socialist to find excuses for taking your money and getting more power. He's very concerned about the state of our parks; he writes indignantly and at great length about Cadillacs and other modern luxuries of the Americans, who nevertheless go to polluted parks. So your money should be stolen from you because Galbraith believes you need more parks.

Further, Galbraith says that if someone wants to buy a second automobile, he must prove to the government that he needs a second one. In other words, the man who earns the money has no right to that money; he must ask Galbraith or the government for permission to spend it. But the government, which lives on our taxes, need not give an account of how it spends our money; it doesn't even need to consult the so-called private sector. The government simply decides that we need parks and schools. (Schools are a convenient excuse behind which liberals always hide.) Galbraith writes that the condition of our schools is bad, therefore we should have fewer Cadillacs.

Of course, the answer is not to give more money to the government, but to take schools, public roads, post offices, and all economic concerns out of its hands. If parks, schools, and other government undertakings are as miserable as Galbraith claims, return them to private enterprise, and they'll be run properly. But the proper (though slightly humorous) answer to Galbraith is for as many of you who can afford it to get brilliant purple Cadillacs (rent them if necessary), drive them around, and show Galbraith that it's *your* money, not his.

The Affluent Society is one of the most outrageous books ever published. That he wrote it is his privilege. What's ominous is that instead of being intellectually ostracized, he's given a government appointment (fortunately in India). [PVA 61]

What do you think of Jane Fonda's ideas and her form of communicating them?

This is simply amusing. I dislike both, of course. Tom Snyder's *Prime Time Saturday* had a good segment on Fonda and her husband [at the time, Tom Hayden], who are going across the country attacking nuclear power and sundry other things, like businessmen. In response to two different questions, she said she doesn't know what she's talking about; she simply feels it. She is not a thinker; she needs to be led. She follows her husband. She implied it's outside authorities that determine what she believes. I don't usually trust her, but I believe she's telling the truth here. As to whether I approve of her ideas, the answer has to be "no," and more emphatically than I can say without going into obscenities—which I disapprove of—or breaking this microphone. [OC 80]

In 1947, AR testified as a cooperative or "friendly" witness before the House Un-American Activities Committee (or HUAC) in Washington, D.C.

At the time you testified before the HUAC, did you support the blacklisting of communist actors and writers?

I do not know anything about a Red blacklist, but I know a great deal about the blacklist of conservatives by the Reds. I am the last person to whom you should address this question, unless you are interested in the truth.

The investigation I was involved in took place in 1947. It was before the McCarthy Era—McCarthy was not involved. This was the hearing at which ten "unfriendly" witnesses were asked about their Communist Party affiliation, and they refused to answer. (Their Communist Party cards were produced at the hearings by the committee's investigators.) Another group of witnesses were the so-called friendly witnesses—friendly to the investigation—and they testified about communist penetration into the motion-picture industry. I was one of the friendly witnesses. Unfortunately, they didn't let me testify as much as I would have liked to. I was the only one who testified about the content of propaganda in movies, and the only movie they questioned me about was a very obvious one, *Song of Russia* [MGM, 1944], which didn't require analysis to prove that it was communist propaganda. I wanted to testify about more complex Hollywood movies that were full of communist propaganda, but they didn't question me about them.

I do not know of any Red blacklisted in Hollywood. I do know, if the newspaper stories can be trusted, that many of those "blacklisted" people, including the Hollywood Ten (who went to jail for a year, for contempt of Congress), were working in Hollywood thereafter under assumed names. They had enough friends in the industry to be able to sell stories under phony names; and today, most of them are back in business. But have you ever inquired into what happened to the *friendly* witnesses? Before we left for Washington, we were put under every possible pressure, short of physical force, by the heads of the Hollywood studios, who did not want us to testify. Why not, if we were opposing communists? They didn't like the issues to be aired. They wanted to soft-pedal the whole thing. There were officials and lawyers for the Hollywood producers pleading with the friendly witnesses to shut up. There was one man whom I won't name [the actor Robert Taylor], who I heard, in a meeting of a conservative organization, tell a certain story. When he was questioned by the HUAC, he told a different story. He softened it. I can't blame him too much, though I wouldn't have done it. But I wondered under what kind of psychological torture he did it.

Further, observe that some of the friendly witnesses at those hearings were famous stars, such as Gary Cooper and Robert Taylor, and they remained working, because the leftists are the greediest people in Hollywood. They want most of all anyone who is box office. So the stars involved in that hearing did not feel any pressure thereafter or experience a blacklist. The real tragedy is what happened to the second-rank people, like Adolphe Menjou, who was a famous character actor, but not a star. He used to work all the time, freelancing in various movies. But he was one of the friendly witnesses, and after that hearing, he could not find work. He made a few more movies, with small roles, and I heard got into financial trouble; so he descended from a prominent position. Or take Morrie Ryskind, who was a famous writer. (He wrote the comedy *Of Thee I Sing*.) In Hollywood, he was getting $3,000 a week, which at the time was top money for writers. He has not worked as a writer one day since appearing as a friendly witness. Writers are dispensable in Hollywood; they were treated quite contemptuously; so the writers who cooperated with the HUAC were the worst victims. Now, junior writers are the most vulnerable people in Hollywood. I know two who cooperated with the HUAC: Fred Niblo Jr.—the son of the director—and Richard Macaulay. They were rising writers, working very well, both men with families, and making about $350 a week. To my knowledge, neither of them worked as a screenwriter again. When I left Hollywood, Fred Niblo Jr. was a laborer at Lockheed in California. This is what happened to the friendly witnesses.

At that time, I was under contract to a movie studio, and my producer [Hal Wallis] was a little more decent than the others. I quit voluntarily some years later, because I didn't want to write for Hollywood anymore. But I don't want to tell you what kind of victim I have been since of a smear brigade and a blacklisting of public opinion. You talk about the blacklisting of Reds. I don't know of one leftist who has suffered for his views; and conversely, I don't know of one pro-capitalist who in one form or another did not have to suffer for his views. [FHF 67]

Please comment on the current campaign in the media reviving the attacks on the Hollywood blacklist of communists: for example, Lillian Hellman's Scoundrel Time, *the [Woody Allen] movie* The Front. *What really happened during that period?*

It is too horrible and too dirty an issue to discuss, and you are looking at one of the victims. I could tell you a great deal about it, but I'd need at least an hour. I'll say only this. All these filthy goddamned communists are boasting about their courage, such as Lillian Hellman, who *was* a member of the Communist Party. How many people died in this country, and in Russia or in Russian-occupied countries, because of Miss Hellman's ideas, God only knows. Nobody could compute the evil of what those communists in the 1930s did. To begin with, they pushed this country into World War Two. What would have been a better policy? Let Hitler march into Russia, as he had started to. Let the two dictatorships fight each other; then the West—England, France, and the United States—could finish off the winner. Then maybe, today, the world would be safe. (Except the ultimate safety of the world depends on philosophy, and nobody has the right ideas.) People like Lillian Hellman were pushing the policy of this country to the left and in support of only one country—not the United States, but Soviet Russia. So were all of "McCarthy's victims." They were either Party members or supporters. In one famous case, a woman was not a communist, but held an important government post and had been a member of eighteen organizations listed as subversive by the attorney general. When McCarthy exposed her, she claimed she didn't know they were subversive. And she had the nerve to work in government. That's what those people were like.

What they were demanding is the right to lie. Nobody prosecuted them for being communists. People didn't want to deal with underground communists. They weren't so openly, and they resented the fact that the government demanded they state under oath whether they were members of the Communist Party or not. That is not interfering with their freedom. There is no freedom to deceive people. If you are being punished by the government for being communist, that's different. But if private employers don't

want to employ communists—if they, properly, consider them enemies of this country, and worse, of mankind—the employee has
no right to lie about it. Yet that's what those wonderful little
martyrs—they were so brave—wanted to do. And they were suddenly forbidden to lie to Hollywood employers.

Now take the other side of the picture. At the Hollywood hearings
of the HUAC, there were the Hollywood Ten—the communists—and
the "friendly witnesses." I was a friendly witness. We were called to
discuss communist penetration in Hollywood. (My particular testimony was about the content of communist propaganda in pic-
tures.) Do you know what's happened to the friendly witnesses?
They did not remain working in Hollywood. I am not a victim in
this respect, because I had a long-term contract, which I later canceled to finish *Atlas Shrugged.* I was not fired for appearing in Washington. I *was* a victim for many years, before *The Fountainhead* was
published, when I couldn't find work in Hollywood anywhere. But
then *The Fountainhead* was too much for them; they couldn't stop
producers from hiring me after that. Gary Cooper, a very good witness against the communists, had a name. But those who didn't
have a name or a contract—younger junior writers, and some
prominent freelance writers—were out of work shortly after the
hearings. Within a year, most of them were not working. Some
were very prominent. For instance, Adolphe Menjou was a prominent actor, but he was freelance. He got fewer and fewer jobs, until
about a year and a half later, when he could find no work. Morrie
Ryskind was a prominent writer—he wrote *Of Thee I Sing* and many
movies and stage plays. He was getting $3,000 a week, and had
more work than he could handle. He appeared as a friendly witness, and thereafter could not find work in Hollywood. The worst
case I know of was the junior writer Fred Niblo Jr. (son of the famous silent film director Fred Niblo). Within a year after appearing at the hearings, he had to work at Lockheed in an airplane
factory.

If someone wants to do something humanitarian, do a research
project on what became of the friendly witnesses. A monstrous
silent blacklist was exercised by those same goddamned communists in Hollywood. Did those talented people who were in demand

suddenly lose their talent? Hollywood producers are cowardly—not as bad as is sometimes claimed, but they don't have strong convictions, and they're ignorant. The communists work their way into every position of influence, and so the friendly witnesses suffered for their testimony, in one way or another. That's never mentioned. [PO6 76]

Why do so many Americans have a paranoid fear of communists?

First, I don't know that they do. Second, I wouldn't call it paranoid fear. If a country is a totalitarian dictatorship—in which one's life, work, future is at the mercy of the government, which engages in the wholesale slaughter of millions—and people are afraid of that country influencing this one, I'd call that a rational fear.

However, opposition to something does not imply a fear of it. Opposing something as evil does not mean one is afraid of that evil. Colloquially, you could say one is "afraid" in the sense that one disapproves, but not in a sense that implies cowardice. For instance, if I oppose smallpox, would you say I'm afraid of it? Well, yes and no. I don't want to have it; but that isn't cowardice. The same is true of those who oppose communism. It isn't fear of communism, as such, or of its power. It is moral indignation—an opposition to the evil of communism.

I will grant you this, however. There are not many intellectual anticommunists. They substitute slogans for serious discussion, which may give you the impression that they are afraid. But even here, I don't think it's true. They are inarticulate and nonintellectual, and therefore ineffective. But that isn't fear. It's indignation—sometimes helpless indignation—against an enormous evil. [FHF 67]

Is communist propaganda the cause of the young Americans' hatred of capitalism?

Probably in part, but it's not the major cause. It isn't a communist conspiracy, however, it's our own "patriotic," perfectly respectable American professors—particularly of philosophy, the social sciences, and the humanities. They arrived at their ideas

without any help from Russia. They're probably losing money by
not being communist agents, because they *are* valuable to the
communist cause. But that's not what's behind them. Immanuel
Kant is behind them—and all of his descendants and consequences. [FHF 71]

Foreign Policy

The Soviet Union

*Did the Russians lose face by backing down in the Cuban Missile
Crisis?*

First, we're not even sure whether the Russians withdrew. We
have no firsthand knowledge. The sole "proof" was an inspection
of covered shapes on ships, which were not boarded, from battle-
ships across a distance. There is no proof. But assume they are
gone. Russia was the aggressor in that case. If she backed down,
that was a good thing for a bully to do. President Kennedy's ulti-
matum was the first time in fifty years that an American president
spoke like an American president. It was magnificent. For once, he
addressed Russia properly; and Russia, like any bully, backed down
when confronted with strength. But Kennedy let the victory disappear into meaninglessness, and nothing happened. He surrendered to the United Nations. Therefore, we didn't win any
concession, merely a gesture.

In the case of Vietnam, we are not the aggressors. We were
drawn in by some kind of Geneva or United Nations agreement.
We went in there in compliance with some treaty, if one can trust
the generalities presented in newspapers, and we are not fighting
for any purpose. Therefore, for us to withdraw *would* be appeasement. But here is what's worse: The idea that this country cannot
defeat Vietnam is ridiculous, and the whole world knows it. But we
are not allowed to use our strength. We're not allowed to take
proper measures—that is, pursue the Vietcong across borders and
into its own territory, and so on. We are fighting with our hands
tied. The idea that America must withdraw from Vietnam is worse
than appeasement. It is a shameful pretense. Further, since the

world knows we are not physically weak, it would be an admission of moral corruption: that we do not possess a primitive dignity that any nation should have—to its own dead, if nothing else—that if it is involved in a war, it should finish it. It must win or be defeated. [FHF 67]

You say the United States alone should control nuclear weapons, not China or Russia as well. Should the United States ever use them?

I would not dispose of the lives of other people. It's improper to put me in the position of commander-in-chief. Ask the question in principle: Is it proper for an individual to defend himself? Yes. Is it proper for a country to defend itself? Yes. Are Russia and China monstrous aggressors, whose first aggression is against their own people? Yes. If so, we should certainly maintain superiority over them. At present, we shouldn't attack them, because we don't have to. But at the first sign of an attack by them, we should fight them by *every* means we have, because it is criminal to kill Americans while not using the better weapons we possess. [FHF 72]

What do you think of President Carter so far, particularly in regard to his claims about human rights in the Soviet Union?

I'd have to say, "No comment"—and then explain why I don't care to comment. I don't trust Carter across the street. During the campaign it was impossible to determine what he stood for; he is continuing that "policy" while president: it's impossible to tell what he is, and what he's after. It's very possible that he is, and is after, nothing.

A friend of mine said (and I'm inclined to believe he's right) that Carter does the following: If his statements in a given field of policy are on one side of the political spectrum, his actions will be on the other. For instance, his speeches on domestic policy are to the left, but his policies so far, fortunately (though probably only temporarily), are not too left-wing. On the other hand, in foreign policy, he makes good statements about human rights, and then hedges the next day and says it doesn't mean he won't negotiate with the Russians. Pretty soon, I expect him to say the Russians misunderstood him: he meant rights but not *human* rights. I'll trust his good statements on rights only when I'm sure he isn't going to sell us further down the river to Russia. But when one could be sure of that, I don't know. [FHF 77]

Do you recognize the Soviet Union's reported military buildup as a threat to the people of the United States of America? And what should individual Americans do about this, or allow our government to do?

The Soviet military buildup is certainly intended as a threat. How effective that threat is, I would not attempt to guess, because Soviet production is so incompetent, so bad, that I don't know what will happen to their atom bombs and whether they will explode before they're loaded on planes. But we certainly cannot rely on their inefficiency. We should be militarily prepared, because, in today's world, any thug can arm himself against us. It's quite possible, and would be logical, that the Soviet Union would be more efficient at producing instruments of death than at any other kind of production. The only thing that would stop them from starting a nuclear war, and that is stopping them now, is, of course, America's superior strength. Therefore, we may and should cut any budget except the defense budget. I want to add that Mr. Carter's policy in canceling the production of certain nuclear weapons is disgraceful. It is truly disgraceful. [FHF 78]

If the United States and the Soviet Union can destroy the world ten times over, why should we spend more on defense?

First, because of scientific discoveries, nuclear weapons (like other kinds of weapons) quickly become obsolete. Second, so long as Russia is manufacturing new weapons, we dare not stay behind. We should be ahead, as we were originally. One of the historic crimes of this country's governments is that they allowed our superiority to deteriorate. But we can't complain about that now; we must correct it. So long as there is the kind of threat that Russia represents, we must extend our ability twenty times over. Finally, I'd rather we blow up the whole world than surrender it to Russia. [FHF 81]

In light of your absolute refusal to surrender to Soviet Russia, is there no intermediate kind of surrender to avoid the end of the world?

There might be, if there were an intermediate state of pregnancy, an intermediate immorality, an intermediate irrationality. In all basic and crucial issues, there are no intermediates. You must stand with Aristotle and me and say: It's either/or. [FHF 81]

The military draft

> *For AR's fullest statement in opposition to a military draft, see "The Wreckage of the Consensus" in* Capitalism: The Unknown Ideal.

What do you recommend for someone drafted into the military?

Morally, nobody can advise a man on a choice of that kind. It's up to him. Legally, it is forbidden to advocate opposing or disobeying the draft. Therefore, I cannot answer. [FHF 67]

I'm preparing a pamphlet opposing the draft and intend to send it to all congressmen. Is this a good idea, and would you support it?

I cannot endorse a work I haven't seen. But your idea is good. Writing to your congressman defending your views as clearly as you can is valuable, as is gathering signatures on a petition, if it is a brief statement expressing your opposition to the draft. But above all, and no matter how brief your presentation, do not omit the words "the draft is a violation of individual rights." Many opponents of the draft carefully avoid mentioning rights. Do not use "individual freedom" or "individual dignity" instead. Such descriptions of the draft are true; but in today's context, they're an evasion.

The draft is expiring in June, so now is the time to write your congressman. Congressmen read their mail; it's the only way they can determine what the country is thinking. The press cannot be trusted. The present preoccupation with public polls is precisely an attempt to take the place of reliable newspaper reporting. My only suggestion is: write politely. Abusive, emotional letters, flinging insults, accomplish nothing. One reason is better than ten insults. [FHF 67]

Since the draft is compulsory owing to the military needs of the country, shouldn't there be a prohibition against profit-making in munitions so long as the draft is in existence?

Certainly not. You do not correct one evil by creating another. If you want to stop this country altogether, abolish profit; in no time we would sink to the level of the rest of the world. Munitions are needed in war so desperately—particularly today, in a war of technology—that you don't dare touch profits in armaments. If you do, our best minds will go elsewhere. They will not work self-sacrificially for their country, particularly in a war like the one in Vietnam.

I agree with one implication in your question: if people advocate the draft, then they should also advocate the abolition of profit and private property and all rights. If you accept the basic principles underlying the draft, you should abolish freedom of the press and every other freedom, because when the right to life is suspended, there's no foundation for any other rights. Incidentally, this is what collectivists are arguing on the basis of the draft. They are encroaching on all our rights, using the draft as a justification. But since man possesses inalienable individual rights, what we should do is repeal the draft, not create new victims. [FHF 67]

Can you explain how conservatives justify the draft?

Because conservatives—if by "conservatives" we mean those who allegedly are against statism and uphold some form of capitalism— are undercut by the altruist morality. Altruism and mysticism are two prominent elements among conservatives. They have no rational philosophical base. So conservatism is full of contradictions. It is impossible to defend capitalism on an altruist basis, and therefore they are forced into contradictions or into avoiding intellectual issues altogether, instead opting for folksy simplicity. There are few conservative intellectuals, and those that do exist are full of contradictions—and not only on the draft. [FHF 67]

Should amnesty be granted to draft dodgers or deserters?

It is improper to discuss this issue while there's a war going on. It's a complex issue. But when men are dying in a war, you cannot promise amnesty to those who refused to fight. I don't blame those who refuse to be drafted, however, if they did so out of genuine convictions (not necessarily religious). If someone opposed the state's right to draft him, he'd be right, and would go to jail. But when a lot of bums declare they don't want to fight *this* war because they don't want to fight Soviet Russia—and that's all it means—then not only don't they deserve amnesty, they deserve to be sent permanently to Russia or North Vietnam at the public's expense. [FHF 72]

The war in Vietnam

If you were Lyndon Johnson, what would you do about Vietnam?

I'll answer you with a historical anecdote, since I cannot project myself as Lyndon Johnson. Napoleon was once asked: "Sir, you are the greatest military genius in existence; what would you do in this situation?" The questioner then described a completely hopeless military situation, to which there is no solution. Napoleon replied: "I became the greatest military genius in the world by never getting into such a situation." [FHF 67]

What is the standard of justice, and how does it apply to the United States' involvement in Vietnam?

The standard of justice is individual rights. I was against the war in Vietnam, but we are not guilty of any injustice except toward ourselves. We are guilty of colossal, stupid self-sacrifice. We aren't guilty of anything with respect to the Vietnamese. Consider what they and the Cambodians are doing now. Did we, by the standard of justice, have the right to interfere in Vietnam? When a country doesn't recognize the individual rights of its own citizens, it cannot claim any national or international rights. Therefore, anyone who wants to invade a dictatorship or semi-dictatorship is morally justified in doing so, because he is doing no worse than what that country has accepted as its social system. It is improper to attack a free country, because it recognizes the individual rights of its citizens. [FHF 76]

Do you consider rational the October fifteenth moratorium on the war in Vietnam?

It is as irrational and immoral as any public act in our history. I am against the war in Vietnam, and have been for years. But I am not *for* the Vietcong or American unilateral surrender. When you know that citizens of your country were drafted and are fighting and dying in war, whatever form of protest you make, do not ask for unilateral surrender. Do not accept compliments from the Vietcong and distribute Vietcong flags. Do anything that supports an enemy during an actual war, *and you are a murderer*. You take on your hands the death of every soldier in Vietnam. If you, as civilians, take the side of the enemy, that is as low and unspeakably immoral as any attitude I can conceive of.

The Vietnam War is the fault of the same liberals and the same policies that today are at the forefront of the *opposition* to the war. The war was the product of Johnson and especially Kennedy, who is now regarded as an idealistic martyr. But Kennedy got us into Vietnam just the same. Republicans and Democrats are in a sense equally guilty, but the Democrats began that war. Look up the speeches of Kennedy and Johnson on Vietnam. Or go further back, and read how the same Democrat-Liberal axis insulted anyone opposed to our entering World War Two as being narrowly patriotic, selfish, and "isolationist." Today, suddenly the liberals are isolationist. Well, this is just too goddamn obvious. If you make any pretense about standing for serious principles, then at least respect your audience. Don't treat them like subnormal children who won't understand that you are holding a double standard: It is proper to go to war to fight fascism, the Left says, but not to fight communism. I say we must fight both or neither.

In my view, we should fight fascism and communism when they come to this country. As to fighting abroad, let us send all the military equipment that we can spare (without sacrifice) to any fight for freedom, whether it's against fascism or communism (which are two variants of statism). But let us never sacrifice American *lives* for somebody else's freedom.

If you want to help, watch our foreign policy and see to it that no administration, Republican or Democratic, ever puts the United States into this position again. Start a movement for George Washington's principle of "no foreign entanglements." The present problems were created by an irrational policy, which is at least fifty years old. You must attack its root and cause. You cannot solve the problem simply by wishing it away. Merely saying, "I want the boys to come back, somehow," is irrational. The problem is: how to end the war without destroying the prestige of America and delivering thousands of people who trusted us—the South Vietnamese—to slaughter. If we hadn't gone into Vietnam, it wouldn't be our responsibility to protect either side. It's their country; let them fight it out. But since we did go in, and asked for and received the cooperation of the local people, to then withdraw and abandon those people, when we have the power to fight, would be monstrous. We shouldn't remain at the expense of American lives; but merely stamping our feet and demanding that our boys come home is acting like a petulant child. [FHF 69]

Didn't the antiwar activists that you criticize play a part in ending the war in Vietnam?

They were spoiled brats looking for publicity and created by the media. They contributed nothing but chaos and disorder. You do not solve serious issues by physical demonstration. If you want to contribute something, think, argue, spread ideas. You teach; you don't sit in the street, obstruct traffic, chant, and look sloppy. That didn't stop the war in Vietnam. [FHF 76]

For more of AR's views on the war in Vietnam, see "The Lessons of Vietnam," in The Voice of Reason.

Innocents in war

What do you think about the killing of innocent people in war?

This is a major reason people should be concerned about the nature of their government. The majority in any country at war is often innocent. But if by neglect, ignorance, or helplessness they couldn't overthrow their bad government and establish a better one, then they must pay the price for the sins of their government, as we are all paying for the sins of ours. And if people put up with dictatorship—as some do in Soviet Russia, and some did in Nazi Germany—they deserve what their government deserves. Our only concern should be who started the war. Once that's established, there's no need to consider the "rights" of that country, because it has initiated the use of force and therefore stepped outside the principle of rights. [FHF 72]

Assume the Soviet Union started a war of aggression; assume also that within the Soviet Union there are individuals opposed to communism. How do you handle this conflict?

I'll pretend to take the question seriously, because it's blatantly wrong. The question assumes that an individual inside a country should be made secure from the social system under which he lives and that he accepts—willingly or unwillingly, because he hasn't left the country—and that others should respect his rights and succumb to aggression themselves. This is the position of the goddamned pacifists, who won't fight, even if attacked, because they might kill innocent people. If this were correct, nobody would have to be concerned about his country's political system. But we must care about the right social system, because our lives depend on it—because a political system, good or bad, is established in our name, and we bear the responsibility for it.

If we go to war with Russia, I hope the "innocent" are destroyed along with the guilty. There aren't many innocent people there; those who do exist are not in the big cities, but mainly in concentration camps. Nobody has to put up with aggression, and surrender his right of self-defense, for fear of hurting somebody else, guilty or innocent. When someone comes at you with a gun, if you have an ounce of self-esteem, you answer with force, never mind who he is or who's standing behind him. If he's out to destroy you, you owe it to your own life to defend yourself. [FHF 76]

Can you defend one country attacking another?

The source of this kind of statement is the idea that nations do not exist, only individuals, and if some poor, noncommunist blob in Soviet Russia doesn't want an invasion, we mustn't hurt him. But who permits governments to go to war? Only a government can put a country into war, and the citizens of that country keep their government in power. This is true in the worst dictatorships. Even the citizens of Soviet Russia—who did not elect the Communists—keep them in power through passivity. Nazi Germany did elect its dictatorship, and therefore, even those Germans who were against Hitler were responsible for that kind of government and had to suffer the consequences. Individual citizens in a country that goes to war are responsible for that war. This is why they should be interested in politics and careful about not having the wrong kind of government. If in this context one could make a distinction between the actions of a government and the actions of individual citizens, why would we need politics at all? All governments would be on one side, doing something among themselves, while we private citizens would go along in happy, idyllic tribalism. But that picture is false. We are responsible for the government we have, and that is why it is important to take the science of politics very seriously. If we become a dictatorship, and a freer country attacks us, it would be their right. [FHF 77]

If an individual who values his life is living in a dictatorship, what should he do?

Get the hell out of there as fast as possible. You cannot live nor maintain any values for long under a dictatorship. There is nothing to do but try to get out. If the whole world became a dictatorship, then all one could do is form a conspiracy—which would probably be discovered in five minutes—and die that way rather than commit suicide. That would be one's only choice. [FHF 70]

The Middle East

What should the United States do about the [1973] Arab-Israeli War?

Give all help possible to Israel. Consider what is at stake. It is not the moral duty of any country to send men to die helping another country. The help Israel needs is technology and military weapons—and they need them desperately. Why should we help Israel? Israel is fighting not just the Arabs but Soviet Russia, who is sending the Arabs armaments. Russia is after control of the Mediterranean and oil.

Further, why are the Arabs against Israel? (This is the main reason I support Israel.) The Arabs are one of the least developed cultures. They are still practically nomads. Their culture is primitive, and they resent Israel because it's the sole beachhead of modern science and civilization on their continent. When you have civilized men fighting savages, you support the civilized men, no matter who they are. Israel is a mixed economy inclined toward socialism. But when it comes to the power of the mind— the development of industry in that wasted desert continent— versus savages who don't want to use their minds, then if one cares about the future of civilization, don't wait for the government to do something. Give whatever you can. This is the first time I've contributed to a public cause: helping Israel in an emergency. [FHF 73]

Does Israel engage in tribalism?

Yes, to a large extent, because it is a socialist country, and it's a country based on a state religion. The idea that a particular race is a special culture is of course tribalism. [FHF 77]

Would you comment on the rights of the Palestinians to their homeland?

Whatever rights the Palestinians may have had—I don't know the history of the Middle East well enough to know what started the trouble—they have lost all rights to anything: not only to land, but to human intercourse. If they lost land, and in response resorted to terrorism—to the slaughter of innocent citizens—they deserve whatever any commandos anywhere can do to them, and I hope the commandos succeed. [FHF 77]

Would you comment on the prospects for peace in the Middle East?

I have nothing to say about that—and I'm not the only one. No one is saying anything that makes sense. The prospects are anybody's guess, and again, the only clearly wrong policy is Mr. Carter's. He is very consistent in that respect. [FHF 78]

On November 4, 1979, Iranian militants attacked the United States Embassy in Tehran and took over fifty Americans hostage. The hostages were released after 444 days.

What should be the U.S. policy in the Iranian crisis? How should we get the hostages back?

Never to allow the country to get into that situation. It's certainly the fault of our foreign policy, and at present, there's no right course of action. It's too late. If we didn't march with force the first or second day after the hostages were taken, nothing we do after that will be any good, and it will take us years to live it down. [OC 80]

Miscellaneous

What do you think of the deposing of Allende in Chile?

The Chileans are still human beings; they did the right thing. Allende had one-third of the country with him; two-thirds supported other candidates. On that basis, he imposed, by so-called peaceful, democratic means, a socialist dictatorship. In terms of human lives in Chile, this meant that a minority had the right to expropriate the property of, and enslave, two-thirds of the country. But nobody has the right to socialism. Even if people are stupid enough to elect a socialist like Allende or a Nazi like Hitler (who got elected with a higher percentage of votes than Allende), no population has the right to vote for the enslavement of other people—any more than they have the right to do it by force. Therefore, if Allende attempted to put something over on the country, I admire the Chilean people for seeing it in time. Of course, this doesn't mean that the people who took over are for capitalism. I'm sure they're not. If there aren't any pro-capitalist political leaders in the United States, how could there be any in Latin America? But at least they aren't communists and don't make alliances with communists. That isn't much, but it's better than Allende—until and unless the new leaders establish a dictatorship, at which time they would be morally equal to Allende. [FHF 73]

What is your opinion of the junta that overturned Allende and tortured and killed thousands?

At present, I don't believe those stories. I want proof from authorities more reliable than extreme leftists. Given what I do know of the junta, I'd say they have no idea what they're doing; and, I don't think they'll achieve much, because the country is too Red. But they're better than the Allende government. [FHF 74]

If present national boundaries were transcended by a political institution, could the different economies of the world better handle their problems?

If you have a disease, does a more serious form of it help? The interdependence of the world is just such a disease. Western countries are all leaning on one another, as bad risks and parasites, and the United States is the only remaining pillar, though it's almost eaten away. So the first step in any solution is to break those foreign obligations, and demand payment for what is owed. If the United States received part of the money the world—and particularly Europe—owes it, we might have a Renaissance in America overnight. The problem is that that money no longer exists. There are only consumers on a more advanced stage toward dictatorship than we are. The fewer ties we have with other countries, the better off we'll be. [FHF 74]

How do you explain the fact that productivity in Sweden is higher than in this country?

They have better press agents. Seriously, I don't believe it. You can prove anything with statistics. I'd sooner believe that they're all walking on their heads—there's some indication of that—than that they're productive, because their best people have left the country. Sweden is on its way into the sewer—if she hasn't already reached it. [FHF 76]

What is your opinion of Henry Kissinger?

I think Mr. Kissinger is one of the most disgraceful and disastrous secretaries of state that we've ever had—mainly because of his philosophical views. He is an admirer and follower of Metternich, who represents the worst of the European approach to foreign policy and to power. [FHF 76]

Is it moral for a businessman to sell goods to our government and to foreign governments, when the source of government funds is expropriated wealth?

It's certainly moral for an American businessman to sell goods to our government, to the extent to which it is moral for him to exist. He cannot accept moral responsibility for actions or policies over which he has *no* control. Government money *is* expropriated funds. Nevertheless, the moral blame falls on the government and on advocates of taxation, not on the businessman. It is not his job, qua businessman, to worry about the source of government funds. But it is his job, politically, to condemn government power and taxation, which today, unfortunately, businessmen don't do.

Whether he should deal with foreign governments is a different issue. You need to judge each case according to the nature of the particular government. It is totally immoral to deal with Soviet Russia, as it was to deal with Nazi Germany, or any genuine dictatorship. [FHF 78]

Should the government of a free society impose embargos on dictatorships?

That's a very technical question. I would answer: if embargos are necessary. If a dictatorship, like Cuba, is a threat to a free country (as a base for Soviet Russia), then there is a demonstrable danger of war, and so the government has the right to impose an embargo on that country, and forbid businessmen to deal with it.

But here's a better approach. In the nineteenth century, the government didn't need to forbid businessmen to deal with bad countries, like South American dictatorships. Instead, the government wouldn't protect citizens who dealt with unstable regimes. The government's attitude was: If you deal with dictatorships, do so at your own peril. The businessmen who did so did not do too well. In modern times, this applies particularly to businessmen who collaborate with Soviet Russia. Unfortunately, big companies helped establish Soviet Russia economically. For details, read Anthony C. Sutton, *Western Technology and Soviet Economic Development: 1917–1930*, a remarkable book on the early history of American business relations with Soviet Russia. It describes how American businessmen helped develop Russian industries, and all but lost their shirts in the process. [FHF 70]

Could you comment on the present Panama Canal debate?

It's a disgrace, because it's a phony issue. It involves playing down to the inferiority complex of a small nation while assaulting our own achievement. The Panama Canal is a great American achievement. The original contract was not only legal; Panama was established with American help because it was thereby able to secede from Colombia. Further, Americans eliminated malaria from the entire isthmus. Before the Americans arrived, it was useless.

Today, the issue is not whether the canal is valuable, or whether we intend to build another. The issue is the abysmal slap in the face to American achievement. Even the defenders of that policy say it is merely symbolic, to flatter the feelings or inferiority complex of South America. So, we should maintain our dignity, which we deserve. There's no reason to give the Panama Canal away. [FHF 78]

Could you comment on America's policy toward South Africa?

South Africa is in a very bad situation. It's like a caricature of the fault in Western civilization generally. The people running South Africa are mystical conservatives. They even have a law forbidding atheism, which I think is worse than their racist policy, as bad as that is. Interestingly, apartheid was established in South Africa not by businessmen but by a liberal government. Poor white labor established those racist laws. The capitalists in South Africa fought against it (but not very intellectually, as usual), since the racist laws are bad for business. The white trash brought apartheid into existence, and it is vicious for everybody involved. However, turning the country over to a lot of tribes, and destroying the white people, is no solution. In fact, there is no solution for a country that far gone. Paraphrasing Napoleon, the solution is for a country not to get into that condition. I don't know what to do about a powder keg in which every party is wrong. [FHF 78]

Racism and Feminism

What is the value of nationalism?

That depends on how you interpret the term. Nationalism as a primary—that is, the attitude of "my country, right or wrong," without any judgment—is chauvinism: a blind, collectivist, racist feeling for your own country, merely because you were born there. In that sense, nationalism is very wrong. But nationalism properly understood—as a man's devotion to his country because of an approval of its basic premises, principles, and social system, as well as its culture—is the common bond among men of that nation. It is a commonly understood culture, and an affection for it, that permits a society of men to live together peacefully. But a country and its system must earn this approval. It must be worthy of that kind of devotion. [FHF 67]

When you consider the cultural genocide of Native Americans, the enslavement of blacks, and the relocation of Japanese Americans during World War Two, how can you have such a positive view of America?

America is the country of individual rights. Should America have tolerated slavery? Certainly not. Why did they? At the time of the Constitutional Convention and the debates about the Constitution, the best theoreticians wanted to abolish slavery right away, and they should have. But they compromised with other members, and that compromise led inevitably to a catastrophe: the Civil War. If you believe in rights, then the institution of slavery is an enormous contradiction. It is to America's honor, which the haters of this country never mention, that people died to abolish slavery. There was that strong a feeling about it. Slavery *was* a contradiction, but before you criticize this country, remember that slavery was a remnant of the politics and philosophies of Europe and the rest of the world. Blacks were in many cases sold into slavery by other black tribes. Historically, there was no such concept as the right of the individual; the United States is based on that concept, so that so long as men held to the American political philosophy, they eventually had to eliminate slavery, even at the price of civil war. Incidentally, if you study history, following America's example, slavery or serfdom was abolished in the whole civilized world in the nineteenth century. What abolished it? Capitalism, not altruism or any kind of collectivism. The world of free trade could not coexist with slave labor. Countries like Russia (which was the most backward) liberated the serfs without any pressure from anyone, but because of economic necessity. No one could compete with America economically so long as they attempted to use slave labor. That was the liberating influence of America.

Now, I don't care to discuss the alleged complaints American Indians have against this country. I believe, with good reason, the most unsympathetic Hollywood portrayal of Indians and what they did to the white man. They had no right to a country merely because they were born here and then acted like savages. The white man did not *conquer* this country. And you're a racist if you object, because it means you believe that certain men are entitled to something because of their race. You believe that if someone is born in a magnificent country and doesn't know what to do with it, he still has a property right to it. He does not. Since the Indians did not have the concept of property or property rights—they didn't have a settled society, they had predominantly nomadic tribal "cultures"— they didn't have rights to the land, and there was no reason for anyone to grant them rights that they had not conceived of and were not using. It's wrong to attack a country that respects (or even tries to respect) individual rights. If you do, you're an aggressor and are morally wrong. But if a "country" does not protect rights— if a group of tribesmen are the slaves of their tribal chief—why should you respect the "rights" that they don't have or respect? The same is true for a dictatorship. The citizens in it have individual rights, but the country has no rights and so anyone has the right to invade it, because rights are not recognized in that country; and no individual or country can have its cake and eat it too— that is, you can't claim one should respect the "rights" of Indians, when they had no concept of rights and no respect for rights. But let's suppose they were all beautifully innocent savages—which they certainly were not. What were they fighting for, in opposing the white man on this continent? For their wish to continue a primitive existence; for their "right" to keep part of the earth untouched—to keep everybody out so they could live like animals or cavemen. Any European who brought with him an element of civilization had the right to take over this continent, and it's great that some of them did. The racist Indians today—those who condemn America—do not respect individual rights.

As for Japanese Americans placed in labor camps in California, that wasn't done by defenders of capitalism and Americanism, but by the progressive liberal Democrats of Franklin D. Roosevelt. [PWNI 74]

Should this country return some of the lands that were seized from the Indians under the guise of a contractual relationship?

As a principle, one should respect the sanctity of a contract among individuals. I'm not certain about contracts among nations; that depends on the nature and behavior of the other nation. But I oppose applying contract law to American Indians. I discuss this issue in "Collectivized 'Rights' " [in *The Virtue of Selfishness*]. When a group of people or a nation does not respect individual rights, it cannot claim any rights whatever. The Indians were savages, with ghastly tribal rules and rituals, including the famous "Indian Torture." Such tribes have no rights. Anyone had the right to come here and take whatever they could, because they would be dealing with savages as the Indians dealt with each other—that is, by force. We owe nothing to the Indians, except the memory of monstrous evils done by *them*. But suppose there is evidence of white people treating Indians badly. That's too bad; I'd regret it. But in the history of this country, it's an exception. It wouldn't give the Indians any kind of rights. Look at their history, look at their culture, look at their treatment of their own people. Those who do not recognize individual rights cannot expect to have any rights, or to have them respected. [FHF 76]

Do you think America is a white racist society?

Certainly not. Do not hold against American society the crimes of a bad and backward part of the country—namely, the South.

The South was never an example of capitalism; it was an agrarian, feudal society. It was the part of the country that established slavery, and had the nerve to secede and fight a war for the purpose of maintaining slavery. (This is an example of when people do *not* have the right to secede.) America fought a civil war to liberate the slaves. The principles of the Declaration of Independence, for the first time in human history, gave individual rights to every human being, regardless of race. [FHF 77]

Could you comment on the upcoming Bakke affirmative action case?

It's like the De Funis case, which I have written on. [See "Moral Inflation," Part III, in *The Ayn Rand Letter*, vol. 3, no. 14, April 8, 1974.] I supported De Funis, and I support Bakke in the same way. If one is not a racist, one should not support reverse discrimination quotas. Racial quotas are vicious in any form, at any time, in any place, for any purpose whatsoever. Affirmative action is vicious; it isn't profiting anybody; it isn't improving the lot of the minorities. It's giving jobs and patronage and pull to the leaders of minority groups, and observe that only the races that got themselves organized get anything out of it (if you could call it an advantage). It's as un-American and unjust as any current movement, and I hope to God the Supreme Court is brave enough to forbid it once and for all. We are supposed to be color-blind, and that's what we should be. [FHF 78]

I notice few blacks in the audience. Would you comment on why so few blacks seem interested in Objectivism?

I'm proud of the blacks who are here, and those who I know personally are interested in Objectivism, because it's much harder today for blacks to preserve their dignity and remain individualists than it is for other groups. But your kind of survey is totally inappropriate. I'm not a racist; I don't try to appeal to certain ethnic groups. I'm interested only in human beings and their minds. Your claim that blacks are not sufficiently interested in Objectivism is an insult to them. I hope you're wrong. [FHF 78]

Could you comment on feminism?

I am profoundly antifeminist, because it's a phony movement. To begin with, it's Marxist-Leninist in origin. It wants to have its cake and eat it too. It wants "independence" for women— government-funded independence, supported by taxes. Extorted from whom? From men, whose equals they claim to be. But men did not get established in this country with the help of the government. If women want to be equal—and of course, potentially, they are—then they should achieve it on their own, and not as a vicious parasitical pressure group. [FHF 78]

What is your position on the Equal Rights Amendment?

I am against it, because it is a dangerous, very dangerous, redundancy. The Constitution (as apart from its amendments) does not make any distinction between men and women. When the Constitution speaks about rights, it does mean equal rights for men and women. Then it is up to the states to pass certain laws that recognize physical, physiological differences between men and women. Those differences do exist. They're not intellectual, they're not moral, they're not an issue of different rights. But they *are* physiological differences. The Equal Rights Amendment wants to repeal a metaphysical fact of reality. For instance, it wants women to be drafted into the army—which I hope all those women libbers would be, except that the country would lose the war if they were. The political power that certain ambitious pressure-group leaders could draw from such an amendment, under the guise of equality, is very dangerous. This is why the Constitution should not be cluttered with nonsense of that kind. [FHF 76]

Could you give us a word about the women's liberation movement?

I'd be the last person to give you that. I'm a male chauvinist. [FHF 81]

CHAPTER TWO

Ethics

Ethical Fundamentals

Do you agree with the widespread philosophical idea that means alone are chosen by reason, while ends are chosen irrationally?

No! I reject the evil idea that choosing ends by reason is impossible. It has destroyed ethics. Everything that I have written is devoted to proving the opposite. Ends are *not* chosen irrationally. We choose our ends by reason, or we perish. "The Objectivist Ethics" provides the essence of my stand on ends and means. [FHF 69]

Is compromise on moral principles evil because of the subjectivism involved?

No. Subjectivism is one of the causes of compromise. The evil is the betrayal of basic values and basic principles, the ultimate result of compromise. Once you compromise and continue that policy, it will be increasingly more difficult to recapture your values. [NFW 69]

How do you respond to someone who says, "Nobody is all bad; even Hitler was nice to his dog"?

You ask him why he has such a poor hierarchy of values that kindness to dogs is considered equal to mass slaughter. You question his knowledge of morality. But such claims—like Stalin was good to his grandchildren, which is considered a plus (though he did murder relatives)—are rationalizations, the meaning and purpose of which I discuss in "The Cult of Moral Grayness." They represent the desire to escape from moral absolutism.

The main issue here is how to pronounce moral judgment—how to weigh certain flaws against certain virtues, which is a complex subject. (In what follows, I assume the importance of moral absolutism and precise moral judgment.) Only approximations can be given. We can name what kind of flaws are so evil (like dictatorship) that nothing else that one does may be regarded as a virtue. The other side of the ledger is more difficult: There is no virtue the possession of which enables you to say of a person that no matter what he does, you'll forgive the act and continue to regard him as virtuous. The hierarchy works differently. If a person has major virtues, more is demanded of him; the standard becomes more severe. [NFW 69]

You assert, as the basis of the Objectivist ethics, man's need for his continued existence. But why should one be concerned with mankind's survival?

My ethics is *not* based on a concern for the continued survival of *mankind*. The questioner is so thoroughly on a collectivist premise that when he hears a pro-man moral code, he assumes it must refer to a collective: mankind. The Objectivist ethics is concerned with the rational requirements of *a* man's survival—of the survival of individual man qua man. The collective survival of mankind is not a consideration in moral questions.

Further, "mankind" is a collective noun, and means only the sum of existing humans. There is no such separate entity called "mankind." When a man lives his own life properly, that is the only contribution to mankind he can make. Any other meaning is collectivist. There is nothing a man must do for mankind in that sense. [OE 62]

Since knowing oneself is so difficult, how can a person be sure he's really happy, and not merely escaping like a hot-rodder from the constant terror of indecision and the lack of direction?

This question illustrates the error in an earlier question (in which the questioner thought ethics applied only to mankind collectively) and is an eloquent proof of why the individual needs the guidance of ethical values for his happiness and proper survival, not mankind's.

On the premise implicit in the question, happiness is impossible. Since man is supposedly in constant terror of indecision and lack of direction, he strives for "happiness" as an escape from this terror. How would he know when he's happy? He couldn't. If a man is tortured by indecision and no direction, then he has not consciously selected his values. If a man has no idea what his standards or goals are, he cannot be happy no matter what he does. Nor could he know the meaning or emotional quality of his actions or reactions. One cannot solve a problem of indecision by asking: "How can I live with my indecision and be happy?" Man cannot properly live with indecision. He must decide what his values are and why, and then what purpose he wants to pursue. When he has chosen a central purpose, that will give him the lead by which he can organize his whole hierarchy of values. Without that central purpose integrating his values, he can neither be happy nor know what will make him happy. [OE 62]

Selfishness and Self-Sacrifice

What do you mean by "selfishness"?

I mean the pursuit of one's rational self-interest. I mean that the central purpose of one's life is to achieve one's own happiness, not to sacrifice oneself to others or others to oneself. "Selfishness" means to live by the judgment of one's own mind and to live by one's own productive effort, without forcing anything on others. [NC 69]

In an earlier answer to a question [see pp. 168–69], you accuse of context dropping the person who says: "I'm going to cheat my aunt out of her money, and then spend it on a library and devote the rest of my time to reading and thinking, which is in my self-interest." What context is he dropping?

He is dropping several contexts, primarily that his self-interest is not determined by whatever he feels like doing. To determine one's rational self-interest, one must include all the relevant elements involved in a decision. The first contradiction he would encounter is the idea of robbery. He cannot claim self-interest if he does not grant this right objectively to his aunt. If he decides to follow his own self-interest but to respect nobody else's, he is no longer on an objective moral base, but on a hedonistic, whim-worshipping one. If so, he has disqualified himself; he is claiming a contradiction. If he wants to maintain rationally his own self-interest, and claim he has a case for his right to self-interest, then he must concede that the ground on which he claims the right to self-interest also applies to every other human being. He could not make a rational case for taking his aunt's property. [OE 62]

Under Objectivism, what would be your social responsibility toward other people?

Rationality and hands off, if you want the briefest formulation. You are not your brother's keeper. You cannot and do not have unchosen obligations; you're responsible for your own actions. You would be responsible for any harm you do to other people. You would be held responsible for any relationship that you enter into voluntarily, for any contract that you break unilaterally. You would have to stand by your word. You would have no right to pass on to others the burden or consequences of your mistakes or failures or whims. In other words, you cannot make other men your victims, and you need not be their victim.

Any help you might want to give others would be your private privilege, but not your moral—and certainly not your legal—duty. If you want to help others, fine, so long as you can afford it, so long as it's your voluntary choice, and so long as you do not claim it as a major virtue or duty. It is good to help others only when you help them on the grounds of the value you see in them. If you see a talented man struggling, and you want to help him financially (and you can afford it), that's not a sacrifice, and would be a good gesture, under my morality. But it's not good to help someone who is suffering as a result of his own evil. If you help him, you are sanctioning his immorality, which is evil. [FF 61]

Is altruism impossible, or is it undesirable?

It is an unspeakable evil. It is impossible for the naive man who attempts to practice it voluntarily; it is possible for altruism's executioners. An innocent man cannot practice altruism—not unless he leaps into the first cannibal's pot he sees, to provide the cannibal dinner. So long as he lives, he cannot be an altruist. But think of what the executioners—the recipients—of altruistic sacrifice can do. Altruism is the sole justification used by every dictatorship—for example, Nazi Germany and Soviet Russia. And it's used in America today any time anyone wants something immoral or unearned. In that sense, altruism *is* possible, as the sea of blood throughout history demonstrates. [FHF 72]

One principle of the Objectivist ethics is: never sacrifice something of greater worth for something of lesser worth. Another is: pursue your rational self-interest. Don't these sometimes clash? Suppose a colleague and I are both being considered for the same job, and I know my colleague is a worthier candidate: he's a better teacher and scholar. If he were promoted instead of me, the first principle would be fulfilled—the worthy would triumph over the less worthy— but my own self-interest would not be promoted. In such a case, should I withdraw from the competition?

Objectivism does hold: never sacrifice something of greater worth in favor of something of lesser worth. But there's an error in your example: the assumption that one candidate has it in his power to sacrifice the other. The candidates for a job do not decide each other's fate. The issue of sacrifice applies only to their employer: he could sacrifice the worthier applicant. He must decide, after judging both men objectively, which one he considers better, and give that man the job. This is *not* a sacrifice of the lesser man. Not giving you a job—abstaining from handing you some value—does not mean that you are being sacrificed.

Now the decision to withdraw your application would be based on a wrong premise—namely, that it is your responsibility to provide employment for your colleague, if *you* consider him better. That's altruism in reverse. An altruist usually says: "If you are better, sacrifice yourself—let the weaker man have the job, since he needs it more." But in your example, you're being an altruist toward the better man. You adopt the interests of your rival and of your employer, and take upon yourself their responsibility, which is an improper enlargement of your responsibilities and powers. You cannot be responsible for running the life or the business of another man. You should not sacrifice yourself for the sake of a better colleague, or for the sake of an employer getting a better employee.

Aside from the issue of sacrifice, I challenge your basic approach in this example. Human abilities cannot be measured in the exact terms implied by this question. Unless there are gross inequalities—one man is blatantly superior to another—you cannot measure the qualifications of every *proper* candidate for a position in the way you suggest; you cannot decide that some applicant is in fact better than yourself. If you can objectively demonstrate that the other person is obviously better, then you should not apply. To avoid such conflicts, never apply for a job in which you *know* some more qualified man will do a better job. Never ask for the unearned. But if you're sure of your qualifications, it is not incumbent on you to measure every small degree of superiority or inferiority in all other applicants. Do your best, follow your own self-interest, and grant the same right to other applicants. But they are not your responsibility. [OE 62]

Is it all life or one's own life that one is morally bound to preserve? Suppose a conflict arises between one's own life and happiness, and that of others. What should one do? For instance, should I let the whole nation go down in ruins rather than give up my own life?

The moral obligation to maintain one's life does not mean survival at any price. Only one's own life is a primary moral obligation—if you want to call it that—because it's the only life over which you have control, the only life you can live, the only life for which ethics gives you guidance. For the same reason that you should value your own life, you should value human life as such. I'd even say animal life has a certain value that man should respect. But that does not mean that you should indiscriminately value the life of every other human, or that you have a duty to sacrifice your own life to others, though you should, rationally, value the life of any human who corresponds to your values.

As for the last part of your question: Metaphysically, we are never put in a position where the life of a whole nation depends on the sacrifice of one man. If that occurred (outside of collectivist fiction), we would be living in a different universe, and so the rules of our existence would be different. Of course, whether a man should die fighting for freedom, as in the American Revolution, is a different issue. Such a man is not dying for the nation. I honor the men who died fighting for freedom in the past, and I honor them when I say I hope they died for their own freedom. Because we profited from their actions, we should appreciate what they did; but it was not their duty to be martyrs for us. [OE 62]

A rational person finds himself in a life-threatening situation, such that unless he kills an innocent man, he will be killed. Under such circumstances, is it morally permissible to kill an innocent person?

This is an example of what I call "lifeboat questions"—ethical formulations such as "What should a man do if he and another man are in a lifeboat that can hold only one?" First, every code of ethics must be based on a metaphysics—on a view of the world in which man lives. But man does not live in a lifeboat—in a world in which he must kill innocent men to survive.

Even as a writer, I can barely project a situation in which a man must kill an *innocent* person to defend his own life. I can imagine him killing a man who is threatening him. But suppose someone lives in a dictatorship, and needs a disguise to escape. If he doesn't get one, the Gestapo or GPU will arrest him. So he must kill an innocent bystander to get a coat. In such a case, morality cannot say what to do.

Under a dictatorship—under force—there is no such thing as morality. Morality ends where a gun begins. Personally, I would say the man is immoral if he takes an innocent life. But formally, as a moral philosopher, I'd say that in such emergency situations, no one could prescribe what action is appropriate. That's my answer to all lifeboat questions. Moral rules cannot be prescribed for these situations, because only *life* is the basis on which to establish a moral code. Whatever a man chooses in such cases is right—subjectively. Two men could make opposite choices. I don't think I could kill an innocent bystander if my life was in danger; I think I could kill ten if my husband's life was in danger. But such situations could happen only under a dictatorship, which is one reason not to live under one. [FHF 68]

Does a person have to be strong (as opposed to weak) to be selfish?

No. This is one of the fallacies of today's prevalent morality, altruism, which holds that man must sacrifice himself to others— that service to others is the moral justification of one's life. This creates the idea that it takes a special strength to live by the judgment of your own mind. But, in fact, all it takes is honesty, whatever your level of intelligence or ability.

The penalty for living unselfishly (that is, irrationally)—for depending on, or sacrificing yourself to, others—is so tremendous, psychologically, that no man has the strength to survive it. As proof, note that most men today live in chronic misery, psychologically and existentially. [NC 69]

If an individual thug is stronger than other men, or a national government is stronger than other people, wouldn't reason make them resort to violence?

Reason involves knowing the nature and the consequences of your actions, and of knowing where your rational self-interest lies. Reason does not mean you can arbitrarily decide that whatever you want is in your self-interest. Some men do this, but that doesn't mean it's rational. To go by reason is not to be guided by emotions or whims.

Reason demands the recognition of human rights. Morality is not based on whim, categorical imperative, or revelation. It's based on the simple fact that man exists by means of his mind. Anything man wants or needs must be produced; man must possess knowledge in order to produce it; reason provides that knowledge. Once you know that, if you then decide you don't want to exist by means of reason and production, but by means of muscle instead—since you're physically strong, you prefer to rob or enslave somebody else—you are contradicting the only base on which you could have any justification for your existence. You are guilty of the most irrational contradiction. The only grounds on which you can claim the right to your own life are the same grounds that support the right to life of every human. If you claim an exception or a double standard, you cannot defend it by reason.

Moreover, a man of self-esteem does not want the unearned: he doesn't want anything from others that he must obtain by coercion—by crime or by government force and regulation. Such a man deals with other men as an equal, by trade. Further, a man of reason plans his life long range. The psychological distinction between a rational man and an evader is that a rational man thinks, plans, and acts long range, while the more neurotic and evasive a person is, the shorter the range of his interests. The playboy or drunkard—the pleasure chaser unable to look beyond the range of the moment—is an irrational neurotic. But no rational person would decide that it's in his self-interest to rob and murder, because he knows that others will and should answer him by the same means.

As for this issue on the level of nations, rationally selfish people do not start wars. Historically, who started them? Woodrow Wilson, a humanitarian reformer, led America into World War One to make the world safe for democracy. Franklin Delano Roosevelt pushed this country into World War Two to save the world and bring everyone the Four Freedoms. In both cases, the state of the world after those wars was infinitely worse than it was before, in precisely those aspects that the humanitarians wanted to correct. The world became more enslaved and experienced a greater spread of dictatorship, poverty, and misery. But most important, in the whole of history, from the Egyptian pharaohs to John F. Kennedy, there has never been a dictator or potential dictator who has justified dictatorship on the grounds of selfishness or individual rights. Only the altruist morality allows a dictator to get away with enslaving people. The dictator must offer his victims some kind of goal and tell them to sacrifice their personal interests to it. Take Hitler: if you read *Mein Kampf* or any other Nazi publications, you'll be surprised to what extent they utter altruistic slogans indistinguishable from communist ones. They despise individualism and "bourgeois" selfishness. What did they ask of the German people? Service to the state, self-sacrifice, the merging of your interests in the great national, racial whole, and so on. I mention Kennedy because I'm very concerned about him: it's a dangerous sign when a presidential candidate tells you he's going to demand sacrifices, without even telling you for what.

Every dictatorship uses the altruist morality to make men sacrifice themselves or bear self-sacrifices. But when someone says you have the right to live for your own sake, but have no right to sacrifice anyone else, you may be sure he's not a dictator. No dictator could last, or even come to power, by telling the individual that he has the right to his own life, and that the state has no right to force him to do anything. Try to project, as science fiction, how a dictator could come to power and then rule without using the altruist morality; it's impossible. By contrast, the Declaration of Independence, which contains the Objectivist morality by implication, says man has a right to his own life, his own liberty, and the pursuit of his own happiness; it doesn't mention service to others. Observe what kind of magnificent, benevolent society resulted. That should be enough to convince you. [FF 61]

You say the predominant trend of nineteenth-century intellectuals was collectivist and statist. But didn't Nietzsche advocate individualism? What's your estimate of him?

It's a low estimate, philosophically. I disagree with him emphatically on all fundamentals. Judge a philosopher by the *fundamentals* of his philosophy—namely, his metaphysics and epistemology. Nietzsche was a subjectivist and an irrationalist. Existentialism claims him as an ancestor, with a great deal of justice. Nietzsche believed that although reason is valuable, it is secondary; man's basic tool of guidance is instinct or blood. Now there is no greater contradiction than a subjectivist calling himself an individualist. An individualist is essentially a man who thinks independently. A subjectivist is a man who does not care to think—who wants to be guided by feelings and "instincts." To survive, such a man must be a parasite on the thinking of others. An "individualist parasite" is a contradiction in terms. (See the article "Counterfeit Individualism" in *The Virtue of Selfishness.*) Incidentally, this is why subjectivists could not stem the tide of collectivism. Politically, Nietzsche was perhaps the most ineffectual of all thinkers. Certain collectivists, like the Nazis, even claimed Nietzsche as their philosophical justification. That was unfair to him; but some passages in his works could be used to justify a totalitarian state (while others would contradict them). Finally, Nietzsche was opposed to capitalism, and contemptuous of the market. [IBA 62]

What is your opinion of humanism?

"Humanism" is like "democracy": a rubber word that can be stretched to mean anything. If you mean, as some do, a belief in man's ability to stand on his own feet, pursue his own values, and achieve his own destiny, then "humanism" is the basic tenet of Objectivism and only Objectivism can implement it. "Humanism," however, is also used to mean that every man is his brother's keeper—that to whatever extent you succeed or do anything rational, you must be penalized in favor of those who (either through no fault of their own or by deliberate dishonesty) have not achieved anything. In that sense, there is no philosophy more opposed to "humanism" than Objectivism. [PVA 61]

Should a nation as rich as ours be indifferent to poor people?

On what we owe others, see "The Ethics of Emergencies" (in *The Virtue of Selfishness*). But let me clarify the use of "indifference" in this context. This question implies that the nation is a collective whole, which experiences emotions such as love, hatred, and indifference. Therefore, it's a loaded question—it assumes a collectivist view of society and human relationships. A nation can be neither loving nor indifferent, because there is no such *thing* as a nation; it is merely a group of individuals. Individuals may be indifferent, but such concepts are inapplicable to a nation. When confronted with the idea of a collective action to be taken by a society, one should ask who is indifferent and which individuals will have to suffer so that other individuals can avoid being "indifferent." Nothing prevents the people of a nation—whether a majority or a minority—from individually helping anyone. Nothing prevents them from feeling compassion, pity, or anything they wish, and using their own money to help whomever they want to help. But no moral principle can justify allowing some men the luxury of feeling compassion at the expense of the wealth, the life, and the effort of others. No one has the right to indulge in "not feeling indifferent" by seizing by force the property of another—who may have good reasons for being indifferent—and giving it away to the poor (whether deserving or undeserving), about whom this Robin Hood wishes not to be indifferent. "Indifference," if it has any meaning in a social sense, means "neutrality." The relevant issues here are rights and justice, not love or indifference.

There is nothing wrong with individuals helping others, provided one never considers it a moral duty. It is not one's moral obligation, because nobody should regard himself as a sacrificial animal. Legally, he may do so, if he wishes; but the Objectivist morality would consider it enormously immoral. [APM 62]

What role should volunteerism (for example, the work of the Peace Corps) play?

It's regrettable that you assign the once respectable word "volunteerism" exclusively to charities. Nothing's wrong with charity work when it's private and voluntary—not public, semiofficial, and enforced by blackmail, like the Peace Corps. The Peace Corps accomplishes nothing and creates a negative image of America. Further, there is an expression Peace Corps officials use that refers to the psychology of the volunteers upon their return to America: "the shock of reentry" (which compares them to astronauts returning from space). What causes this shock? Those selfless little altruists claim they joined because they want to help undeveloped people. They do manual labor—or become great white fathers and lord it over helpless savages—and in exchange, they expect big jobs in government or private industry when they return to America. That's selflessness for you. [FHF 67]

What do you think of the idea of working for the family of man?

My main objection is literary. I object to bad metaphors like "the family of man." They're dangerous when taken seriously. To equate mankind with one's own family is to rob both terms of any meaning. You can want to work for your family, because it's *your* family, and your own choice. That can contribute to your happiness, and supporting your family can be within your power. But mankind is not a family. Historically, it has never behaved like one—except perhaps like the worst kind of family. And you have no control over and no choice about what happens to mankind. You cannot have much interest in literally every member of the human race; there are billions of people. You cannot serve billions of people the way you can support your own family. You cannot do anything *for* them. But metaphors of this kind allow you to do things *to* them. You can enslave them and prevent them from living their own lives. All you can properly do for mankind is: leave it alone. [FHF 67]

Is it your obligation to try to reform society?

It's not my obligation, it's my choice. Why do I choose to try? If I want a society in which my rights are respected and I am free to pursue my happiness, I cannot push onto others the job of establishing such a society. If I can contribute to its establishment, I should do so. The same is true for every man interested in the kind of society he lives in. It is certainly in my rational self-interest to live in a free society and not in a dictatorship. Therefore, I work to reform society primarily for myself, and secondarily for those I value. What I do will also benefit mankind—that's the consequence of every rational achievement—but that is not my purpose. [FHF 67]

As an opponent of welfare, what do you propose to do with welfare recipients?

They're not my property to dispose of. [FHF 74]

Do you oppose young people being concerned with the welfare of others?

Taken broadly, yes. I do not believe people should be primarily concerned with others. Every man should be concerned with himself and with his development into the kind of human being fit to live in a society with others. In college, a person is not yet properly developed and is in no position to undertake to help others. Helping others should not be the goal of his life. It is not a moral duty. If and when he can afford the time to help others, nonsacrificially, it is not wrong for him to do so. But by that time, he should contribute money, not time or work, to help the poor.

Incidentally, I do not believe that the poor are social victims. Environment does not condition man; if it did, mankind would never have survived. The worst environment in this country is luxury compared to what the rest of the world lives in. If a man cannot rise out of poverty here, he couldn't survive in the rest of the world. This does not mean that the poor are evil. They may be victims of misfortune—these are the so-called deserving poor. What should be done about them? Voluntary charity by those who can afford it nonsacrificially. There is enough money for that in this country, which has always given generously—in fact, too generously. Charity organizations can hire professional social workers to help the poor. It is not the job of some young power luster or sacrificial altruist to be concerned with helping others when he himself is not yet a formed individual. [FHF 67]

What do you think of the masses—not the groveling masses, but those people who have no talent, but want to earn a living?

No human has no talent. Every human, if he uses his mind, has talent to that extent. He shouldn't be pretentious and aspire to more than he can understand and produce with his own mind. But there's no such thing as a worthless human being—unless he makes himself such. There is no such thing as "the little people." But let's suppose there is a group of people of such limited intelligence that they really are helpless. If you're concerned with them, you should be a greater advocate of the exceptional man than I am (if that were possible) because it's only by means of the work of the better minds—and only in a free society—that helpless people (*if* they exist) can survive. They couldn't survive in a more primitive society. They could survive only in an industrial society, which requires freedom.

But why is anybody entitled to our concern, interest, and sympathy simply because he is undistinguished? If there are helpless people—and that's your choice of words, not mine—why should we be interested in them? We should be interested in the talented, intelligent, hardworking, ambitious people who want to carry their own weight and make something of themselves. That's the overwhelming majority of Americans. [FHF 72]

What do you think of Albert Schweitzer?

To paraphrase Howard Roark, I don't think of him. [FHF 67]

I take it, from reading The Fountainhead, *that you have a low opinion of social workers. What is your opinion of doctors and nurses?*

I do not oppose all social workers. Both Howard Roark and Peter Keating are architects: there are good and bad men in every profession. What I am opposed to is the collectivist-altruist kind of social worker (like Katie from *The Fountainhead*). That sort is frequently encountered, but that doesn't mean all social workers are frustrated little tyrants.

But why ask me about doctors and nurses? My guess is that since I don't think human beings should be sacrificial animals, you think I'm opposed to any profession that helps others. Doctors and nurses are desperately needed, and a great deal of skill and knowledge goes into making both. (I would not place them in the same category as social workers.) But I do reject the collectivist-statist idea that doctors should be regulated and controlled (for example, under Medicare) because others need them. I don't insult doctors by assuming they are self-sacrificial animals. When they are good, they deserve all the money they make. No good doctor goes into medicine to help others altruistically. He goes into it to fight disease. He is a scientist. He is for life; not to help others, self-sacrificially, while hating his job. That type never helps anybody. [FHF 68]

How do you account for the apparent unselfishness of those doctors and nurses who work under extremely difficult conditions?

The answer is contained in your question: "apparent unselfishness." Good doctors and nurses are never unselfish. They had to be selfish to become competent at their profession, which doesn't mean they are indifferent to the welfare of their patients. They don't practice their professions for the sake of their patients, as a sacrifice, but because this profession interests them. They are no more unselfish than anybody who takes part in an exchange economy. If you sell books or wait on tables, you have to satisfy your customers by holding high standards and offering values. If their standards agree with yours, you make a trade, each party doing so for his own sake. The same applies to doctors. Since they deal with matters of life and death, they often put themselves in great discomfort, such as being awakened in the middle of the night. But since their purpose is human health, it's not a sacrifice for them to rush to save a patient. If a doctor said, "I prefer to play poker for another half hour, so I won't budge," then he doesn't like his profession, let alone his patients. [FHF 70]

Abraham Maslow claims to have found that self-actualizing men—the kind of men you like—were assisted by an altruistic attitude. Could you comment?

I've written countless words on altruism. I've read such experts on it as Plato, Kant, Hegel, and Marx, and I've opposed their arguments. I am not interested in Maslow's "arguments," though I know them. He is so much on the fringe—so primitive and irrelevant—that they're nothing more than arbitrary pronouncements.

Now, you are free to say anything when I'm not around, but do not, in my presence, ascribe to me a liking for the kind of people that Maslow projects. The kind of people I like are in my novels, and some exist in real life. (I could name them briefly.) Don't ascribe any other "likings" to me. [FHF 70]

The Ford Hall Forum is having financial difficulties, owing to the rise in speakers' fees. You have not sought to take advantage of this. Isn't that altruistic?

How do you know what a particular speaker charges? In any case, your main error is the assumption that the only possible value one can derive from any activity is financial, and thus anyone who wants to be a speaker does so only for a high fee. That's placing your self-interest very low. Public speaking is a difficult job, which no one should undertake for money, because it's too much work and you can't make a fortune.

Is my purpose altruistic? No. In any proper deal, you act on the trader principle: you give a value and receive a value. Your question implies that unless I collect a fortune (which I'm collecting in other ways) I have no interest in spreading my ideas. That would mean that I have no interest in a free society and in denouncing evil, though my audience does. That's an impossible contradiction. If I accepted it, I wouldn't be worth two cents as a speaker.

I have a profoundly selfish interest in the freedom of my mind, knowing what to do with it, and therefore fighting to preserve that freedom in this country for as long as I am alive—and even beyond my life. I don't care about posterity; I care about any free mind or independent person born in future centuries. [FHF 73]

When a person collects unemployment benefits, it is charged against some particular ex-employer, whose rate of compulsory contribution to the state automatically increases. Does Objectivism view receiving unemployment benefits the same as receiving scholarships?

Yes. Government controls create unemployment. No matter what happens to your employer, if you are out of work today, why should you protect him and starve? There cannot be individual responsibility for something that is the government's fault. In any situation where the government creates a hardship that pushes you into a position of martyrdom, you are morally justified to take advantage of whatever money is offered to you, provided you don't spread the kind of ideas that created the trouble. [PO10 76]

What do you think of the special education programs wherein retarded children are educated alongside normal children?

I think it's monstrous, as is everything they're doing to feature or favor the incompetent, the retarded, and the handicapped, at an impossible expense. The retarded should not be allowed to

come near children, who cannot—and should not have to—deal
with the tragic spectacle of a handicapped human being. When
the children grow up, they can give it some attention, if they're interested; but it should never be presented to them in childhood,
and certainly not as an example of something they must "live
down" to. [FHF 81]

*Why is so much money spent on helping children with mental
problems, and so little on bright children, who would have more
possibilities?*

I have been saying for years that before we help the helpless—
who can only be lifted a little—we should see to it that we help the
talented children, the child prodigies, who need support desperately. They don't need financial help; what they need is freedom
and private schools in which they'd be free to rise as fast as possible, without being held down to the community standards of the
average child. The people who prefer to help the mentally weak,
and neglect or actually hinder the talented, are the most unjust,
evil people on earth. [FHF 73]

Applied Ethics

Abortion

*How do you define a human being? What are your thoughts on the
morality of abortion?*

A human being is a living entity; life starts at birth. An embryo
is a potential human being. You might argue that medically an
embryo is alive at six to eight months. I don't know. But no woman
in her right mind would have an abortion that late; it's very dangerous for her. So nature is consistent with the interests of both.

For my position on abortion, see "Of Living Death" [reprinted
in *The Voice of Reason*]. I'm in favor of abortion, of birth control, of
sex as such, as an absolute right of the parties involved. The right
of a living human being comes above any *potential* human being. I
never equate the potential with the actual. Moreover, if you argue

that a potential human is entitled to life, then we are all murderers every moment we're not in bed trying to reproduce. [FHF 71]

Why do you support abortion?

Because I support individual rights, and no state, community, or individual has any right to tell a woman what to do with her life. An embryo is not a human life, and one of the most disgusting frauds today is the enemies of abortion calling themselves "pro-life" when they advocate the rights of an embryo—an unborn entity—but refuse to recognize the rights of the living person: the woman (and, for that matter, the father). [FHF 73]

When does a human organism become an individual? At conception, at birth, or at some other time?

At birth. And let me answer the unstated context of your question, because it's obvious. The fact of birth is an absolute—that is, up to that moment, the child is not an independent, living organism. It's part of the body of its mother. But at birth, a child is an individual, and has the rights inherent in the nature of a human individual. Until the moment of birth, the child is physically the property of the mother. It is debated that at some time before birth the child becomes conscious. I don't know; this is for science to determine. But what is not debatable is this: a human embryo does not even have the beginnings of a nervous system until a number of months (around three, I believe) into the pregnancy. At that point, the embryo is perhaps potentially conscious. And beyond this time, abortion becomes dangerous to the mother. Nature is apparently more consistent and more benevolent than certain ideologies. But before that point, there is no rational, moral, or semi-humane argument that could be made in favor of forbidding abortion. Only the worst kind of medieval mystic could defend such a view. Outlawing abortion is a crime against all women, and particularly against the thousands of victims who die every year wherever abortion is forbidden. Because when it is forbidden, women go to quacks who perform abortions under unsanitary con-

ditions. This is what social hypocrisy condones. A piece of tissue—
an embryo—cannot have rights. It is no surprise that an ideology
that denies the rights of adult human beings is concerned about
the rights of an unborn piece of matter. [FHF 67]

*Some women have abortions to prevent the birth of mentally re-
tarded children. Is the opposition to such abortions a version of
altruism, and is its motive the worship of mindlessness?*

The opposition to this kind of abortion is not an example of altruism. It is almost an abnormality within an abnormality. It is the
psychological abyss from which altruism comes, but it is not altruism in its pure form.

Altruism is the view that man should live for others. It does not
imply, as such, that we should sacrifice everyone to the subnormal.
(In fact, many altruists would advocate destroying these children
because they are of no use to society.) For instance, communists
are altruists. They want to enslave and sacrifice everybody because
they think (or pretend to think) that this will benefit everyone in
the future. It is just a temporary sacrifice. There is at least the pretended (and maybe, in the young, the accepted) notion that these
are sacrifices for everybody's good, so that a very mistaken, evil
premise of the good is present.

But in the opposition to these abortions, there is no pretense at
anybody's good. The motive of an advocate of this view is not social
benefit. What distinguishes this from altruism is precisely the view
that sacrifice *as such* is the value—sacrifice for the sake of sacrifice,
not for anyone's good. Of course, this is the *implicit* result of altruism, but it is not the explicit theory; and not everyone who
preaches altruism or subscribes to it in part would accept it. Therefore, to say that this is a variation of altruism is honoring the position
too much. It is much lower morally.

Anyone who speaks of the mentally retarded knows that a retarded child is not capable of taking care of itself. He knows that
the child's parents (particularly the mother) will be tied to that
child for life. When one keeps this in mind, altruism becomes almost too clean a concept by comparison. The sacrifice of the men-

tally healthy to the mentally deformed is unspeakable—it is a sacrifice without recipients. In that way it is a more evil, more metaphysical view of life than altruism. Its purpose is not to have some man sacrifice himself to others, but to have man sacrifice himself. The more useless the sacrifice, the better.

The view that abortions should not be permitted to avoid the birth of mentally retarded children is not the worship of mindlessness. It is hatred for the mind, which is not the same thing. If someone says the mentally retarded should be helped and, therefore, all the resources of society should be devoted to educating them, that is the worship of mindlessness. But the opposition to these abortions involves sacrificing the rights of the living to the desires of something that is not a thing. It is the worship of the non-thing. The horror here is that this view advocates using a deformed fetus as a means of enslaving or destroying the men who have intelligence. It is precisely because it is not even a conscious entity, but something neither human nor animal, that one could not say that the advocate of this view worships the mentally retarded. If he did, he would be half a degree higher in hell. Although there *is* an enormous evil in those who worship simple-minded people over geniuses, there is still some degree of semi-plausibility: they want to protect helplessness. But when somebody wants to protect the desires of an unborn object, then you know the motive is neither the worship of the embryo nor pity for the less endowed. It is hatred for the mind as such.

But the issue here is wider than the mind. That hatred of the mind is involved is obvious. That an advocate of this position would politically seek to enslave the mind is undoubtedly true. But the main motive is hatred for man and happiness. Hatred for the mind is only a springboard. Such a person does not want man to be happy, and he knows that the mind is necessary for man's happiness and values.

This is real man hating, for which altruism serves as a rationalization. Not every altruist is necessarily a man hater. Conceivably, in the Middle Ages, among the ignorant, or today, among the very young, there could be the error that sacrifice is for everyone's happiness. Certainly, anyone who would think about it would not hold that idea for long, but in a lower level of development (when men live in something like the Dark Ages), there is some plausibility in assuming that if we all sacrifice for each other we would all make each other happy, because conditions are so inhumanly hopeless and men do not know what to do about it. But this is not the same as advocating bringing a tortured, nonhuman creature into existence and sacrificing the living to take care of it. That is a capsule of pure evil.

What is particularly horrible about this position is that there is no concern shown for the parents (particularly the mother). In all cases of "normal" (not openly pathological) altruism, when somebody demands self-sacrifice from one group for another, he can point to a rational need (like the helplessness of children). But a mental (as opposed to a physical) cripple is a horror to deal with, and to a mother it is the constant horror that it is her child, only it is not human. The cruelty of this view is that it is utterly unconcerned with the feelings of a healthy mother. To be made to live for a subnormal, mindless child whom one cannot face is sacrifice and drudgery without a goal. It is the person's own values and chance for happiness that are being destroyed. [NFW 69]

Lying

If you are discussing an issue with somebody, is it proper not to volunteer the whole truth?

That is a very vicious form of lying. There are many situations in which you don't have to answer, particularly certain family situations. If you disagree with your parents—and incidentally, you should never attempt to convert them—and you don't want them to be unhappy, don't answer, or if they force the issue, answer the minimum. That's all right. What I regard as vicious is when you agree to discuss an issue with someone, yet you do not tell the whole truth. That's more misleading than simply lying, which is bad enough. It's especially evil to claim honesty when you are deceiving somebody. This is why the oath you're asked to take in court is so wise: You're supposed to tell the truth, *the whole truth*, and nothing but the truth. [PO8 76]

Did you say that we don't have to tell the whole truth to our parents, if it made them unhappy?

No. Someone's unhappiness is not a proper standard; it's an emotional standard, and is thus irrelevant in judging what to do. One shouldn't lie to one's parents to protect them in a fool's paradise. You should either tell them the truth or refuse to answer. For example, if they suspect a love affair and you don't want to admit it, say you'd rather not discuss it. Don't say, "No, I'm perfectly virtuous," which only does violence to your own convictions. The fact that something will make a parent or friend unhappy is no reason to lie to them.

The only exception (which doesn't apply here) involves doctors withholding the truth from their patients. There are cases where, if a patient doesn't know the seriousness of his illness, he'll be more likely to recover. Here it's up to the doctor to judge the evidence. But that's not a question of making a patient unhappy. Happiness is no justification for dishonesty. [PO9 76]

Moral sanction

John Galt said: "The evil of the world is made possible by nothing but the sanction you give it. Withdraw your sanction. Withdraw your support." But didn't he also say that the looters want you to break their rules so that they can control you? How can a person withdraw his support without losing his freedom in the process?

The line you quoted was Galt's. (The second point, incidentally, was not Galt's but Dr. Ferris's, though it is true.) What Galt meant was philosophical sanction: do not accept your enemies' ideas; do not compromise with today's trend; do not pretend to approve of today's ideas for some ulterior motives. But what do you mean in asking how one can withdraw support without losing freedom? About which country are you talking? The United States is in bad shape, but not so bad that you lose your freedom for refusing to share the ideas of your enemies. If you have in mind paying taxes, that's way down the line of importance. That's not how you support today's government; you support it every time you tacitly accept collectivist-altruist-statist slogans or ideas. [PO12 76]

I heard from a group of students of Objectivism that ethics no longer requires saints. Could you comment?

I have tried very carefully not to sanction any group, so that I sometimes offend innocent students of Objectivism rather than sanction a single guilty one. In intellectual matters, this is important. Why are they students of Objectivism, if this is what they do? Until they really learn Objectivism, it's too early for them to make moral pronouncements. You graduate from being a student when you no longer have to use the name of your teacher. They are not helping Objectivism.

There is nothing wrong in using my ideas, provided you give me credit. You can make any mixture of ideas that you want; the contradiction will be yours. But why name someone with whom you disagree in order to spread *your* misunderstandings or falsehoods?

Now, to what does the concept "saint" refer? If it refers to a religious figure, then it can't be appropriate to Objectivism, which is an atheistic philosophy. But the word also has a secular usage: "saint" means a person of perfect moral character—a moral hero—and that is what Objectivism requires of its novices and buck privates. I want nobody but saints, in the moral sense. This is open to each man according to his ability.

Do not accept anything that didn't come from me as in any way representing Objectivism. If you want to know what Objectivism is, learn it from me and my publications. Nobody else can speak for me—and if he doesn't want to speak for himself, you know what to think of him. [FHF 71]

Is it true you canceled some subscriptions to **The Objectivist** *because of letters certain subscribers wrote to you?*

I don't read those letters, but my office has instructions and carries them out. I don't cancel subscriptions if someone disagrees with me—that's his loss. But I do when the letters are rude and crude. It's not an issue of ideology, but of manners. I reject the modern conception of manners; I don't have to engage in conversation with, or offer a service to, anyone who doesn't know how to disagree with me politely. [FHF 71]

Improper questions

This question is going to sound silly. . . .

Never apologize for your own thoughts, and don't estimate them for me in advance. [NFW 69]

Why does your generation exhibit so much more fear than my generation?

No personalities, please. You aren't a psychologist, and I'm not here to be analyzed. You may object to my ideas; you cannot pass judgment on my state of emotions. Besides, you're wrong. [FHF 69]

One of my professors said your arguments lack substantiation. Could you comment?

Let me explain what is improper about this man's question, and why I won't answer *him*. Some time ago, there was a little scandal in Washington involving Hamilton Jordan, who had insulted the wife of the Egyptian ambassador. This ambassador said something very wise: "The person who repeats an insult is the person who insults me." That's my response to this questioner. He had no business repeating such a vicious lie to me—not in private, if he knew me, and certainly not in public. I am not broad-minded enough to listen to every kind of swill.

Now, I'll answer the audience generally. Anyone who knows my writings or lectures knows that I give more clearly thought out and logical reasons for my views than anybody today—and I mean anybody. [FHF 78]

Paul Samuelson, a Keynesian economist, in Newsweek *and elsewhere has criticized Alan Greenspan and you. What is your opinion of Greenspan and of Samuelson?*

I'd be happy to answer that question if it's asked by someone else, in a different context. In the way in which it's asked, I will not answer it, on principle. Here's why: If you saw that Samuelson's comments were derogatory, why get up in public and announce it to me? You are acting as Samuelson's transmission belt or press agent, whether you intended it or not. In effect, you are asking: "Some so-and-so has attacked you and a friend of yours; what do you think of your friend?" I won't give you my opinion of Mr. Greenspan in such a context. As for Samuelson, you could have determined my opinion of him yourself from the remarks that you read. [FHF 68]

What's your reply to conservatives who say your philosophy is akin to socialism, because both are dogmatic and materialistic?

I don't argue with mystics. I never answer the smears of *National Review,* and on the same grounds, I won't answer you. [Questioner apologizes, and says he didn't intend any smear.] Since you apologize, I'll tone down my response and point out the smear. To call my philosophy, which demands the absolutism of reason, dogmatic— which means "arbitrarily taken on faith"—is the most profound smear. If you didn't intend it, I'll take your word for it; but then be awfully careful of sources like *National Review.* [FHF 70]

Miscellaneous

Please elaborate on your claim that we should not try to convert our parents. Does this apply to our teachers as well?

I did say you should not try to convert your parents. This doesn't mean you should never discuss ideas with them; but don't try to *convert* them. Your parents may be neutral about your ideas, or even sympathetic; but if they are antagonistic, so long as they don't force their ideas on you, you should not try to persuade them. No matter how right you are, they will always see you, their child, as a little boy or girl. It is practically impossible, psychologically, for a parent to regard his child as a full adult. To a parent, there will always be the impression of that little one who first began to acquire a personality. No matter how adult you are and how properly your parents treat you, that image of the child always remains. Suppose that little one suddenly undertakes to teach the parent something. The parent, if he's decent, will be profoundly affected by the thought that he must guide the child, and suddenly the child reverses the tables and wants to guide the parent. That is more than a rational person could absorb. If it upsets your parents, you would be at fault.

Always remember your parents' context in regard to you, and also that (unless they are monsters, which do exist, but rarely) your parents are a value to you. It's wonderful if they are both a personal value, through the accident of parenthood, and an intellectual value, through sharing ideas. But if they don't share your ideas, it's not your place to condemn them. You can express disagreement and politely give them your reasons for holding different ideas, but do not pass judgment vocally. You can't avoid passing judgment in your mind; but don't tell your parents: "I regard you as wrong, irrational, and dishonest." That's an improper method of arguing with anyone; in regard to parents, it is unnecessarily and irrationally cruel. Therefore, make it clear to your parents what your ideas are, and after that, give them the privilege of voluntary association, as you want for yourself. If they are interested in continuing a discussion and would like to try to persuade you, continue it. If not, and doing so merely makes them feel helpless and confused, leave them alone in the realm of ideas.

However, you should not let your parents force their ideas on you. Here age is relevant. If you're old enough to maintain yourself and do not accept your parents' financial help, and if the concessions they demand from you are serious, then leave their home and maintain a friendly relationship. If you are too young to stand on your own, however, and what they demand is not a major violation of your ideas, then agree as a courtesy. They want to help you in an area where they think you're wrong. If it's not an important

issue to you, allow them the privilege of not worrying about the results of their support. Don't ask them to violate their ideas; don't
permit them to violate yours. With both parents and child willing
to be rational, it's easy to establish a civilized relationship without
cruelty on either side.

This principle does *not* apply to your teachers. They have no
moral claim on you. If you disagree with a teacher, whether you
should try to convert him depends on your respect for his rationality. Remember, a lot of teachers—particularly anti-Objectivists—
are not very moral, and they may take it out on you. Saving their
souls isn't worth getting lower grades. Therefore, if you're in their
power, in a sense, don't do anything, intellectually, except say "Yes
sir" and get your union ticket—your diploma—as quickly as possible. [PO9 76]

When entering a profession, should one aim to be better than every- one else?

You shouldn't enter any profession with the idea that you must
be better than anybody. This is true today, and would be true in an
Objectivist Atlantis. *Never* make your job an issue of comparisons or
personalities—for example, "I am better than Mr. X." Say you're a
writer. Your approach should be: "I have something important to
say, and *I* am saying it." Period. Let the chips fall where they may.
Maybe somebody is better; maybe somebody is worse. Chances are
that if you operate on this premise, you'll be better than 99 percent of the people in your field. If you allow being better than others to be a conscious aim, then you're passing judgment on your
work before it's completed. You're evaluating something that does
not yet exist, which is a contradiction. First produce something;
then evaluate it according to objective standards. If somebody is
better than you according to these standards, you learn from him.
It's an inspiration. But if many people are worse, don't take pride
in that. That's too bad. The most tragic position is to be alone
among incompetents.

Incidentally, there's no standard by which to measure yourself
professionally, except in very general terms. Take writers, for ex-

ample. Within the group you regard as good, some may be best on certain occasions, and others on other occasions. Many issues are involved: how important is the subject to a given writer, how carefully has he worked on this particular assignment, and so forth. Man has free will; nobody works automatically. Therefore, there is no such thing as one writer who is always superior to every other. This is true of journalists, great literary figures, and also philosophers. [NFW 69]

Love and Sex

Can you comment on Erich Fromm's views on love?

His book *The Art of Loving* presents, as proper, the view of love that in *Atlas Shrugged* I give to the villain James Taggart. Fromm, like Taggart, says that love must be causeless. (His book came out before *Atlas Shrugged*, but I didn't take this conception of love from him.) [*Atlas Shrugged* was published in 1957, *The Art of Loving* in 1956.] It's fascinating to what extent the logic of his wrong premises work. He says that if you love a person for certain virtues or values, then you're being commercial. But you should love a person without reason; otherwise, your love is a trade—it's capitalistic—and capitalism is the enemy of love.

Capitalism *is* the enemy of his idea of love, although capitalism wouldn't bother with him. He can indulge in any kind of love he wants, and if he wants unearned love, he must have his reasons. But that is the opposite of what I advocate. Proper romantic love is based precisely on what he regards as commercial, namely, on justice—on a proper response to the values you admire in a member of the opposite sex. Love is a response to values, and must be earned by means of your virtues. [FHF 68]

In **Atlas Shrugged,** *Dagny Taggart has romantic relationships with three men. If romantic love allows for more than one person, what does this do to monogamy?*

I resent the nonsensical implication that Dagny Taggart in *Atlas Shrugged* is promiscuous. She had three men in her life, not simul-

taneously. Where have you been all your life? Not only is this permissible, it's virtuous. Marriage is not the only proper form of romantic love. There is nothing wrong with romantic affairs. There
are reasons why a couple cannot marry; for example, they could be
too young. That is not promiscuity, provided the relationship involves strong feelings based on serious values. As to more than one
love, remember that men have free will. The Catholic Church advocates indissoluble marriage; I do not. Man is not omniscient. He
can make a mistake in his choice of partner, or his partner may
change through the years, and so he falls out of love. For example,
take Hank Rearden and his wife, Lillian, in *Atlas Shrugged*. He was
in love with her at first, because he thought she was a certain type
of woman. She deliberately faked the kind of image she thought
he wanted, and he eventually became disappointed. He was wrong
to have a secret affair with Dagny—not because of the sex, but because of the lie.

Relationships with many men—not at the same time—is appropriate, but unlucky. Of course, if one is unlucky too often—if one
makes constant mistakes—one must check one's standards. But as
a principle of romantic love, a single, lifelong romance is not the
only appropriate romantic relationship. That is the ideal. If a couple achieves that, they are extremely lucky, and have good premises; one can't make that the norm.

The standard of romantic love is the seriousness of the feeling
and the values it is based on. [FHF 68]

**In Atlas Shrugged, *Dagny Taggart jumps from one man to an-
other, and they're all good men. How can there be any stability in
your concept of romantic love?***

If you find somebody you value, and then find somebody you
value more, you don't necessarily fall out of love with the first person and fall in love with the second. Love is a response to the values one finds in another person; but that doesn't mean that
though you're in love, that will necessarily change if you meet
somebody better.

In *Atlas Shrugged*, Dagny had three men in her life. (By today's standards, you'd call her repressed; I would not.) Three men in a woman's life is not "jumping from one man to another." In her first two romances—Francisco d'Anconia, then Hank Rearden—she was not committed to the man as her one and only love. In the case of Francisco, they were too young. In the case of Rearden, he had philosophical problems and he was married. Neither relationship was begun on the understanding that it was her final choice. And because she was not fully committed, when she met John Galt she was free to realize that he was exactly the type of man she had always hoped to find. She was emotionally and intellectually free to fall in love. If her relationship with Hank Rearden, say, had been different, and they were both fully committed to romance—if they were married or living together permanently—she would still have responded to Galt by finding him attractive and appreciating his value. But that appreciation would not have developed into real love. She would not have left Hank Rearden. [NC 69]

Is an open relationship consisting of one man and two women immoral?

Not necessarily, though usually it would be. One would need to know the situation and their motives. (This is Noel Coward's *Design for Living* in reverse. In that play, two men and one woman live together.) It would be moral if he didn't choose them both at the same time. One situation is where a woman who is married disappears and is presumed dead; her husband—who always loved her—remarries, and then she reappears. If they are honest and they all understand the arrangement and agree to it, then it's possible for it to be proper.

As a general principle, be very careful about passing judgment on the romances of others. Don't pass judgment unless you *know* something is improper, and so don't wish to deal with the person. If you are not personally involved, don't pass judgment. You have to know a lot about both persons before you could do so. Don't judge the personal life of others too lightly. It's a difficult subject, and you must be scrupulous about what you regard as objective evidence. [FHF 68]

AR regarded the male, by the nature of his anatomy, as the prime mover in the act of sex.

Will you comment on what makes the male the dominant sex?

No, because I would have to discuss the psychology of the sexual act. That's a proper subject for doctors and psychologists, but the psychology of sex is not my great interest. Try to figure it out. [FHF 71]

Could you explain the difference between male and female sex roles, and its connection to your position on a woman president?

I have written an article on this subject ["About a Woman President," reprinted in *The Voice of Reason*]. I think it would be improper for a woman to be president. The kind of woman who would agree to be is in some respect neurotic. I am opposed to women's lib. I believe in masculine superiority passionately, enthusiastically, delightfully—not intellectual or moral superiority, but sexual and romantic superiority. If you don't understand this, then I'll reluctantly say: I'm sorry. [FHF 77]

If there is no intellectual difference between men and women, and no moral difference, what other kind of difference could there be, and why would this make it wrong for a woman to run for president?

The difference between men and women is *sexual.* In the sexual roles, it is proper for a man, who is the stronger sexually, to be worshipped, and it is not proper for a woman to be worshipped, and the woman who would even conceive of such a thing is not a woman. [FHF 77]

Is priestly celibacy advocated as a form of birth control?

It isn't so much birth control as a declaration that sex is evil or unworthy of the man who dedicates his life to God. In modern times, the Catholic Church claims that celibacy is not intended as a disparagement of sex, but simply aims to enable a priest to be dedicated exclusively to his calling—to his duty to God—so that he is not distracted by love for woman or family. That's an unlikely reason; but if it is the reason, it's a miscalculation, because a happy marriage *helps* a man or woman in any serious devotion. If God existed, He would not regard romantic love as evil, so there's no reason priests shouldn't marry. But in fact celibacy is one of the oldest and most profound indications of the Catholic Church's antagonism toward sex. [FHF 68]

Is a girl's impression of her father her impression of manhood?

God help womankind if it were! That's a completely unwarranted Freudian conclusion. Incidentally, I'm not being autobiographical here—that is, I don't mean to imply that I had a bad impression of my father—quite the opposite. What I mean is that a rational person would never form his first impression of men or women from his father and mother. First, nobody forms an abstraction from just one concrete. You need at least two of something. Second, the moment you know more than one man or one woman, Papa and Mama acquire a status in your eyes totally separate from everybody else. "That's just family; that's not people." A child very early on makes a distinction between his parents and everybody else. [FW 58]

Humor and Morality

Humor doesn't play a major role in the lives of your fictional heroes. What is the role of humor in life? Do comedians have a value to an Objectivist? What does an Objectivist find humorous?

This is a dishonest question. I'm answering it as an example of philosophical detection. I said before that I'm sometimes asked questions on issues about which there can be no philosophical stand, and here's a good example. What does an Objectivist find humorous? How in hell would I know? Philosophy cannot give you a principle by which you decide what is humorous. As to the value of comedians to an Objectivist, that depends on what kind of value, to which Objectivist, and above all, which comedian.

The dishonesty here is the idea that humor does not play a major role in the lives of my fictional heroes. You're goddamned right it doesn't. Show me a person in whose life humor plays a *major* role. In the old days, there used to be short films, usually comedies, called the spice of the program. That's what humor is, a spice. Proper humor can be amusing and enjoyable, just like good food and tennis. They're valid pursuits. But are these major issues in life? Not unless you're a chef or professional tennis player. I would exclude careers; but anyone who thinks that sports is a major interest has to check his premises.

Now, what is humor? Humor is the denial of metaphysical importance to that which you laugh at. A classical example: you see a snooty, well-dressed dowager walking down the street, and she slips on a banana peel. What's supposed to be funny about it? It's the contrast of the woman's pretensions to reality. She acted very grand, but reality undercut her with a plain banana peel. That's the denial of the metaphysical validity or importance of the pretensions of that woman. Therefore, humor is destructive, which is proper, but its value and morality depend on what you're laughing at. If you're laughing at the evil in the world—provided you take it seriously but occasionally permit yourself to laugh at it—that's fine. But if you laugh at the good—at heroes, at values, and above all, at yourself—you are a monster.

Whenever I hear someone say there is no humor in my novels or heroes, this is what is meant. There are funny passages in all my books that I know have caused readers to laugh out loud. But there isn't one line that laughs at my heroes, my values, or anything good. Recall an important distinction I made in *Atlas Shrugged*: In her childhood, Dagny observed that Francisco and her brother James both laughed often, but they laughed in different ways. Francisco laughed as if he saw something much greater than what he was laughing at. James laughed as if he wanted nothing to remain great. The kind of people who say there is no humor in my novels say it about every work I like, including *Cyrano de Bergerac*, which is a tragic comedy. It is a very witty play—and also tragic—but the humor is always directed at human weakness or evil, never at Cyrano himself.

The worst evil you can do, psychologically, is to laugh at yourself. That means spitting in your own face. Anyone looking for humor as a major issue is looking for that. Such a person doesn't think it's funny when you laugh at him—that is, at villains—but he wants you to laugh at yourself, and will be happy and at home only with another character like himself, spitting in his own face. Leave them to it; but if this is what you're looking for, my novels are not for you. [PO11 76]

You have said that it is inappropriate to treat evil humorously, if you know that it is an actual evil. In this connection, what do you think of the movie Ninotchka?

Ninotchka is an excellent movie. It is brilliantly done, and yet, when I saw it for the first time, although I could admire it technically, it depressed me enormously. The reason is that the subject is not funny. Recall that when Ninotchka returns to Russia from Paris and describes her beautiful hat, her roommate asks, "Why didn't you bring it?," and Ninotchka answers: "I'd be ashamed to wear it here." The roommate replies: "It was as beautiful as that?" The audience chuckles, but this is not funny. It's very eloquent, and typical of the Russian atmosphere. It's a good, realistic line, and for that reason it's not the subject for humor. Moreover, I assume the film's creator is anticommunist, because ideologically the film *is* anticommunist. Yet observe: by treating the issue humorously, he left you with an element of sympathy—with the idea that the evil is unreal. Ninotchka escapes from Russia, as do the three funny commissars. Then, in a clever touch, the movie ends with one of the three starting up trouble with the other two all over again. What does this scene do to the reality of the evils they are supposed to symbolize? It makes you feel, "Oh, yes, Russia; that's *Ninotchka*"—a good-natured disapproval. It makes you feel that these Russians are naughty when in fact they are evil. In that sense, *Ninotchka* is a morally inappropriate movie.

Artistically, *Ninotchka* is well done. But to enjoy it, you must evade (at least for the duration of the movie) the nature of its background. The same would be true if you transposed *Ninotchka* to Nazi Germany. How would you feel about a movie that joked about the concentration camps, and in which some good-natured guard or torturer from a camp finally escaped from Germany. It wouldn't be funny or appropriate. [NFW 69]

CHAPTER THREE

Metaphysics and Epistemology

Philosophy in General

Apart from basic moral premises, is it ever proper to speak of an **Objectivist** *position on an issue? Shouldn't one's own mind be the sole determinant of one's stand?*

This is not an honest question. What does the questioner think a basic moral premise is: "A is A," "thou shalt not steal," "try to be honest"? That's not enough. The basic premises of philosophy are the axioms. But there is an enormous distance between philosophical axioms and the actions of your life—so many issues and subissues, so many questions and consequences—that anyone who thinks his own mind can handle these without the help of principles cannot be interested in principles, philosophy, or his own mind. He's interested in his whims. Objective, rational positions—that is, principles and their application—are not a violation of one's mind, but an aid. If it is proved to you why a certain course of action is right, and according to what premises, then your own mind is saved a lot of time. It is thereby much easier to consider a case and evaluate it than to do so by yourself from scratch. This is the function of philosophy: to save time.

But if this questioner thinks his own mind should be the sole determinant of his stand on an issue, I'll ask him by what standard, and by what right? Right is a moral—that is, philosophic—concept. Why should *his* mind be the sole determinant? Is he properly equipped? No. He would have to be a professional philosopher, and then per-

143

haps by early middle age he would begin to be qualified—that is, to pass judgment on issues strictly on the strength of his own mind alone, unaided by anyone else's philosophy. He would need to return to the pre-Socratic philosophers. Anyone is free to originate his own philosophy if he can do it. But then he must start from scratch. He must define his premises and objectively demonstrate that his system is right. Then he can practice it on his own, with his own mind as the sole determinant of his actions.

The alternative is to adopt a few slogans or commandments, and assert: "That's enough, I'll decide the rest by whim." The serious error here is the failure to differentiate between principles and their application. What philosophy gives you are principles, which are abstract. What philosophy doesn't tell you is how to *apply* those principles to the events and the choices of your life. In regard to concretes, your mind *is* the sole determiner of what to do. Nobody can or should help you. Your own mind must decide how to apply principles. In a dilemma, are you going to betray your moral principles or be faithful to them? What principles apply in this case? What is the right course to take? Your mind must answer these questions, not derive every philosophical position. You may agree with a philosophical position or not, but you need the guidance of principles.

I'll mention here the opposite error—the other side of the failure to understand the dimensions, nature, and place of philosophy. I have in mind questions I'm asked about the narrowest concretes, for example, "What is the Objectivist position on the latest movie?" You can criticize a movie; you can indicate certain philosophical strengths or weaknesses, but there can be no Objectivist (or any other philosophy's) position on a movie. There can be an Objectivist position on an esthetic issue, such as romanticism versus naturalism. There, philosophy speaks, not one's own mind devoid of principles.

So remember that philosophy deals with broad abstractions— with principles—which underlie other conclusions, other knowledge. It's a *philosopher's* job to provide you with these principles; it's *your* job to apply those principles to your own life. Philosophy will foreshorten the difficult problem of knowing what to do in complex situations. Philosophy is the guide; you are the traveler. Remember this whenever you're in doubt about what is or is not a philosophic problem. [PO10 76]

You say it's wrong to be a parasite living off of others. Can't a person use another man's ideas, or must he think solely on his own?

It's not wrong to accept an idea originated or discovered by another, provided you don't accept it on faith, but conclude by your own rational judgment that it is true. In this respect, philosophy is in the same position as the physical sciences. It's not wrong to accept a scientific truth discovered by someone else. If you go into medicine, for instance, you need not discover everything from scratch. But whether it's science or philosophy, you cannot claim to know or understand or accept an idea if you merely memorize it or take it on faith. You must use *your* mind—your rational judgment. Man is the only species that can transmit knowledge. It is proper to learn from others, provided you don't claim authorship. You learn from those who went before you, and then you originate your own ideas when and as you can. [NC 69]

I have the idea that I need unanswerable knowledge—that if one objection can be raised to my position on some issue, then I have to answer it before I can make any other point. But if I answer objections on politics, then I have to answer all the questions on morality that underlie them, and then the questions on epistemology underlying them, and so I can never begin. What's the solution to this problem?

This is a good case for man's need of philosophy. What you describe is exactly what one needs for every subject and every science. You need answers to all those questions, and the only science that can provide them is philosophy. This is why we all need philosophy, regardless of profession. Those questions will come up if you want to be thorough, and they will always be reducible to philosophical principles.

But (and this is an important "but") here's what you must

clearly distinguish: you must answer every *legitimate* question; you *cannot* answer the irrational. You cannot answer questions pulled out of thin air on the "Why not?" premise. For example, "How do we know that existence exists, and it's not all a dream?" Or, "Might life that is not life *as we know it* exist on other planets?" If something exists on other planets that has some characteristics of life, but that is not "life as we know it," then it's a different phenomenon and we'll deal with it when we encounter it. If a high school smart aleck asks such questions, it might be worth pointing out his mistake. But if an adult asks them, you need not answer, because they're unanswerable—not unknowable, but improper.

In deciding which questions to answer, the responsibility is yours: You must determine (nonarbitrarily) what questions are illegitimate. You must be able to say (if questioned by a rational person) why you regard a question as inadmissible. For instance, "Who created the universe?" is inadmissible. This is the archetype of the kind of question that comes from a nonphilosophical context. How do you decide objectively what's an illegitimate question? When you reduce a question to its underlying principle, if it contradicts a philosophical axiom, it's illegitimate. There's a difference between discarding an improper question built on a contradiction, and discarding a question because you dislike it or because an answer doesn't immediately come to mind.

If a question is legitimate, though mistaken in some aspect, you must answer it. But if it comes from the denial of philosophical axioms, you do not. That is the pattern of all questions in modern philosophy. For example, "If you created a being that is in every way like a human, how would it act?" It isn't difficult to answer these questions, because you stop the speaker at the beginning. If it's something in every respect like a man, then it will act like a man. Do not twist your brain every time somebody asks such questions. Once you've trained yourself to identify from what premises a given question comes, you'll be able almost automatically to trace it down to its premises and to say it is irrational. That is the only necessary answer.

Suppose you're writing an article on politics. You need not answer every possible moral question, though you must be clear about fundamental moral principles, because that is the base of your politics. For example, suppose "How should children treat their parents?" or "Should parents beat an obstreperous child?" occur to you. Such questions do not pertain to politics, so you need not answer them to write an article on politics. But they do pertain to morality, so if you wanted to answer them, you'd have to think of the appropriate moral principles.

If at any time a *legitimate* question arises that throws doubt on your fundamentals, then drop everything (short of a medical emergency) and answer that question. If you notice that something you believe contradicts your other convictions, then you cannot function until you solve that problem. Such a question must be handled immediately, because you're in moral and epistemological danger every moment you take a step without resolving the issue.

You'll find that the more you allow yourself properly to question your premises, the firmer they'll become. [NFW 69]

You criticize today's cultural leaders, and claim they are trying to take away our values. But if philosophy is at the root of contemporary culture, aren't they victims of philosophy?

I didn't say that today's cultural leaders are all trying to take away our values. That would be too conscious a process on their part. My objection is that they have no values to offer, and yet occupy positions of leadership that demand the knowledge of values, a commitment to rational values, and the communication of values.

Outside of philosophy, today's cultural leaders—artists, politicians, writers—are victims of bad philosophy. But they are not entirely innocent victims. The situation *within* philosophy is somewhat different. The destruction of values—and specifically of the source of values, reason—was deliberate on the part of the archvillain in the history of philosophy: Immanuel Kant. The same is true for his followers and lesser disciples, though they are mixed cases. Some are victims and killers simultaneously; others are plain victims—but not fully innocent victims, to the extent to which they continue to spread such evil and are afraid to speak the truth. A man is not innocent if he goes into an important profession, knows he lacks the requisite ability, and fakes conviction while ignoring the evidence. However, I would not consider a philosopher evil if he said the following: "There are many fundamental questions to which we have no answers, though we know what these questions are and should attempt to answer them, since philosophy plays an important part in human life." Such a man would be, if not brilliant, at least honest—and more brilliant than most philosophers today. But this is not what contemporary philosophers do. While preaching skepticism, they permit themselves outrageous dogmatic pronouncements. For example, the chairman of the Philosophy Department at UCLA dogmatically announces that there are no answers and never can be. How does he *know* that? This kind of statement is deliberate. [AR is referring to Donald Kalish, whom she quotes in her lecture "Our Cultural Value-Deprivation," reprinted in *The Voice of Reason*.] I consider such men guilty and not victims. [FHF 66]

Besides Aristotle and Ayn Rand, have any other philosophers identified important philosophic truths?

Yes, Thomas Aquinas. He brought the philosophy of Aristotle back to Europe, at the end of the Middle Ages. He was the intellectual father of the Renaissance. He was valuable in clarifying and developing many Aristotelian ideas. But he was a monk. At that time, you could not be a thinker if you weren't religious. There's even a suspicion that he wasn't religious (though historically, that's not known). He wrote on philosophy and religion, and he attempted to reconcile the two. This unleashed philosophy from religion and so in time, of course, philosophy won, because he was Aristotelian—an advocate of reason. He was not a mystic, but you still can take only half of him as a value: the secular, Aristotelian part. His religious treatises are errors or a cover-up, I don't know which.

In a sense, there's only one philosopher: Aristotle. He made some errors—he couldn't be omniscient—but he covered all the essentials. Some lesser truths were identified by philosophers of less value. For instance, John Locke did some valuable thinking, based on Aristotle, in politics. He was the teacher of the Founding Fathers. But this is only politics; in metaphysics and epistemology, Locke was disastrous. He departed from Aristotle and denied that we can perceive reality. In this respect, he opened the gate to a lot of trouble from modern philosophers.

So if you speak in big terms, I'd rather Dr. Peikoff said it, but since I'm his stand-in tonight, take the three As: Aristotle, Aquinas, and Ayn Rand. [PO6 76]

Metaphysics

What do you mean by the nature of reality—if there is such a thing—and where can I find it?

If you don't know, how do you expect me to understand your question? And who is asking it? If you ask me an illegitimate philosophical question about the nature of reality, and I answer, "It's raining outside," that would represent a refusal to recognize your question. But if I answer you correctly—that is, take logical cognizance of your question—that constitutes the recognition of the nature of reality, of facts, of what exists.

The nature of reality is a broad subject that I cannot discuss here. You can find the answer to your question in my writings and especially in *Introduction to Objectivist Epistemology*. This might give you some idea of what is meant by "the nature of reality," which today's colleges won't give you. [FHF 67]

Is there room in your philosophy for God?

No. My philosophy includes only what man can perceive, identify, and demonstrate by means of reason. It doesn't permit the invention of "facts," or the acceptance of anything on faith—that is, without rational demonstration. But there is no evidence for any kind of God, afterlife, or mystical dimension. [NC 69]

How can you account for the universe without God?

What do you mean by "account for the universe"? If you mean "explain what the universe consists of," that's the job of the special sciences, not philosophy. But if you mean "explain the existence of the universe," my reply is: the universe does not need an explanation. "Universe" means "everything that exists"; but "everything that exists" requires no explanation. Existence exists, and only existence exists. Existence, as such, does not require an explanation; it requires study. We need to know what exists, and the nature of what exists. But the attempt to explain the "source" of existence—of the universe—involves a contradiction. Where do you stand, intellectually, if you attempt to explain existence? You, the observer, are part of existence. [NC 69]

How can you account for life and the wonders of the universe on the basis of accident or chance, without the concept of design?

I suggest you identify the meaning of every concept you use. There is no design in nature. The consistency of nature, the fact that nature follows certain laws, is not a product of design, but of the Law of Identity—the fact that things are what they are. Since contradictions cannot exist—since an existent cannot be itself and not itself at the same time—the result is an orderly, non-contradictory universe. In material nature, nothing happens by chance *or* by design—that's a false alternative. They happen according to the Law of Identity: things act and interact according to their natures. This is *not* chance. Chance is a concept pertaining only to human ignorance. When we don't know the causes of some event, we say it happened "by chance." [NC 69]

What is the Objectivist conception of time?

There can be no such thing as an Objectivist view of time, any more than an Objectivist view of the solar system. This is a scientific question, unless you put it in a philosophical form: "Does Objectivism hold that time is absolute, as Immanuel Kant held? Does time exist apart from entities?" My view is, in effect, Aristotelian. Aristotle's position is (in my words) that there is no such thing as independent time or space. The universe is finite, and the concept of time applies to the relationship between entities. Specifically, time is a measurement of motion, which is a change of relationship between entities *within* the universe. Time cannot exist by itself. It exists only within the universe; it does not apply to the universe as a whole. By "universe" I mean the total of what exists. The universe could have no relationship to anything outside itself: no motion, no change, and therefore, no time. [FHF 68]

Is it proper to study something that has no connection to human life?

Suppose someone discovers a plant on the dark side of the moon, and given our present knowledge, it cannot have any effect on human life—on agriculture, food, and so on. *If* this were true, there would be no reason to study it. *But*, such a discovery is impossible, because the universe is one; everything is connected. So scientists ought to study such a plant if it existed. [NFW 69]

Free Will

Doesn't free will contradict the idea that man has a specific identity?

It's almost blindingly self-evident that the philosophical fundamental being ignored here is the Law of Identity. This is a good example of what questions you need not bother answering, since they contradict philosophical fundamentals. The guideline for anyone tempted to ask such a question is: Do not rewrite reality. On what grounds did someone decide that choice contradicts identity? That is an arbitrary construct of determinism.

I first encountered a similar issue in college. Some professor declared: "We must decide whether we're spiritualists or materialists, because the universe cannot contain opposite elements. So either everything is spirit or everything is matter." I was about sixteen, and thought: "Of course, I'm for matter." That seemed the rational answer. It took me a couple of years before I asked the following question: "On what grounds did he decide that reality must be one or the other?" Then I discovered the principle of rewriting reality, and that was very helpful. You'd be surprised how many errors consist of rewriting reality. Kant is the archetype. He does it more, and more openly, than most philosophers. He decides (on a primitive, rationalistic basis, à la Heraclitus and Parmenides) what reality has to be, and if it doesn't correspond to his demands, then reality is wrong—not his demands.

You must ask on what grounds do we decide what reality has to be. You know that reality cannot contain contradictions, and you know that one of the first things you learn, after infancy, is that there are inanimate objects *and* conscious entities. You know yourself—that you have a body and consciousness. That is the empirical self-evident proof that there is both matter and consciousness in the universe. All of your knowledge of man's nature rests on these primaries—that existence exists and consciousness exists. If you drop either of these axioms, you'll encounter contradictions everywhere. And you'll be guilty of using a stolen concept if you claim that the universe is all consciousness or all matter. This is the attempt to prescribe what you think in logic *should* be the nature of reality. But you have no right to any concept of reality or logic unless the material of your concepts came from reality—from the evidence of your senses.

By what reasoning does anyone claim that identity means only material identity, and that human consciousness contradicts the Law of Identity because it operates by choice? Free will is self-evident through observation. Further, it can be demonstrated by as many arguments as you care to muster. Everything you observe about human consciousness tells you that it operates by choice: not only your introspection, but also your observation of other people. So you put yourself in this position: You observe that matter exists and that consciousness exists, and that consciousness operates by choice. Is it a contradiction to hold that we have firm identities *and* the capacity for choice? Ask yourself: "Choice about what?" We don't have a choice about our own *nature*—its identity is firm—but about our *action*. There are no grounds in reality for claiming that freedom of action contradicts the Law of Identity.

This is what I mean by reducing questions to see whether they correspond to or contradict basic axioms. For practice, I recommend Kant's *Critique of Pure Reason*. Read it and observe how often Kant rewrites reality.

Unless he identifies this issue, a conscientious person might feel it's up to him to answer impossible questions. The unstated assumption behind this attitude is that nobody could be as dishonest and irrational as some of these philosophers are: "If a philosopher like Kant spent his life creating a huge body of knowledge, he probably had some legitimate reasons, which I don't see. Surely he isn't a total fraud." If you proceed on that premise, you're lost; the result will be skepticism, unearned guilt, and self-doubt. The more you study Kant, for example, the more helpless you'll feel: "Oh, what's the use? Man knows nothing—at least I can't know, and I am too tired to pursue the quest. There is something wrong with philosophy, there's something wrong with Kant, but I am unable to untangle it, and therefore logic is impotent, reason is impotent, and Kant is right for him, and I am right for me, only I don't know what's right." That is the ultimate result of granting this kind of benefit of the doubt.

Don't give anyone the benefit of the doubt if your first impression is that he's irrational. Don't discard him on an impression; you may be wrong. Be patient enough to see the first admission of mysticism or the first non sequitur. When you get it in his own language (which is the fairest procedure) you can forget all about him. You need not study all of his evils. If you are a philosophy teacher, you might have to help your pupils untangle the particular evils; but for your own information—for the clarity of your own convictions—once you arrive at the conclusion that someone is a mystic (that some part of his philosophy, by his own statement, is not subject to reason or is beyond reason), then he has saved you the trouble of considering anything else that he says. [NFW 69]

Is the choice to focus a rational choice?

No, it's a primary choice—that is, you won't be rational if your mind isn't focused. But conversely, once you've acquired the rudiments of reason, you focus your mind consciously and volitionally. But how do you learn to focus it originally? In the same way an infant learns to focus his eyes. He is not born with his eyes in focus; focusing his eyes is an acquired attribute, though it's done automatically. (I'm not sure whether it's entirely automatic; but from what we can observe, no volition on the infant's part is necessary.) Why does he learn to focus them? Because he's trying to see—to perceive. Similarly, an infant or young child learns to focus his mind in the form of wanting to know something—to understand clearly. That is the beginning from which a fully conscious, rational focus comes. [FHF 72]

What is the difference between concentration and focus?

Concentration means undivided attention on some particular task or object, which includes but is more than focus. It is an attention, an activity, devoted to a particular subject. Focus is more fundamental. You need to be in focus in order to concentrate, but focus is the particular "set" of your consciousness, which is not delimited by the particular task, object, or action that you are concentrating on. You have to focus on something, but focus is not the continuing task you are performing. It isn't tied to the concrete object or task. It remains the same no matter what you're focused on. It is the "set" of your mind. It is a strictly epistemological concept, whereas concentration is more an action concept. The latter includes the idea of focus, and of a particular task that takes longer than a moment, because you don't concentrate for a second. Concentration implies a duration or time. [PO6 76]

People seem somewhat consistent in character. If the choice to think is primary, can there be some quality that endures in a person that enables one to predict what his choices will probably be? Must one's predictions be limited to how a person will act, since a moral person's premises and psycho-epistemology will tend to lead to better action, given any level of focus, compared to an immoral person's premises and psycho-epistemology?

Never attempt to predict what someone will do. You can establish a strong probability. If you know a person well enough to know his basic premises, then you can say with assurance that the chances are he will make the right choice, if he understands a given situation. But you can't say that with full confidence, because you can't even say it about yourself. The choices you make require a specific action of your consciousness: a decision, a choice, when a particular issue comes up. Sometimes you may make the wrong choice, or you may lack the strength or courage to make the right choice. If you can't make predictions about yourself, you can't make them about others. If you know a person is moral, you can expect his actions to be better than the actions of an irrational person. But the idea of attempting to predict human action, in the way you would predict an eclipse, is improper. You cannot and need not predict human actions that way. If you know the general trend of a moral person, his basic premises, he may make mistakes and even evade particular issues, but he'll likely come out right in the long run—he'll correct his errors. That's all you can say about another person, and about yourself, too. [PO6 76]

How does one translate the desire to write into the will to write?

That's a psychological question, but a friend who read this question with me wrote under it the perfect answer: Try hard. [OC 80]

Is it possible for someone to accept the Objectivist philosophy—or any philosophy—and thereby act much as one would through a conditioned reflex, without thinking?

Man cannot act on the basis of conditioned reflexes. The concept of a conditioned reflex does not apply to human psychology. It is a meaningless package deal, with no application to the conceptual, intellectual functions of man. There are automatic functions, reactions, and ideas in a man's mind, but they are ideas that were conscious at one time and became automatic. [FHF 67]

Is man a social animal? Can he develop only in society?

Man does live in society, not on a desert island. But that does not mean society "develops" him. The expression "develops in society" implies that man *is* a social animal. I believe no such thing.

The issue here is: What is primary in a man's development, society or his own mind? Of course, his own mind has primacy. Society cannot make or unmake him. An immoral society can mangle him and make it enormously difficult for him to develop properly psychologically. A rational society can help a man's development a great deal. In a mixed society, the best minds and those who are strongest morally might withstand the pressure from society, whereas the average person will find it beyond his individual independent capacity and give up. Society cannot form a person. It cannot force him to accept ideas; but it can discourage him. Nevertheless, that doesn't make man a social animal. [FHF 67]

Epistemology

Theories of truth

In Objectivism: The Philosophy of Ayn Rand, *Leonard Peikoff writes: " 'Truth,' in Ayn Rand's definition, is 'the recognition of reality.' In essence, this is the traditional correspondence theory of truth: there is a reality independent of man, and there are certain conceptual products, propositions, formulated by human consciousness. When one of these products corresponds to reality . . . , then it is true." A widespread alternative theory of truth is the coherence theory, which AR discusses below.*

*My question is about the criteria of correspondence as a test of truth. An idea that corresponds to its object is true, but how do we determine whether an idea in fact bears a **perfect** correspondence to its object? Doesn't this require some criterion besides correspon-*

dence? Further, in asserting a correspondence between an idea and reality, don't we need some test to determine the precise degree of similarity between what we think and what exists?

The error here is the idea that something other than correspondence is needed to establish correspondence. Take the same error in a different realm: If you say someone is beautiful, you'll need a criterion other than beauty to establish beauty. But if you've established that beauty is, say, a perfect harmony of elements, then you don't need something other than beauty to establish that someone is beautiful.

To establish correspondence means to establish the similarity between, or the identity of, A and B. What other criterion do you need? If you introduce another criterion, the first thing to go is reality. The questioner regards his ideas as something separate from reality. This is extreme rationalism. How are you going to determine the precise degree of similarity between what we think and what exists? Will you say, "My ideas correspond to reality about one-tenth of a percent"? When you speak of ideas, to be exact you must be able to say what in reality your ideas refer to. In using concepts—the minimal tool of ideas—unless you can indicate what's designated by your concept, you have no moral or epistemological right to use it. You must first know what your concept refers to in reality. If you know how to use concepts and organize them into grammatically correct sentences, then you know what it is your sentences denote in reality. The questions you must have in your mind constantly are: "What am I thinking about?" "What am I talking about?" Draw no conclusion until and unless you can point to the facts of reality and say, "I have concluded this about that." That's the test of correspondence. For instance, if you see somebody picking another man's pocket, and say, "This man stole another man's wallet," that's correspondence to reality. If, however, you see this and say: "I don't know; I can't be sure what I saw," then your statement does not correspond to reality.

No special criterion is needed to establish correspondence. What's needed is reality and the proper kind of intellectual identification. Your thinking is not a separate attribute or collection of

Platonic objects that you compare to reality. The idea of the degree of similarity between what we think and what exists is Platonic. Proper thinking is a mental identification or classification of what exists.

Another dangerous Platonic element in this question is the notion of *perfect correspondence.* Be careful in using "perfect." It's applicable in the realm of ethics; but in the realm of cognition, it is extremely dangerous. It's a mystical concept. What would "perfect correspondence" be? According to some mystical uses, it would have to be "omniscience"—knowing everything about some object. But that's not how the human mind works; that's not rational epistemology.

In regard to correspondence to reality, you need only be concerned with two simple rules: In drawing a conclusion you claim is true, you must have (1) included everything relevant to your conclusion, and (2) omitted nothing relevant. In other words, you have considered everything open to your knowledge about a given fact or set of facts, so that when you say, "My conclusion is true," you have used all of the knowledge available to you and have not indulged in any evasion. These are the only rules for establishing that your conclusions correspond to reality. But the real test is what is out there in reality, not some double criteria based on preconceived ideas somehow formed in your mind and detached from reality.

Look at reality. If you find you have ideas detached from reality, that's a sign of rationalism. [PO6 76]

In her epistemology, AR upholds a contextual approach to knowledge. Absolute truths exist and are attainable—certainty is possible—but always in a specific context.

What is the difference between the concept of contextual absolutes and the coherence theory of truth? Is the coherence theory an instance of rewriting reality?

It's a difference of life and death. The coherence theory of truth holds that any set of claims that is coherent—that is, does not contain a contradiction—is true. You need not refer to reality; you merely present a consistent case, and if there aren't any inner contradictions, that establishes the truth of your case. That's pure rationalism; it posits a mystical absolute that sits somewhere in another dimension, above this world. The father of the coherence theory of truth is Hegel, who is not exactly an advocate of contextual absolutes.

The coherence theory is certainly a case of rewriting reality. It simply says: "Go ahead and rewrite, and if you can somehow avoid a contradiction, then your rewrite becomes reality." In fact, you can't avoid contradictions if you attempt this, but you can get as involved as Hegel did. [PO6 76]

Reason and rationality

How can you use reason to prove that reason is valid?

The concept of proof is based on and derived from the concept of reason. It doesn't exist outside of it. I cannot discuss epistemology in detail here, so I'll refer you to Galt's speech, and indicate my answer briefly.

First define what reason is. Reason rests necessarily on the self-evident information provided by your senses, that which you perceive—not on your sense data or sensations, but on your percepts (sense data integrated by your mind or your brain, automatically). That is the start of human knowledge. That must be taken as self-evident, because that is the content of your consciousness, and you cannot talk about consciousness without identifying the fact that your consciousness starts with the perception of entities of the material world outside of you. Then you have to know what reason is, and reason involves the formation of abstractions by means of specific and absolute definitions, abstracting from your perceptual material that which you have observed certain entities to possess in common or that which differentiates certain entities.

The concept of proof is hierarchically dependent on the concepts of reason, axioms, and evidence. To prove something is to go by means of logic down to a fundamental axiom or perceptual starting point. (For details, see my works and Aristotle's.) To speak of "proving reason" or "proving the laws of logic" is a contradiction in terms. Reason and logic is that by which you prove something; they are primary. You do not prove the laws of logic; they are implicit in your first sensation. The Law of Identity is perceived by you the first time you perceive a blob of light. But it takes a lot of perceptual and conceptual knowledge to get you to age twelve or fifteen, by which time you can understand or identify the Law of Identity in conscious, conceptual terms. But implicitly, it was there long before. [FF 61]

Could you explain the dichotomy between reason and emotion?

I deny the existence of any reason-emotion dichotomy. To state my position briefly, emotions are the product of your thinking or your evasions; they are the result of your rational faculty, and are created by you either consciously or subconsciously. Emotions are a subconscious response, but are directed by your conscious mind. So there is no dichotomy. Friedrich Nietzsche and the hippies, for example, believe there is a dichotomy, and they do so in order to place emotions above reason. When you reverse the relationship of reason and emotion, and decide your mind must serve your wishes, you create an inner conflict—a dichotomy between your reason and your emotions. Such a dichotomy is created in an irrational man and by an irrational culture. [FHF 69]

In The Romantic Manifesto, *you state that artistic creation and rational cognition are different methods of using one's consciousness. Would you explain the difference? For example, is artistic creation a subconscious pictorial process, while rational cognition is conscious and verbal?*

Rational cognition is conscious and verbal. Unless your knowledge is in verbal form, you don't really know what you've concluded, and you won't be able to retain it. But artistic creation is not subconscious and pictorial. It's pictorial for the visual arts, but not for the others. The difference is that in artistic creation, you're not bound by reality in the strict sense of the word. Reality is your material, your foundation. It sets the limits for you. It tells you what you can selectively rearrange or re-create. In that sense, it's a consequence of cognition. You have to observe and know something about reality before you can begin to rearrange it. In artistic creation, you rearrange what you know about reality, and even if you do a great deal of this subconsciously, you always check the process consciously.

In rational cognition—to be severe—I'd say *you* don't exist; you're merely a mirror, except that you must direct the process by which you grasp the reality outside yourself. In rational cognition, you are not a creator or rearranger, but a passionately honest observer, and there is no standard and no other emotion involved, except a love for the truth, which is the only standard for a process of rational cognition. It is totally existence-oriented. [PO11 76]

Many philosophers, including Kant, use logic to arrive at their conclusions. How can we be sure that by using reason we can arrive at satisfactory conclusions?

First, even if the whole world agreed or disagreed about everything, that wouldn't mean or prove anything about logic. The mere agreement of everybody on an idea, or the fact that there are ideas on which men cannot agree, doesn't prove that these philosophers were logical or honest. You can't take that on faith about anyone. How you determine whether a given philosophy is true is by your own conscious use of logic, and it's not a guaranteed process—you are not infallible. Learn how to reason, and then you'll know what to accept. If you make a mistake, reason will allow you to correct your error and to learn more. Outside of your reason, you have no means of knowing anything. If you concluded that man can know nothing, one look around would refute you instantly, because you could see how far man has come, and that he needed knowledge to get where he is. In fact, you needed knowledge to arrive at your question.

As for Kant, there can't even be a presumption of innocence. His system is so consistently wrong and illogical, and mistakes of that size cannot be made accidentally. His philosophy is calculated for one purpose: to destroy man's mind. Everything in it is subordinated to that end, and in that sense, he's "logical"—like a criminal is logical in his undertaking. [PWNI 74]

I thought you and Emerson were both champions of individualism, so I was surprised by your remark [in "Philosophy: Who Needs It"] about Emerson's "very small mind." Could you comment?

I'm glad you asked this. Individualism is not a philosophical, nor even a political, primary. It is a concept which, to be valid, must rest on a valid epistemological and metaphysical base. Emerson was an archenemy of reason; he believed in a form of supernatural mysticism. He was a "transcendentalist"—a variant of European Romantic philosophy, which held that we should worship the will as against reason. I consider it emotion worship.

I am primarily a defender of *reason*, not of individualism or capitalism. I defend capitalism because I'm a defender of individualism; I defend individualism because I'm a defender of reason. That's *my* epistemological base, not Emerson's. A man doesn't have the right to do anything he pleases. If he acts on whim, nature quickly destroys him. A man has the right politically to act and think like an Emerson, but it is contrary to reality and to reason.

So never confuse me with a thinker like Emerson—or Nietzsche, who is a much greater mind. Nietzsche also advocated individualism, and he wrote some (literally) beautiful passages in defense of the individual. But he was a mystic. He regarded Dionysus, the god of emotions, as above Apollo, the god of reason. He believed in a malevolent universe: reality is set against man, though the superman will act against reality somehow (even though he can't succeed) and can trample over others for his "selfish" end. But what's his selfish end? Blank-out. Nietzsche never defines a proper morality of selfishness. In fact, he said the superman is "beyond good and evil." But selfishness doesn't consist of sacrificing others to yourself; and I reject altruism, which is sacrificing yourself to others. Man is not a sacrificial animal. My morality begins by dropping the idea that men are, by nature, enemies of each other. The interests of rational men do not clash, so I disagree with Nietzsche about a superman versus the inferior men. Every man should be free and entitled to whatever he can earn, provided he doesn't get it through physical force. If his values and ideas are bad, only he will suffer.

If you want to compare me to anyone, there's only one philosopher whose influence I admit—and proudly—and that is Aristotle. I disagree with some of his philosophy, especially his cosmology (but then cosmology is not a proper part of philosophy). I disagree with certain Platonic influences in some of his works. But I agree with all of his essential points. So, if you want to pigeonhole me, it will be an honor to belong to the same class as Aristotle. [PWNI 74]

Isn't it hard to view objectively the ideas you've grown up with and reject any that are false?

No, not if you accept the premise that reason is the only justification for accepting any idea. If in childhood you accepted some ideas on faith or by conformity, they may be important to you emotionally. But they don't affect your mind unless you permit them to. Once you know that rationality consists of perceiving things correctly, it is not difficult to correct any wrong ideas or premises you have. The difficulty is that sometimes these wrong ideas create psychological problems. But if a person has psychological difficulties, it's not impossible to correct them. And if he doesn't correct them, he sentences himself to a life of misery, since he is acting against reality. [NC 69]

During the Apollo 11 moon launch, I sensed that people felt something like "species solidarity." Is there any sense in which people should feel such solidarity?

If there is any "species solidarity"—a proper community of values among people—it is precisely a technological achievement that can produce it, because such an achievement tells you: Here is what reason can do, and you have the same faculty. You don't have to go to the moon, but if you invent a new matchbox you are using this faculty. Reason is the life power in man. If you know that you possess a magnificent and limitless faculty, that will lift you up and be the basis for feeling a certain self-esteem (but not species self-esteem). The Apollo 11 launch was just such a big, unprecedented demonstration of what reason can do. [NFW 69]

Is there a good reason for going to the moon?

Yes, the extension of knowledge. Every rational endeavor expands knowledge. Further, I hope there is a relationship between the Apollo program and our military, for in the future, space exploration could have enormous value for self-defense. Remember, savages much worse than those at Woodstock claim to be traveling into space. If they are, we should try to beat them to Mars next, and fast. I don't think the Russians can make it; but as long as they are trying, and there are corrupt men of intelligence even in that cesspool, we are morally obligated to try for the sake of self-defense. [FHF 69]

You quoted a farmer from Woodstock who said that because of the destruction of his property, if the hippies came back next year, he would burn down his property. Is this rational?

Yes. A man works hard to make a living, and his property represents years of his effort. He then sees it taken over and destroyed by savages—middle-class, college-bred savages, who are worse morally than innocent jungle savages. If such people descend on his property and destroy everything it took him years to build, he cannot continue that way. So if the authorities do not protect him, I would advise him to burn his place down—especially if he could get national attention by doing so. I understand that the victims are thinking of suing the city and the festival corporation. If they do, I wish them luck. [FHF 69]

Irrationality

What is the most dangerous philosophical concept a man can follow?

A single concept? If I have to make a choice, I would say irrationalism, because it involves everything else. [FHF 78]

What is wrong with the prevalent philosophy today?

Three basic ideas: (1) *Irrationalism.* Men no longer respect reason or believe it's valid. This is the result of the philosophy they have been taught for at least the past two hundred years. (2) *Altruism.* This moral theory holds that the only justification for a man's existence is service to others. (3) *Collectivism.* The view that the individual has no rights, that a collective (society or some other group) holds all rights and may dispose of any individual as it pleases, and that its power over the individual is unlimited. Irrationalism, altruism, and collectivism are the three fundamental evils of today's dominant philosophy. [NC 69]

Aren't men basically irrational, and hence always seek happiness from what is irrational?

No. Rationality is a matter of choice; reason is a volitional faculty; man has the choice to think or not. Therefore, man basically is neither rational nor irrational. He can choose to be either. Further, it is impossible for a man to find happiness in the irrational, since the irrational is what's contrary to reality—it's the insane or the impossible. Many men have tried to "find happiness" in the irrational (they're responsible for the present state of the world); that doesn't mean all men do. [OE 62]

In the question period last week [PO7 76; see p. 70], you voiced a strongly pessimistic view of the future. How can you say you're glad to be old, when one of the most important concepts of Objectivism is that irrationality must never be taken seriously?

What in hell gave you that impression? I've never even hinted at the idea that one of the most important philosophical concepts is such a childish piece of inaccuracy. The most important parts of my philosophy are my theory of concepts, my ethics, and my discovery in politics that evil—the violation of rights—consists of the initiation of force.

The only passage that I can imagine gave you this impression—and if so, it makes me angrier, and hurt—is Dagny's line to Galt: "We never had to take any of it seriously." That's one of the most beautiful passages in my novel qua fiction. But it is light-years away from "Irrationality is never to be taken seriously."

I've written that one problem with Americans is that they don't believe in the reality of evil. You better take evil and irrationality seriously: not in the sense of regarding it as important—not in the sense of letting it determine the course of your life or your choice of career or other key values—but in the sense of not evading its existence. You should do everything in your power (though not at the price of self-sacrifice) to counteract evil and irrationality, which requires taking it seriously. But that is not the meaning of this line from *Atlas Shrugged*.

Now, why did I say I'm glad to be old? Because I'm tired of fighting low-grade irrationality. I don't mind fighting serious, philosophically important instances of irrationality—if there are any left. But I *almost* feel like Leo in *We the Living*, who said he could muster the heroic in his soul to fight lions, but not to fight lice. He gave up too early. But I have put up a long fight, and have fought every crucial evil that I have observed. To fight somebody like Carter is boring. I think it's a fair division of labor if I leave the fight against irrationality to you. [PO8 76]

Do irrationalists—for example, the existentialists—claim to be totally against reason?

Not most of them. Herbert Marcuse and William Barrett, for example, would say they are for a *higher* kind of reason. They support the hippies, they'd claim, because the hippies are really the incoherent, advanced guard of a higher approach to reason. They'd say the hippies are simpler and closer to the voice of God, in the way some cultures regard the half-wit as a holy man. Hippies, on this view, are moved by special revelation, by means of LSD. (Timothy Leary started a cult that held just that.) Irrationalists need that kind of excuse. They wouldn't say: "I know exactly what you mean by reason, and I am against it." That is the impotence of evil: it must pay lip service to the good, particularly on the issue of reason. Kant and Hegel and all the worst destroyers of the mind, of individualism, of freedom, had to claim that there is a higher reality, a higher reason, a higher freedom. They don't dare proclaim that men are better off without their heads. [NFW 69]

Is Existentialism an important philosophy?

Not in the grand scheme of things, and not even journalistically. It's important only as a symptom of a diseased culture. When people revert to mysticism and call it philosophy, they have less significance than somebody like Kierkegaard, who (unlike most Existentialists) was at least religious. Any school, like Existentialism, that goes into mysticism explicitly is no longer a philosophy. Their precursor (though it's less fashionable today) is Zen Buddhism. Existentialism is a disease in the history of philosophy. Such movements have appeared throughout philosophy's history.

Preserve the perspective of the ages. Aristotle and even Plato are significant today; Marx is not. He is significant politically, but not philosophically. He's a footnote to Hegel. Similarly, you can't call Sartre or Heidegger philosophers. (Heidegger says things like "nothing nothings.") These are modern aberrations. Politically, Existentialism is a good excuse for people like Marcuse, but he is hardly a philosopher. [NFW 69]

Can the assassins Sirhan Sirhan and James Earl Ray be said to have in some sense used logic and rational judgment?

No, both are examples of complete irrationality. They are obviously irrational—even judging from their actions and statements, apart from the assassinations. For instance, Sirhan was a student of mysticism, and claims to be able to control matter mentally. Ray was a criminal: a man who lives by force. Neither qualifies as rational by any stretch of the imagination. "Rational" does not mean "rationalizing." Anyone can lie to himself and invent reasons that out of context appear logical to him. "Rational" refers to a policy or principle arrived at in the full context of everything relevant to a given action. The first rule of rationality is that if you value your life and believe you own it, you must recognize the same right in others. You cannot prove that *you* have a right to *your* life but that another man does not. So there is no logical argument by which these assassins could prove that they have the right to take another man's life. Sirhan Sirhan, James Earl Ray, and Lee Harvey Oswald have a great deal in common, psychologically. Apparently, all three killed to get attention. That's a confession of an abysmal lack of self-esteem: the desire to be noticed, to gain attention regardless of one's action, to be famous as a monster. Their psychology is as evil as anything displayed in public for some time. [NC 69]

Isn't the Machiavellian who plots to cheat his wealthy aunt out of her money using his reason more fully than the simple soul to whom no such machinations would ever occur? Isn't the clever gangster using reason more fully than the gangster's victim?

The Machiavellian schemer may be using *logic* within a narrow range. He tries to determine logically how to rob someone. Logic can be used out of context, and you can analyze whether a man used his mind logically or not, regardless of the morality of his action. But that is irrelevant to the issue of rationality. The primary meaning of "rationality" is: context-keeping. A man cannot be rational out of context, though he may be "logical" out of context, in a particular case. Logic is a method; rationality is a mental attitude—a use of one's mind that does not permit a single act of evasion, and therefore does not permit context-dropping. Rationality is not a selective attitude. A person cannot be fully rational about some issues but not fully rational about others. Rationality is an absolute. Therefore, anyone who drops context in the sense given in these examples would not be rational according to Objectivist morality. [OE 62]

Contradictions do not exist. So what happens in a mind holding a contradiction?

Mental deterioration. A man's capacity to hold contradictions does not mean contradictions exist in reality; they exist in the mind. You must distinguish between existence and consciousness. What happens in reality if you attempt a contradiction? The classic example: Two objects cannot occupy the same place at the same time. You can try to defy this by causing two cars to drive at full speed toward one another. The result of this attempted contradiction is destruction. The same occurs in a mind that holds contradictions. [PO6 76]

Is it proper to judge the psychological motives of a person based on his ideas?

Some magazine did this to Barry Goldwater during the 1964 campaign. The evil there was that psychologists tried to arrive at a verdict on the psychology of a man they had never met, which is just as improper professionally, if not worse, than a doctor diagnosing a medical disease in somebody he's never met. The same applies to any psychologizing about a person's ideas.

The only way to attempt this properly would be to identify a philosophical idea, and ask what could be the psychological motive of anyone holding it. If you wanted to expose a psychological aberration, you'd need to analyze what's wrong with an idea and then demonstrate that only improper motives A, B, and C could lead to anyone holding such an idea.

To discuss the psychological roots of certain evil or irrational ideas in this way is proper, because you are dealing solely with the implication of an idea that's available to you; you are not passing judgment on a person. To deduce the motives of a man from his writings is improper and nonobjective, because there could be ten million motives for the same kind of action. For example, you couldn't list all the possible motives a man might have for committing murder. The same goes for every other psychological evil. You cannot deduce a man's motives from what he says, except in the generalized way I described. But even then, you shouldn't make a claim about the *only* possible motive, because a special aberration or combination of psychological errors is always possible, which you couldn't judge simply from what someone said.

Further, it is also improper to try to prove that a true idea came from good premises; you can't even be sure about good statements. That's proper only when you try to tie philosophy to psychology abstractly. [NFW 69]

Don't I have the right to be irrational?

There is no such thing as freedom or rights that stand above and against reason and reality. Your rights are based on reality and derived by reason from the observation of reality. You don't have the *moral* right be irrational. Of course, in a free society you can do whatever you want, however irrational, so long as you don't violate the rights of others. [FHF 69]

Epistemology and chess

Do you like chess?

I could never play chess. I resent it on principle. It involves too much wasted thinking. Chess is all "ifs," and if there's one thing I cannot do mentally, it's handle anything more than two "ifs." In chess, you must consider hundreds of possibilities, it's all conditional, and I resent that. That is not the method of cognition; reality doesn't demand that kind of thinking. In cognition, if you define the problem clearly, you really have only one alternative: "It is so" or "It is not so." There is not a long line of "ifs"—and if your opponent does this, you will do that. I can't function that way, for all the reasons that make me a good theoretical thinker: it's a different epistemological base. Chess requires a different mental process—where you're willing to play with intangibles, and nothing has a firm identity. A isn't A; every A is conditioned by hundreds of possibilities. That is a different universe.

Observe that chess experts have no idea of anything else. Chess becomes a substitute for philosophy or a profession. It is a way of life. They use their minds to play chess, and are like absentminded professors in everything else. They have no idea about life. In its extreme form, that psycho-epistemology takes over, and incapacitates a person for living. I don't mean you shouldn't play chess moderately. If you enjoy it, that's fine. But I don't think it's an intellectual game. Chess involves too much effort under conditions that are not the cognitive conditions of reality. It is the deliberate exercise of a mind in a non-A vacuum. That's my objection to it.

I hear that scientists are trying to get a computer to play chess. If they can do that, then you shouldn't waste your mind on the game. If this is possible, it justifies my personal theory about chess: computers are wonderful for mechanical, not creative, work. [NFW 69]

Isn't the psycho-epistemology used in chess similar to that used in certain military or business decisions, where there are a large number of factors and alternatives to take into account? A chess player doesn't literally look at every possibility. He knows automatically that ninety percent of them are out; then he looks at the remaining ten percent. Aren't you in effect saying that to choose a romantic partner, you must decide between two billion women? But you don't, because you can eliminate on principle a great number of them.

I understand that to be a good chess player you must be able to project hundreds of possibilities. I assume an experienced player automatizes certain connections, but I wouldn't have the incentive to learn. For example, in choosing a romantic partner, you can reduce the issue to essentials: you want virtues or values A, B, and C, and everything else is optional. You don't weigh every detail against major virtues or major flaws. Chess involves the opposite.

Now business is similar to chess only in the following way. The businessman has to consider a lot of "ifs," but he also has the essentials organized hierarchically: what must be considered first, and then what are the subdivisions and the lesser decisions to make. (This, incidentally, is why there are few great businessmen.) In a sense, we all do this when we spend money. We don't consider every detail. We project approximately: what can we buy, and should we spend this money now? But we do it by essentials. We don't make every decision on the premise that an opponent is going to make any one of a thousand possible actions against us, which we'll then have to counteract.

The nearest to chess might be the military, but even then you act according to certain essentials. But in chess, there are no essentials. Every move is a detail, which you must gauge according to your intentions and your guess about your opponent. It's the guess about one's opponent that I cannot accept. A businessman does not *concentrate* on what his competitors will do. He concentrates on what *he* can do—and incidentally on whether any particular threats or new products are coming up. And there are big rewards at stake, as there are in the military.

Finally, as far as complexity goes, chess is nothing compared to philosophy, wherein you must organize a large number of concretes into categories, decide on your basic categories, and then prove all of it. We must all do this. To the extent that you have convictions, you must weigh various existing systems or create one of your own, and decide what your convictions are. But the reward is your life; there is an incentive for doing this kind of thinking. It is not simply the complexity, but the unrewarded complexity, that makes me dislike chess. [NFW 69]

In your "An Open Letter to Boris Spassky," you claim that enthusiasm about chess is in some ways an escape from reality. Does this apply to professional athletes?

No. If men become professional athletes, that improves their skill in the relevant respect. If a man is a champion runner, he runs well outside of sports, too. The paradox in chess—which is supposedly an intellectual sport—is that the men who go into it professionally destroy their capacity for intellectual understanding in any other field. This isn't necessarily so, and there's nothing wrong with playing chess for relaxation; but chess grandmasters are usually naive, helpless, and mystical in the other realms of life. They concentrate their intellect on one particular activity, which doesn't improve their intellect for the rest of their existence; it does the opposite. For example, take Bobby Fischer. I saw him on TV and was startled by the intelligence he projected—which makes his behavior more tragic. A man with his ability should not be traveling to communist Yugoslavia and joining cults. For a man of his brains, that's not innocent. His behavior is obviously an escape. [FHF 72]

Epistemology and education

In The Man Who Laughs, *Victor Hugo describes a group of criminals— the comprachicos—who steal children, disfigure them, and then use or sell them as clowns, jesters, and sideshow freaks. AR wrote an essay entitled "The Comprachicos" in which she describes—as a modern spiritual equivalent—progressive education's mutilation of the minds of children.*

What suggestions do you have for a parent eager not to destroy his child's mind?

The best antidote is Montessori education, which I mention in "The Comprachicos." The Montessori system deals primarily with nursery school—that is, it gives a proper foundation to a child, after which he will be safe and impervious. So if you send him to the worst of today's high schools, he may not be happy, but it won't affect him if he's had Montessori training. Besides Maria Montessori's own writings, I'd recommend Elizabeth Hainstock's *Teaching Montessori in the Home*, which provides practical advice for parents on how to start your child on the Montessori method, and how to help him thereafter when he goes into public schools.

I understand Montessori groups are beginning to develop high schools based on the Montessori method. This would be the greatest and most hopeful movement in this country so far. What's wonderful about the Montessori movement is that it's completely grassroots and unplanned. Groups of parents started schools for their children because they were appalled at what is taught in "progressive" nursery schools. There's no vested interest behind the movement. It's spontaneous and is spreading with marvelous results. Not all Montessori schools are fully reliable. Some are slightly mixed or try to combine two different systems. Still, your child will learn more in such schools than anywhere else today. [FHF 71]

Is it important to explain to a young child, while in a Montessori nursery school, the importance of thinking? Wouldn't this help him avoid the difficulties he might encounter in public school?

No. You cannot explain to a child of six or under what thinking is, or why it's important. By the time a child goes to public school and begins elementary school, he's still too young to understand. He is certainly too young to hear a theory about it, which requires a great deal of conceptual development. You shouldn't begin to explain theory until he's an adolescent. If he's very precocious, and brings up the subject, you might teach him a few principles. But that's not what Maria Montessori does. She does something much more important: she trains a child's method of thinking—what I call psycho-epistemology. Her system is consciously aimed at developing the conceptual ability in a child's mind. It is an achievement of genius. She writes that what she wants to teach a child is not any particular ideas, but the method required to acquire ideas—to bring order into a child's mind, so that he won't feel like a confused stranger in the world. She wants to train a child's ability to deal with cognition—with concepts—which is precisely the ability "progressive" education is out to destroy. There's no guarantee that a child will think the right thoughts. The proper method of thinking is the protection Montessori provides a child against what they get in public schools. With some assistance on the child's part—because nothing is automatic—he has a good chance, because he grasps how to deal with percepts and then concepts. That's what the Comprachicos are destroying. [FHF 71]

In a university, what should be the relationship among faculty, students, and the administration?

First, there should be an agreement between faculty and administration—an agreement that does not exist today—that teaching in the university will be intelligible. A fundamental epistemology—with rules of logic, presentation, and what is taken as evidence and explanation—should be established, so that teachers do not confuse their students epistemologically. Students should not have to memorize and recite what they cannot understand. Universities should be places where students learn to understand.

Assuming that kind of rational base, students should agree to go to the university for one purpose only: to study. It's fine if students have a number of elective courses, particularly as they approach graduation. But students should not have any voice in the administration of the university or in the nature of the curriculum. A young man entering college is not qualified to know how a subject should be taught or by whom. Nor is he qualified to select representatives who can so decide for him. Students cannot run a university.

As to the balance of power between the administration and faculty, that varies—and properly should vary—from university to university. There is only one general rule that ought to be established: nothing should be forced by law on anybody. A student is free to leave a university if he doesn't like it; he can go to another. The same should apply to administrators and faculty.

Finally, as a general principle, a university must be an institution of learning, science, scholarship. It should *not* be a political institution—a political voice. This is a bad idea found in European countries that are not distinguished by freedom historically. [FHF 67]

If there were any aspect of this country's behavior that you could change, what would you change?

The universities, of course. I don't know whether you'd call that *behavior*. I wouldn't think in terms of people's behavior, because behavior is only a consequence. You have to think in terms of people's *ideas*. So if I had a magic power to change things fast, I would change the philosophy departments of today's universities. [FHF 78]

In light of your criticism of the academic world, why do you advise college students to stay in school?

Because you should never help your own destroyers. The goal of the type of educators I criticize—who are a majority today, but don't have a monopoly—is to defeat the mind. They can achieve this in two ways: by your weakness and submission while in school, or by forcing you out of school. They either cripple the best minds, or deprive them of an education.

There are two reasons you need not quit: (1) There are still some good teachers, and (2) Man is not a determined being; his education can help him or hinder him, but it doesn't make or break him. Therefore, he can remain impervious to the influence of his educators, if he does some clear and critical thinking on his own—that is, if he neither accepts his teachers on blind faith nor criticizes them blindly. If he doesn't agree, let him answer in his own mind why he disagrees. If his teacher is hopelessly intolerant, the student need not make himself a martyr; but he still learns (even in reverse), preserves his mind, and gets his diploma.

Incidentally, I graduated from the University of Leningrad. No conditioning that you are subjected to could compare to what I went through (and I'm glad you don't have to go through it). You can survive today's schools. [FHF 71]

What accounts for the collectivist orientation of most American universities?

The influence of one man, the destroyer of the modern world: Immanuel Kant. Every university is under his influence. Every school of philosophy—in one form or another—is Kantian at root. That's the real danger to the Western world. [FHF 74]

Miscellaneous

What is the main unresolved philosophical issue that your philosophy has not dealt with?

A technical one, which I'd like to formulate if I don't die too soon, but it's a hard job: the principle of induction—of how to think inductively. We need a proper statement of induction. Aristotle provided some leads, but there's been no full presentation of the subject. [OC 80]

Could you discuss the cardinal principles of the philosophy of science?

No. A subject like the philosophy of science would require several volumes, which I have not written, though I have certain ideas on the subject. It's a special undertaking that cannot be addressed in a question period. If you want some leads, read *Introduction to Objectivist Epistemology*. If you can't pursue them, you'll have to wait until I or someone else works it out, if we do. But the leads are there. [FHF 76]

Could you comment on Objectivism's impact on psychology?

I don't know, except to say that based on the more obvious phenomena in psychology, it's had no effect whatever. Most people in psychology don't seem to know that the mind exists, and so could not know what Objectivism is. [FHF 78]

Is it possible to think in images, rather than with words? I have in mind the mental process in which an architect projects in his imagination a view of a particular space, and works on that image in his mind. Isn't an image like a word—a perceptual concrete that can stand for an idea?

No. The only image that can stand for an idea is a written or printed word. That's a visual symbol. But the image of a concrete has nothing to do with thinking. An image can be the *object* of thinking, but you can't think *by means* of images. What an architect or any visual artist does is much more complex, and cannot, except as a bad metaphor, be called "thinking in images." It isn't thinking; it's imagination. Imagination can make use of a mix of images, sounds, and words; it's an entirely different process. But imagination, creativity, or anything rational cannot take place unless the creator uses words. It's pleasant to indulge your imagination, and let your mind roam, but until and unless you can translate the images into rational terms, you're in trouble. An architect isn't good if he can't translate his spatial imagination into actual words, and in effect say, "I'll build a building of such-and-such size, and put the stress on height," and so on. He must translate his plan not only into language, but into *engineering* language, which is mathematical and extremely precise.

Aside from creative imagination, what one does without words most of the time is simply despair and court disaster; it's not thinking. In using concepts, words are merely arbitrary symbols. The word "table" is not the concept "table"; it helps one to hold that concept in mind. The word gives identity to the concept, but it isn't the concept. The concept is our understanding of what that word stands for. A concrete image cannot do that. [PO6 76]

Is "common sense" a valid concept?

It has two different meanings. The original, Aristotelian meaning is that "sense" which integrates the evidence of your five cognitive senses—that is, forms a percept. But the general meaning is rational thinking by a person who does not know the philosophical standing of his thinking. Common sense is a simple form of rationality—the non-self-conscious use of logic. It's a valid concept, and a very good thing to have. [PO6 76]

Is there any validity to the technique of the devil's advocate?

Yes, it's very valuable. Playing devil's advocate means assuming a role opposite to your own conviction; advocating ideas the "devil" would throw at you. This technique trains you to answer every objection to your position. It's a good way to test your ideas, because if you encounter an objection you can't answer, you better find the answer or correct your thinking. [PO6 76]

What's the difference between a person who is well trained in his field and someone who is exceptional?

The exceptional person has premises leading to an active mind; he doesn't rest too easily at any one level of his own development, and he doesn't take too much as given. Now, we cannot achieve everything at once. We must always take some things as given until our development permits us to question them. But the exceptional person acts on the premise: "I must find things out for myself; I must go beyond what is now known." The well-trained, but unexceptional, person acts on the premise of taking things as given: "This is an established profession. It has demanding standards, and it takes a lot of work to comply with these standards. I'll fulfill all of the requirements set by my profession. I'll learn everything required. I'll read the appropriate journals and be as good a practitioner as any." That is the premise of stagnation. That type of person can achieve his goals and be competent; but in five or ten years his profession will have left him behind.

I'm not saying it's never proper to accept the standards of your profession. But this is a beginner's premise. It's fine for the beginner to hold that the expected standards are valid, and to comply with them. But it's when one knows the essentials—what's been discovered so far—that the distinction between the men and the boys appears. The man will want to go a step further; and if it's more than one step, so much the better. The exceptional man does not stand still and does not take the acquisition of knowledge from others as his permanent state. [NFW 69]

Could you write a revised edition of **Introduction to Objectivist Epistemology** *for people with an IQ of 110, or will it remain available only to people with an IQ of 150?*

I'd prefer that people raise their IQ from 110 to 150. It can be done. [FHF 67]

CHAPTER FOUR

Esthetics, Art, and Artists

The Nature of Art

What is art?

Art is the re-creation of reality according to one's values. By "re-creation" I mean neither copying reality nor creation in a mystical sense. I don't mean going contrary to reality or indulging in fantasies. I mean (paraphrasing Aristotle) creating what could be and ought to be. "What ought to be" implies that the re-creation is according to the artist's values. "What could be" means that which is consistent with reality as opposed to fantasy. Fantasy is a legitimate form of art, but one must know how to use it within a rational framework. Proper fantasy must be consistent with reality. Therefore, when I say a writer re-creates reality, I don't mean he creates a mystical fourth dimension or something else incompatible with actual facts. [FW 58]

> *AR is not here ruling out science fiction, which—in* The Art of Fiction— *she says is rational when it serves "some abstract purpose applicable to reality."*

What is the purpose of an artwork?

It presents reality according to a certain set of values. Every other human productive activity is utilitarian in that the product is not an end in itself but a means to an end. If you make an auto-

181

mobile, it's for transportation. If you write a journalistic article, it's for conveying information to people. But when you create a work of art, the purpose is the work of art itself. Now a work of art is not an end in itself in the sense that a person might write a book or paint a painting just because he feels like it. There's a reason why a man wants to look at a painting or read a book. The purpose of all art is the objectification of values.

A person's response to a work of art will have a lot to do with his attitude toward human values. But the reason why in reading a story or looking at a painting we feel it is an end in itself is that we don't want to experience that pleasure for any other purpose but the pleasure itself. And the nature of that pleasure is precisely the fact that we are observing an idealization of values. [FW 58]

What if you take a statue—which is a work of art—and attach to it an electrical bulb and a lampshade, thus creating a lamp? Is this a work of art or an object with a utilitarian purpose?

It's both. You could say the object as a whole is no longer a work of art because it serves a utilitarian purpose: to give light. But you could also say that part of the object was at one time, and is now (though a lamp stand), a work of art, because it represents certain aspects of reality—a human figure, say—according to the artist's basic values. [FW 58]

Can an artist create art divorced from his values—take, for example, a naturalist writer who simply presents reality as it is?

It is inconceivable that an artwork could be divorced from values, whether or not any artist claims otherwise. For instance, the naturalist school claims that values don't exist and that therefore they don't include values in their art. What they overlook is the fact that values cannot be separated from any human activity. In this sense, anything man does is a matter of choice. He can do it or not. He decides whether he'll do it, and if so, how. It is impossible to create a work of art without some kind of selectivity directing one's actions. A man writing a book must decide what to include and what to omit, and how to present what he includes. Every time a man exercises a choice, he is directed by some kind of values (conscious or not). He cannot escape the fact that he must make a choice.

When you attempt to re-create reality—whether it's a painting, a statue, or a novel—you must decide what aspects of reality you're going to use. Directing your choice will be your philosophical core of values. You have no choice about whether to have a philosophy. The choice is whether you know your philosophy and have chosen it consciously—or whether you are at the mercy of your subconscious, of chance generalizations and undigested abstractions accepted on faith from others without any clear understanding and decision on your part. [FW 58]

Must all art be about humans and human values?

Since the purpose of a literary work is the re-creation of reality according to the author's values, it must be a story about humans, because although a human can value animals or inanimate objects, that would hardly be the proper subject matter for a literary composition. One could write an essay on nature or a beautiful description of nature, but there your values and views on nature will not form a story. Your primary values are those affecting yourself and therefore other human beings. Your view of men is involved whenever you create a literary composition. I can't here go into detail about how this also applies to all other forms of art, though the connection there is not as direct. I'll simply mention that even in painting landscapes without human figures, an artist is actually presenting his view of human values. It is his human perspective on nature. [FW 58]

> In "Philosophy and Sense of Life" (in The Romantic Manifesto), AR writes: "A sense of life is a pre-conceptual equivalent of metaphysics, an emotional, subconsciously integrated appraisal of man and of existence."

In evaluating a work of art, does the sense of life portrayed have any weight? For example, is a work of art that inspires a rational

*man to achieve rational values greater than a work of art that bril-
liantly illustrates an improper sense of life?*

Yes, if their esthetic means are roughly equal. (You cannot
measure to an inch which of two artists is a better stylist.) But assume that two artists are equally good stylistically, but one presents
something great and inspiring, the other something bitter and
malevolent. The first would be greater. But you must judge them
esthetically first. [PO11 76]

*Many people claim to like all kinds of music, painting, and so on.
How is this possible, if art reveals their implicit sense of life? Are
such people insincere?*

I'm sure they're sincere. This might mean that they like all
kinds of art or that they like none. A consistent sense of life—one
that makes a person like certain artworks and recognize his own
view of the universe—is a rare achievement. There are few people
whose tastes are motivated by consistent values. It's already a great
psychological and moral achievement to have a clear-cut sense of
life.

Therefore, people who like everything can be explained in either of two ways: (1) They have not observed or experienced
enough artwork to care much, so that they have a general, almost
childlike, interest in all art as a spectacle, but they've never defined what they like in particular. This is fine; it tells you something about their sense of life—it's still in the process of
formation and they don't value much; or (2) they truly have no
values, and therefore everything appeals to them equally, because
nothing appeals to them too much. Remember, for most people,
sense of life is formed by accident and subconsciously. They don't
know what they like or dislike. They may have good reasons why
they like a certain work of art, and yet feel guilty about it. Or they
may force themselves to like something because it's convention-
ally acceptable.

So many combinations of premises are possible that you can't
make a rule applicable to everyone who claims to like all kinds of

art. You can say the same about people who claim they only like "romantic" art or—be careful here—"Objectivist" art (if there were such a thing, which there isn't). You cannot always be sure what a person's premises are; most people are inconsistent.

(Before you deluge me with questions about there being no such thing as Objectivist art, let me add: My novels are Objectivist, because I translated my sense of life into conscious terms. I can't say that about anyone else's novels. Further, no such formulas necessarily apply to other fields of art. For example, my husband's paintings are exactly in his field what my novels are in mine, but I'd never call it "Objectivist painting." No such term is appropriate.) [PO11 76]

How would one define one's own sense of life, and in how much detail? Would one use words like "happy," "sad," or "sensitive"? As an example, could you describe the sense of life of the character Scarlett O'Hara in Gone With the Wind*? Does a novelist need to know the sense of life of his characters?*

The fundamental mistake in this question is its treatment of sense of life as if it were a conscious, rational conviction. I've always stressed that a sense of life is not a conviction, but an emotional sum arrived at subconsciously. This is why man cannot be guided by a sense of life alone; he is helpless without a conscious philosophy.

You define your sense of life by introspection; however, if you're interested in identifying your sense of life, you don't start by defining it. Begin by defining the causes of your emotions. First learn to identify the exact nature of what you feel (and why) in any instance. Learn to be at home with your emotions. Learn to identify *in conscious words* (not approximately) what you feel and why. Once you've become acquainted with yourself emotionally—when there are no longer any great mysteries—then you can try to identify your sense of life.

Sense of life is predominant in two realms: sex and art. In sex, sense of life wouldn't be as clear to you, since it's harder to identify your own sexual reactions. So the best and perhaps only way to identify sense of life is by observing your reactions to art. (This is not a shortcut; it's pretty difficult.) Observe what you feel in regard to art and why. Select particular novels, paintings, and perhaps sculpture, because those are easiest to identify conceptually. (Music is very important, but very difficult to translate into firm concepts.) Observe yourself as honestly as you can. You are the only judge, jury, prosecutor, and defender of your esthetic reactions. When you feel a strong emotion about some work of art, ask yourself what you like about it and why. That might give you some idea of your basic metaphysical convictions, because what a sense of life presents is your metaphysics, but in the form of emotions, not conscious convictions.

Now, words like "happy," "sad," and "sensitive" are superficial. When people speak of a tragic sense of life, that's a foreshortening. There may be any number of opposite senses of life that could be called "tragic." You need not characterize your sense of life; what's important is to ask yourself: "Are my subconscious ideas right or wrong? Do I consciously believe them, or have I made a mistake in my childhood?," and then translate your sense of life into conscious convictions. Once you've reached the point where you have identified the essentials of your sense of life, you'll know you're succeeding when there is no clash between your conscious convictions and your subconscious, sense-of-life emotions.

How much detail is necessary? Sense of life doesn't deal with details, just as emotions don't. It deals with philosophical fundamentals. Therefore, if you know in sense-of-life terms what you feel about the nature of reality, cognition, man's nature, and his morality, that's sufficient to know your sense of life.

In the light of what I've said, it is of course impossible to name the sense of life of fiction characters. You *might* name the sense of life of your closest friend—though I doubt it. You may, after some years, know approximately the sense of life of the person you love, but nobody beyond that. You cannot *judge* the sense of life of another person; that would be psychologizing. Judge their philosophical convictions, not whether their feelings match their ideas. That's not for you to judge; it's of no relevance to you.

In art, you can say I like this artist's sense of life, even though his conscious convictions are different or opposite. But then you're not concerned with his psychology but with the ideas expressed in his work. It's impossible to tell the sense of life of a character of fiction. What you need to determine are his convictions—his basic views on life. Incidentally, I think Scarlett O'Hara had a pretty cheap, social metaphysical view of life. [In "The Argument from Intimidation," in *The Virtue of Selfishness*, AR writes: "A social metaphysician is one who regards the consciousness of other men as superior to his own and to the facts of reality."] *Gone With the Wind* is a fascinating novel, which I like very much; it's an excellent example of romantic fiction. But the characters in it are atrocious.

A novelist need not—and cannot—know the sense of life of his characters. He needs their conscious convictions.

Speaking of one's inability to know another's sense of life, now might be a good time to make a request: Please don't send me records or recommend music. You have no way of knowing my sense of life, although you have a better way of knowing mine than I have of knowing yours, since you've read my books, and my sense of life is on every page. You would have some grasp of it—*but I hate to think how little.* I hate the painful embarrassment I feel when somebody sends me music they *know* I'd love—and my reaction is the opposite: It's impossible music. I feel completely misunderstood, yet the person's intentions were good. Nobody but my husband can give me works of art and know infallibly, as he does, that I'll like them. So please don't try it. It's no reflection on you or on me. It's simply that sense of life is *very* private. [PO12 76]

In presenting the fundamentals of esthetics, is the subject of nonobjective "art" important?

No. Fundamentals are important. The connection between art and epistemology is important. That applies to all art. But nonobjective "art" is unimportant. It's important *today,* as a symptom of cultural disintegration. But it would not have been important a hundred years ago, and I hope it will not be important a hundred years from now. [NFW 69]

Literature

Ayn Rand's fiction

In "The Goal of My Writing" (in The *Romantic Manifesto), AR writes: "As far as literary schools are concerned, I would call myself a Romantic Realist."*

What do you mean in calling yourself a Romantic Realist? Which of the writers that you like are also Romantic Realists?

My school of writing *is* romantic realism: "romantic" in that I present man as he ought to be; "realistic" in that I place men here and now on this earth, in terms applicable to every rational reader who shares these values and wants to apply them to himself. It's realistic in that it's possible to man and applies to this earth; it's romantic in that it projects man and values as they ought to be, not as statistical averages.

The writer I consider my closest ancestor literarily is Victor Hugo. He is a romantic writer who presented values as they apply to human life. He's one of the few who attempted—"attempted" hell, I apologize—who *wrote* a great novel in contemporary terms, *Les Misérables*. Offhand I can't think of another romantic novel presented in realistic terms. His other novels take place in earlier periods, but *Les Misérables* is a novel of Hugo's own time and society.

O. Henry is a romantic writer with a strong sense of values translated into concrete action in the modern period, in almost journalistic terms. Yet he never presents a "realistic" study of the characters he creates; he presents essences. He presents wealthy men, working girls, and con men tremendously idealized or stylized. They are not statistical copies of the people he saw. They are creations out of his own abstraction of what human beings could be and ought to be. The overall moral message of O. Henry is: "Isn't life interesting?" That's the benevolent universe element in him. He presents not what people do statistically but what people could make of life if they were imaginative. [FW 58]

Why do you consider yourself a Romantic Realist?

I consider myself a romanticist, and believe my values are relevant to and possible on Earth. I deal with realistic issues in a romantic way. "Realism" and "naturalism" were once considered interchangeable, though I use "naturalism" for novels that are plotless and based on a deterministic metaphysics. So if I called myself a romantic naturalist, that would be a contradiction. But "realism" means "based on reality," and doesn't imply naturalism or determinism.

Joseph Conrad also called himself a Romantic Realist. I don't like him, but I think he is correct in so labeling himself. He treats his novels realistically, but not naturalistically. So even though my values are quite different from his, I agree with that designation. He expressed his values and, in that sense, he was a romantic—only his settings and characters are much more realistic than I'd ever select. But he was not a naturalist. [NFW 69]

In your fiction-writing course, you say that We the Living has your best plot. Could you explain why this is so?

Yes, because it's a simple story. A plot is a purposeful sequence of logically connected events. *We the Living* has a narrower theme, and therefore has almost a classic progression of one event leading to another—with a definite subplot, the story of Kira's cousin Irina—and it's one event depending on the other. The events are interconnected almost as tightly as the plot of a good detective story.

Anthem has no plot at all. *The Fountainhead* and *Atlas Shrugged* have plots, but on so grand a scale, and with so many involvements, that they are not as perfect one-line plots as in *We the Living*. *We the Living* has the best single-line plot, and it's the easiest on which to learn what a plot is. So it's better to start with a novel like *We the Living*—even to read it, let alone write it—before coming to *Atlas Shrugged*. [PO11 76]

Throughout her life, AR maintained what she called the "Benevolent Universe Premise"—the conviction that we live in a world in which

*man can succeed and achieve his values, and where evil is ultimately
impotent.*

**If the universe is benevolent, why does Kira die at the end of We
the Living, *just as she's about to escape?***

This is concrete-bound. [In "Let Us Alone" (in *Capitalism: The
Unknown Ideal*), AR describes the concrete-bound mentality as the
"inability to grasp principles, to distinguish the essential from
the nonessential."] I did not sit there and decide arbitrarily to let
Kira die. A novel isn't written that way. If you want to know about
anything in a novel, ask what its theme is. The theme of *We the Living* is the individual against the state. I present the evil of dictatorship, and what it does to its best individuals. If I let Kira escape, I
leave the reader with the conclusion that statism is bad, but there's
hope because you can always escape. But that isn't the theme of
We the Living. In Russia, a citizen cannot count on leaving or escaping. Someone who does escape is an exception, because no
borders can be totally closed. People do escape, but we'll never
know the number of people who died trying. To let Kira escape
would have been pointless. Given the theme of *We the Living*, she
had to die. [PO8 76]

**Was Howard Roark, in The Fountainhead, *based on Frank
Lloyd Wright?***

Absolutely not. Some of his *architectural* ideas were, as was the
pattern of his career. I admire Wright as an architect; but as a
person—as a character—Roark's philosophy is almost the opposite
of Wright's. [FHF 74]

**Why did you choose architecture as the central profession in The
Fountainhead?**

The theme. I wanted to show individualism and collectivism in
psychology: Roark versus Toohey as the two extremes. I had to
show how this works in a creative profession. I chose architecture

because it combines science and art. It involves a great deal of engineering and esthetics.

After choosing architecture, I did a lot of research on it, in order to originate dialogue that would sound true to the profession. It's funny that I still receive fan mail inviting me to speak on architecture. People assume I love the subject, but I don't. I like architecture as an art. But after *The Fountainhead*, it had no special meaning to me—less so than music or painting. I'm glad if I convinced people that I like it, but what I actually did was translate into architecture what I felt about writing. My research material for the psychology of Roark was *myself*, and how I feel about my profession. [NFW 69]

In The Fountainhead, *why did Dominique act as she did against Roark? Particularly, why did she marry Peter Keating?*

I explain that in *The Fountainhead*, through Dominique's own words, but I'll elaborate. Dominique's error is one from which many good people suffer, only not in so extreme a form. She was devoted to values, was an individualist, had a clear view of what she considered ideal, only she didn't think the ideal was possible. Her error is *the malevolent universe premise*: the belief that the good has no chance on earth, that it is doomed to lose and that evil is metaphysically powerful.

Many people make that mistake, and the reason is that they form their conclusions by statistical impressions. As a person grows up, he looks around and certainly sees more evil than virtue. So he is disappointed more often than pleased; he's often hurt and sees a lot of injustice. And with each generation, given the present culture, it gets worse and worse. By emotional overgeneralization from these first impressions, a great many people whose basic premises are good decide to become (in effect) philosophical subjectivists. They conclude that their values can never be shared by others or communicated to others, and therefore that they can never win in reality.

That was Dominique's mistake. She acted against Roark because she was convinced that he should retire and never open himself up to be hurt by the world—that he shouldn't attempt to fight the world, because he was too good to win. Observe that her actions against Roark were in fact superficial: she did not create any major damage to him, and she never would. But her actions implied a great compliment to him: her understanding and valuing of him as a great man and a great creative talent. It was the misguided application of her estimate of the world that caused her to do what she did.

Why did she marry Peter Keating? Because he was the least worthy of her. It was her symbol of rebellion, in this way: She never made the mistake of thinking that since the world is evil, she must make terms with evil and try to be happy on those terms, as Keating and Wynand tried. She was too good for that. She would not seek happiness in a world she considered evil. So she married a man she could not love or respect, as a symbol of her defiance and desire *not* to seek anything in a world as low as she thought it was. Well, she learned better. By the end of the book, she discovered why she had been wrong, and why Roark was right. Before that, Roark did not attempt to stop her. He was right to conclude that she must correct her error herself.

If you translate this abstraction into less extreme forms, I'd say that most men share Dominique's error in some form or another. You may not try to stop the career of the person you love; but any time you have a good idea or an important value, you will tend to repress it. You'll tend to feel "This is good and I know it, but nobody else will understand me; nobody else will share it. Why be hurt?" Any time you experience an emotion of that kind, you are acting on Dominique's error, and you'd better correct it. [FF 61]

AR wrote the screenplay for the film version of The Fountainhead *(Warner Bros., 1949).*

The climax in your novel The Fountainhead *seems to contradict the climax of the movie version. Did you have any control over the film?*

If you were any kind of dramatist—if you understood literature and the difference between a novel and a screenplay—you'd take your hat off to me for what I accomplished in that movie. [FHF 70]

In Introduction to Objectivist Epistemology, *AR describes an experiment that established that crows could deal with only three units at a time. She points out that man, too, can deal with only a limited number of units. This fact about human cognition is sometimes referred to in Objectivist literature as "the crow epistemology."*

How does the principle of the crow epistemology apply to the presentation of ideas in your novels?

By the time I come to an abstract speech, I've given you all the concretes required for you to draw a conclusion—and then I draw the conclusion. I present the concretes at a certain pace so that you don't have to take in the whole theme all at once. This is why *Atlas Shrugged* is so long: I give you certain concretes in action before I explicitly and at length mention the abstraction they're based on. [OC 80]

In The Art of Fiction, *AR makes the following suggestion: "do not use slang in straight narrative."*

At the end of Part 2 of Atlas Shrugged, *Dagny "rents" a plane, writing "a check for fifteen thousand dollars . . . as deposit against the return of the Sanders plane—and . . . another check, for two hundred bucks, for his [the airport attendant's] own, personal courtesy." Given your views on slang, why did you use "bucks" instead of "dollars"?*

Look at the context. It's not fully narrative. It's written as a paraphrase of what they [Dagny Taggart and Owen Kellogg] told him. It's paraphrasing the kind of dialogue that went on between them and how they assured him that they're on a special mission from mysterious authorities, and he thinks of Washington, and so forth. When I use "bucks," it was precisely to give coloring to a condensed synopsis of an actual conversation, and this is the terms in which *he* would think of it. And what was achieved is a stress on the lack of dignity of the man and the whole procedure. He gives to total strangers a $15,000 airplane for a two-hundred-buck bribe.

That's why I used the word, and that doesn't contradict what I said about slang. [FW 58]

> *In* The Art of Fiction, *AR says: "It is proper to laugh at evil . . . or at the negligible. But to laugh at the good is vicious."*

You've said that one should never laugh at the good—for example, at heroes—but there's a scene in Atlas Shrugged that's funny, though the humor seems to be directed at Dagny. She is in the valley, and after coming across an automobile manufacturer who runs a grocery store, a judge who runs a dairy farm, a writer who works as a fishwife, and so on, she meets a man who "looked like a truck driver," and she asks: "What were you outside? A professor of comparative philology, I suppose?" The man replies: "No ma'am . . . , I was a truck driver." Could you explain this joke?

It's Dagny, for a moment, who is contradictory, so the joke is on her. She has made a mistake in judgment. She concludes that since everybody in the valley is something more than what he's doing at the moment, and since this man looks like a truck driver and is doing unskilled labor, he's undoubtedly a professor. Therefore, it's her judgment that one is laughing at. But it's not malicious humor, because it's not an important error of judgment. That's good-natured humor. Dagny is having an unusually good time in her bewilderment, so if she makes a mistake of that kind, it underscores the benevolent preposterousness of the whole situation. That's why one can afford to laugh at it.

The same is true of Noel Coward's "Mad Dogs and Englishmen." In effect he's saying: "How irrational the Englishmen are! When everybody else collapses, they still go out in the sun dressed formally." Is that an insult to the English? No, he's laughing at the natives snoozing there, *not* at the English. [FW 58]

What characteristics would you seek in an actress playing Dagny Taggart in Atlas Shrugged?

Katharine Hepburn as she was in her first movie [*A Bill of Divorcement* (1932)], but about five years older and with somewhat better ideas, so that she could understand the role. Nothing less would be ideal. [FHF 73]

In **The Romantic Manifesto,** *you write: "It is impossible for young people today to grasp the reality of man's higher potential, and what scale of achievement it had reached in a rational or semi-rational culture." Is this true for all young people? Can reading about the past or reading a novel such as* **Atlas Shrugged** *provide a grasp of such reality?*

I had in mind the daily reality of living in a culture, which is almost incommunicable. Some novels can communicate it, but that's not the equivalent of actually living in such a culture. As to *Atlas Shrugged,* you have to omit it from consideration, because one always omits the role of one's own work in discussions such as this. If I'm discussing the state of the culture, I won't say, "It's rotten and depraved, but remember, my novels are different." That's not my function; it's yours. [PO11 76]

How did you select the names of your fictional characters?

My characters are not named after real people. I made long lists of first and last names for both heroes and villains. I like certain combinations of sounds musically, and selected those. Observe that my characters' names have similar combinations of sounds. Incidentally, I didn't deliberately choose to have the names of the characters Roark and Rearden begin with an "R." That was pure accident. [OC 80]

Why haven't you written any fiction in the last twenty years?

I have a serious dilemma. I don't write historical fiction or fantasies, and it's impossible to write heroic, romantic stories in today's setting. The world is in such a low state that I couldn't bear to put it in fiction. I am trying to get around that difficulty, but I don't know whether I'll succeed. If I don't write another novel, this is the reason. Look around you. [FHF 77]

Other writers

What plays do you recommend?

The top three plays are: *Cyrano de Bergerac, Cyrano de Bergerac,* and *Cyrano de Bergerac.* It is without a doubt the greatest play in world literature. Edmond Rostand's other plays, which are not well known in this country, are also excellent. I'd also recommend Friedrich Schiller, an early Romantic writer. Unfortunately, there are no good English translations of his plays; but even so, the translations that do exist will give you some idea. Henrik Ibsen is not uniformly good, but he's a marvelous craftsman. [OC 80]

In "What Is Romanticism?," you say Nathaniel Hawthorne's **The Scarlet Letter** *is a great work of romantic literature. Why do you like it?*

I regard it as great for the same reason I admire the novels of Dostoyevsky and Hugo. Hawthorne has an abstract theme, and he dramatizes it perfectly. He has created an unbearably dramatic situation. His theme is the problem of guilt, which he never resolves, though he protests against it [that is, the Puritan conception of guilt]. But observe what he projects: for the theme of guilt, he selects the rigid religious background of the Puritans—people with the strictest ritualistic morality—and for drama he creates this conflict: A married woman (Hester Prynne) has an affair with a minister, who is devoted to his religion. Hawthorne then proceeds to use the theme properly. He gets all the drama possible out of that situation. For instance, the minister must ask her to reveal her lover, and she doesn't name him. Given his position, he must lead the community in ostracizing her. She is made an outcast and penalized for her sins, and he keeps silent.

Who is in the worst position of the three main characters?

Hawthorne indicates it's the minister. His idea is that Hester was guilty, but that she made up for it by preserving her spiritual dignity. The minister was guilty and collapsed, because he lied and hid his guilt. The husband is guilty because he is motivated by vengeance and hatred. Hawthorne's message is that hatred of the guilty is not the answer; but he has no solution. I remember one line, from the end, which seems to indicate what he wanted to say. Hester thinks there is something wrong with the laws on love and sex, and someday people might be liberated from them. She doesn't know by whom, but perhaps by some woman who would not be as tortured by the pain as she is. I think that's the author's overall conclusion: there's something wrong with the Puritan moral ideal, though morality is necessary; and somebody someday may discover the solution.

It is a tremendous achievement to state such a theme, and then have a very dramatic conflict expressing its essence, in a story in which the suspense is terrifying, and the three main characters each commit a different error. That's why I regard it as one of *the* great novels, because of its integration of theme and plot: the action expresses the theme very dramatically. (*The Scarlet Letter* has one literary flaw, which is minor compared to its values: Like many nineteenth-century novels, it is written in straight narrative too often.) [NFW 69]

Do you consider Dostoyevsky a naturalist or a romanticist?

He's in between—though essentially he's a romanticist. He's "in between" only in this sense: what he presents is the evil; he never successfully presented a hero. He belongs to the romantic school on two counts: (1) plot structure, and (2) the moralistic attitude—that is, he presents men as volitional beings. He never suggests that his villains couldn't help it (though he doesn't preach how they could have helped it). His whole approach is: this is the kind of depravity that man should not become. There is always a "should"; in that sense he's a romantic. [FW 58]

What do you think of Terence Rattigan? Do you consider him a romanticist, and specifically, is he a romanticist who uses conventional characters?

Rattigan is a repressed romanticist, and incidentally, a very good writer.

The Browning Version has a good, though subdued, plot. It seems naturalistic, but it has a well-constructed, romantic plot. In that sense, Rattigan is closest to Ibsen. The trappings are realistic and on the verge of naturalism, yet it is never naturalism. In *The Browning Version*, the professor is not a grand hero. But neither is he a conventional man. Nor is the relationship between the professor and the boy conventional. It is beautifully presented. Rattigan seems very sensitive to the devotion to values in human psychology; but all he can do is express this devotion. He has no philosophy with which to express values. That's why I don't consider him a writer who presents heroic actions by average men. The conformist touches are simply thrown in. He is not a romantic with conventional characters—he is better than that. The same is true of *The Winslow Boy*. It's a historic event presented realistically, but it's very abstract.

Rattigan employs dramatic characterization by essentials, and is concerned with the characters' values. *Separate Tables* is beautifully done and romantic, although it has all the trappings of naturalism. It involves characters at a run-down resort hotel, and not one of them is treated naturalistically. They represent certain psychological abstractions, and are very beautifully done. It has *almost* no plot; yet there is action integrated into the theme. It has what I call a rudimentary plot. Something is resolved at the end. All the complex relationships—including the poor girl and the posturing man, and the central male character and his ex-wife—are resolved in action, even though it is not a fully integrated action leading to a climax. It's a series of small climaxes.

What I've said applies to his screenplays as well. *The V.I.P.'s* is brilliant as writing. The characters in *Breaking the Sound Barrier* are not entirely conventional men. The industrialist is not conventional in regard to his profession; neither is the young pilot who finally breaks the sound barrier. They are conventional in regard to their personal lives, and that is Rattigan's great error. There is something strange about *Breaking the Sound Barrier*. I've seen it several times, and I have the impression that Rattigan presents his industrialist and pilot as concerned about their grandchildren or baby's diapers, and so on, only because he wanted somehow to anchor his characters to earth. But his heart wasn't in it; he obviously didn't know how to present heroes in regard to daily life or human relationships. All the relationships in the movie seem to be thrown in as side details, and they had a negative effect on the total film. Rattigan's focus was so obviously on their professions alone that I had the impression that he was asking the audience for forgiveness, in the same way the old industrialist begs his daughter to remain with him. It was as if Rattigan were saying to the audience: "I'm not inhuman; I do appreciate human relationships, only I don't know what in hell to say about them. I'm interested in man the producer." I'm putting words in his mouth, but that was my impression.

Judging by his works that I have read or seen, he is not good at presenting the conventional. He's at his best presenting the unusual (though not always heroic), for example, the professor in *The Browning Version*. [NFW 69]

I have a hard time classifying some novels or stories as either romantic or naturalistic. For example, your short story "The Simplest Thing in the World" (which you say doesn't have a plot) and the novels of Sinclair Lewis seem to share characteristics of both schools. Could you comment?

Don't be a classicist. [In "What Is Romanticism?" (in *The Romantic Manifesto*), AR writes that classicism "was a school that had devised a set of arbitrary, concretely detailed rules purporting to represent the final and absolute criteria of esthetic value."] Don't set standards pertaining to romanticism and others pertaining to naturalism, and make them rigid absolutes, so that to be romantic, a work must have plot, free will, and so on, and to be naturalism, it must have determinism, slow movement, and so forth. That's not true. You cannot classify novels that rigidly. Any number of cross-breedings and mixed premises might not fall into either category. What you can say is that the (implicit) premise of free will and the purposeful progression of events (a plot) are the distinguishing characteristics of romantic literature, whereas a plotless story that concentrates on characterization and the statistical is deterministic and therefore naturalistic. Those are the extremes. Every story has some elements of both—*in the details.*

My presentation of Howard Roark is as romantic as any story could be; no architect in real life is literally like him. But the conflict between him and the traditional architects is historical; I didn't invent it. From that aspect, you could say *The Fountainhead* is naturalistic. Many people think Roark is Frank Lloyd Wright because Wright *did* fight the traditional builders and had a hard time. But apart from that, he's totally different from Roark. That's an element of naturalism, but *The Fountainhead* is *not* a naturalistic novel.

Sinclair Lewis is essentially a naturalist, yet his novels occasionally contain romantic touches. What do I consider romantic touches? When he projects certain values that he did not get from statistical observation—they are *his* way of expressing something. You could say that's romantic. In *It Can't Happen Here,* there's a bad mixture of romanticism and naturalism. Nevertheless, it's a very good novel.

In every work of literature, you'll find elements that, taken out of context, could belong to either school. Naturalism would include everything that corresponds to *some* kind of concrete issue or event in real life; romanticism would include any abstract projection of values. But no intelligent (or even stupid) naturalist could exist without values. And nobody can write about a nonexistent planet; everybody will write about something here on Earth. [Even a science fiction novel set on some fictitious alien planet must project values that the author believes are applicable to man on Earth.] Classify a work of literature by the overall metaphysical view presented in the total work. Never hold out for one element—not even plot. [NFW 69]

Is Cervantes's Don Quixote a romantic novel?

Don Quixote is a malevolent universe attack on all values as such. It belongs in the same class with two other books, which together make up the three books I hate most: *Don Quixote, Anna Karenina,* and *Madame Bovary.* They all have the same theme: Man should not aspire to values. *Don Quixote* is usually presented as a satire on phony romanticism, but it isn't. It's a satire on all romanticism. As for its literary category, it's a precursor of naturalism (though it isn't written naturalistically). But philosophically—if you could call it philosophy—it is plain evil.

You might even be against reason, if you are a mystic, and make some kind of semi-plausible or barely explicable philosophy out of that, because you stand for mystical values. You are mistaken, but you are a valuer. For example, I wouldn't call Plato a nonvaluer, even though he placed his values in another dimension and preached Hell on Earth. He was dedicated to what he regarded as values. But plain cynicism is not philosophical—it is a denial of philosophy. A cynic holds that man is helpless, nothing is of any value to him, and the one mistake is to hold strong values. He is dedicated to an anti-value viewpoint. "Skeptic" and "cynic" are the only philosophical designations for this outlook; but those are not actually schools of philosophy. They are schools dedicated to the destruction of philosophy. *Don Quixote* is in just that school, philosophically. [NFW 69]

Is Hemingway a romantic writer?

That's apparently what *he* believed, but I don't consider him one. He's a naturalist posturing as a romantic. I originally planned on including him in "What Is Romanticism?," but he's not significant enough. By modern standards, he's a good writer technically. From the perspective of history, he's third-rate. He's way below Sinclair Lewis and John O'Hara.

I say he's a naturalist posturing as a romanticist, because there's no value projection in his books, and no value abstraction in his characters. In general, he's not too good on characterization. He's

better on atmosphere—the Hemingway viewpoint: a vulgar Byron-
ism disguised in American terms. This is his only value: the terse-
ness of expression. Its emptiness is more apparent in his imitators.
But he at least could carry it off with a degree of eloquence.

His overall style is that he's tough, he's brief, he's a man of action who represses everything and faces the malevolence of life.
But what is he repressing? Nothing. Take his two most romanti-
cized novels: *A Farewell to Arms* and *For Whom the Bell Tolls* (the two
I've read). The heroes and heroines in both are cardboard figures.
They're as bad in their terms as the worst courtiers and swash-
bucklers of third-rank romanticists. There is no characterization. I
challenge anyone to show me what passages—what actions and
dialogue—give some idea of the character of the hero and the
heroine in each novel.

In *For Whom the Bell Tolls*, the hero wants to fight for the Span-
ish Left. Why? Unless you know that's a cultural bromide of the
1930s, you won't find any reason in the book. It's simply self-
evident that one fights for the Left. Is that characterization? Even
a communist deserves better characterization than that. To present
a man's political outlook, you must indicate why he holds those
ideas (rightly or wrongly). But Hemingway indicates nothing. The
hero simply fights, and dies at the end. As for his heroine, he apparently wanted to project her innocence. She was raped by Nazis
during the Civil War, but she is spiritually innocent; she's never
been in love. So when she and the hero have their first love scene,
he kisses her and she remarks, "I always wondered where the noses
would go." Is that characterization, or is it a preposterous statement a child wouldn't make? In both *A Farewell to Arms* and *For
Whom the Bell Tolls*—and particularly the latter—it's clear that Hemingway did not know women. What he projects is his own idealized
version of a woman—only it's the ideal of a high school boy. There
is no characterization, and the way he expresses his love scenes is
embarrassing.

Hemingway is a good example of an author with a malevolent universe outlook. In deciding whether an author has such an outlook,
unhappy endings are not conclusive. I have an unhappy ending in *We
the Living*; Hugo has an unhappy ending in almost every novel. But

we don't have the same sense of life—the same metaphysics—as Hemingway. Sometimes it's hard to judge whether a writer is malevolent universe. If the hero or heroine is defeated while fighting for his values, that is not necessarily malevolent universe; it may be simply the recognition of the fact that happiness is not guaranteed to man. It is possible to man, and of intellectual and moral significance, that he may be defeated. But observe: In Hemingway, the disaster happens by pure chance. That is the infallible test. In *For Whom the Bell Tolls*, they accomplish their purpose and are about to retreat, and a chance bullet kills the hero. There was no metaphysical necessity—and no element *of his job*—that caused his death. If he died heroically blowing up the bridge, that's not necessarily an indication of a malevolent universe outlook. But if he is killed gratuitously, after his purpose is accomplished, that's Hemingway's way of saying: "Man is doomed."

This is even more obvious in *A Farewell to Arms*, a book I loathe. It's an ugly book. The hero and heroine fight whichever problems they have; there's no plot; and near the end, the girl dies in childbirth. Now death in childbirth, though possible, is certainly an exception. Why did Hemingway include this? It's connected to nothing in the story; it's totally gratuitous. That is an indication of pure malevolent universe. What in life may be an accident in a novel becomes metaphysical. This alleged great love is defeated by an accident. Whenever a novel resolves its story by having somebody die of an illness—unless the illness is connected to his values or the fight for his values—that's an indication of the author's malevolent universe outlook.

Incidentally, *A Farewell to Arms* is supposed to be a presentation of a great love, though I don't know of one sentence in it that represents love. What remains in my mind as typical, the supposedly strongest expression of love between them, was the following: The girl (a World War One nurse) tells the hero (a soldier) that she'd like to have known all the girls he ever slept with; and if he had gonorrhea—she uses the vulgar term, "clap"—she'd like to get it from him. To make that an expression of great love is so sickening that it cannot be an accident. That's all that I remember of the book's presentation of characterization. My remembering only that is not proof of anything; but you can see why such a touch would wipe out everything else. It's not romantic. One could write about any horror, even leprosy, and keep it romantic. But one wouldn't write about love that way. [NFW 69]

How would you rank the following naturalists: Upton Sinclair, John Steinbeck, and Theodore Dreiser?

I'd question whether Sinclair's books are literature. He writes bad propaganda pamphlets. He's a dreadful writer, stylistically, and there's no characterization. It's like Soviet literature at its crudest. Steinbeck is above that. He can write on a certain pretentious, naturalist level. He is very overrated, because in that period he was about the best naturalist there was. I would hang Theodore Dreiser somewhere between Upton Sinclair and literature. He really cannot write. Quite apart from content, his works have no structure or style. He has the kind of "style" I'd reject in a high school essay. He is an accident: in certain bad periods, some people acquire a status they don't deserve. Dos Passos is not a very good writer, but I'd still classify him on the lower rungs of naturalism. But Dreiser goes over the line even if judged by plain, grammatical skill, if nothing else. [NFW 69]

Do all naturalists write about the lower classes?

No. Most today do, but that wasn't always so. For instance, the nineteenth-century Russian naturalist Turgenev wouldn't touch a proletarian. He's an enormous phony. In Russia, he's considered a second-rate classic; but I don't think he's even fourth-rate. He writes about genteel aristocrats; you need a Russian *Who's Who* to read him. Nevertheless, his books are pure naturalism. He appears to be more romantic because he writes about the Russian soul and the meaning of life. But he's not dealing with big issues; he's merely copying the kind of class that existed at the time he wrote. The same is true of F. Scott Fitzgerald: He's a naturalist describing the "lost generation" (a term he coined). He doesn't write about the gutter. He *seems* idealistic because he deals with the aimlessness and alleged aspirations of the intellectuals of his period; but he's still a naturalist. Anton Chekhov and Henry James are two other naturalists who select intellectuals or the upper class for their subjects. Tolstoy is the great naturalist: he covers the whole gamut, from peasants to Napoleon. [NFW 69]

In **The Romantic Manifesto,** *you say that Leo Tolstoy's* **Anna Karenina,** *though good as literature, is the most evil novel ever written. There seem to be two criteria involved in calling this the most evil novel: One, the theme is fundamentally evil; two, such an evil theme is expressed by a great unity of plot, theme, and characterization. Is this a correct understanding of your position?*

No. The questioner uses "evil" as if it were an esthetic judgment. It isn't; it's a moral judgment. I didn't say it's the worst novel esthetically because its theme is so evil. On the contrary, I said it's a good work of art (not great) for what it's preaching, but it's preaching evil. (Incidentally, *Anna Karenina* has no plot. Don't give it an honor it doesn't deserve.) It's not its technical competence that makes it evil, but the consistency of its hatred of man's happiness. That's its theme: the evil of the pursuit of happiness. The novel is full of statements to the effect that even if society is wrong, it is your duty to live as society wants you to live; if you don't, and you pursue your happiness, you will be punished monstrously. [PO11 76]

Given what you say about **Anna Karenina,** *is it true that for a novel to be monumentally evil it must first be great esthetically?*

Not really. This is still a confusion between ethics and esthetics. Modern novels are bad art (and some aren't even art) and as such, they're on a lower level of art than *Anna Karenina.* But in a way—and this pertains more to morality than to esthetics—it is true that if you go "below zero"—that is, into the negative evaluation—then the closer to zero you are, the better. For instance, take the same evil theme written by Tolstoy or by some modern writer. The modern writer couldn't even communicate his evil theme, so you could give him, say, a –5; Tolstoy deserves a –100 or more. It's –100 because he presents his theme much better, much more convincingly, and therefore it is potentially more dangerous. But this is not an esthetic issue; it's the mathematics of morality.

The same is true in politics. Take two dictators, Mussolini and Hitler. If Mussolini is a –50, then Hitler is a –50 billion—because he's a monstrous creature, and because of the degree of destruction and cruelty he perpetrated. There's not much difference between them morally, but because of Mussolini's premises or policies, or by sheer accident, he was more inept as a total dictator. Hitler was more able—and Stalin even more so, because he had a bigger country and more people to murder. So as for dictatorship (which is a moral negative), the more efficient a man, the more evil he is. Therefore, concerning moral negatives, the better you are, the worse you are morally—and this applies to Tolstoy.

But this is not a literary judgment. Literarily, I understood Tolstoy's message and gave him credit for how he carried it out; but it's a monstrous message. A lesser novel, *Madame Bovary*, has almost the same theme, only it's less metaphysical and more journalistic. It's not evil, it's disgusting. Whereas Tolstoy says no one should pursue happiness, Flaubert says a woman should not be romantic, which is a narrower version of this theme. To that extent it's a less evil, and more inept, novel than *Anna Karenina*. [PO11 76]

Could you explain why modern naturalistic novels do not deal with fundamentals as well as romantic novels?

Take a novel like *By Love Possessed*, by James Gould Cozzens. Implicit in it is the idea that reason is helpless. The hero is allegedly a man of reason, which consists of never giving in to his emotions, feeling nothing, and being "sensible" (that is, a cautious middle-of-the-roader). When he does occasionally give in to his emotions, the result is disaster, which underscores the hero's imperfection. But the questions the author never answers are: What is reason? Why do the characters view things the way they do? Did they have to? Such issues aren't dealt with, because the author's first premise is: here are characters as they are—as I have observed them to be—

and given that they are the way they are, this is what I think is logical for them to do. And there is a certain logic to that approach, given the author's premise. But there is no question of defining the elements of human nature with which any author should be concerned, such as: (1) the nature of reason and emotion, and (2) if certain characters are the product of their background, who made that background? A naturalist cannot deal with fundamentals. [FW 58]

What do you think of Mark Twain, as a writer?

He is a very good writer, though he's not a favorite of mine. In my childhood, I loved *Huckleberry Finn* (in a Russian translation), but not *Tom Sawyer*. Today, I enjoy reading him sometimes; he's very witty. But I don't agree with his sense of life, and he was a well-meaning socialist. [FHF 77]

Is it possible to write a completely humorous work that still upholds one's values? I have in mind Alice's Adventures in Wonderland.

Alice's Adventures in Wonderland is humor and fairy tale mixed, and could be classified with benevolent stories (though I have certain reservations about parts of it). But in general, you could include it under benevolent humor, with O. Henry's short stories and Oscar Wilde's comedies, for example. It doesn't seem to be destructive. Alice herself is supposed to be the good, and what is satirized is the irrational (predominantly, not exclusively). It's an odd little work: a lot of it is good, while other parts seem to undercut it. [FW 58]

How would you classify Lost Horizon, by James Hilton? Isn't it a fantasy, since they live so long in that utopia?

It's a sociological utopia, which is not strictly speaking fantasy. The longevity is merely a symbolic projection. I couldn't disagree more with its philosophy, though literarily it is a legitimate work.

The symbol there is that if people are on what the author considers the right premises, then they get extremely long life and other advantages. Mystics, who despise Earth, are always eager to get long life and unending supplies of wine, milk, and so on. [FW 58]

If you are familiar with the recent novel or TV film series **Roots,** *would you care to relate it, or the reaction of the public or the critics, to your thesis tonight [tribalism]?*

That's a point I wanted to discuss. But it's a complicated point and I had no room for it in my lecture. I have seen only the last three installments of *Roots* on television and am reading the book now. The three installments that I did see were magnificent. They were beautifully written, beautifully directed, and particularly brilliantly acted. It was not a racist story in any way, not as it was presented on television. The author's intention in his research for his book was to trace his own ancestry, however, and in that form, yes, it is a very bad form of tribalism. But this is a mixed case.

The author may have had the idea that it is important to know one's physical ancestry, but this is his mistake. What he produced is much better than his idea. He produced an image not just of his particular ancestors, but a representative image of the black people in America from an aspect that had not been presented before. And he did it very convincingly. I am, as I say, judging by the last three installments of the television script.

Now, what was it that the television film presented? It presented black people as *moral* heroes. Here were people, totally helpless, caught in slavery with no way of escape. And they, the main characters, preserved the idea that they were morally right and their persecutors were morally wrong. They maintained the idea that the right was on their side: they had a right to freedom. This was made particularly clear in the character of Kizzy, the daughter of the original head of the family in America. This—the moral conviction of your own right under every kind of evil and terror (which the blacks lived under)—this is the essence of morality. If people in Soviet Russia had an attitude like Kizzy's, there would be no Soviet government left today. The moral message of *Roots* is:

Even when circumstances beyond your control make you completely helpless existentially, you are still free intellectually and morally; and if you hang on to your moral conviction no matter what happens, you are saved, at least spiritually; that is ninety percent of the battle.

This, I think, was the appeal of the television film. And I think that black people who are enthusiastic about the film sense it. It is very unfortunate that the meaning ascribed to *Roots* is "know your own ancestors," and that black audiences, as well as people of other races, are now running to fortune-tellers, trying to find out who their great-great-grandmother was.

Ancestor worship *is* an essential part of racism and tribalism. But that was not the actual meaning of the television show. What came across was a national legend, the creation of a myth about the black people in America, a myth in the best sense of the word, created by one man, the author, Alex Haley, who deserves credit for it, whether this was his intention or not. The black people never had a mythology, at least not in this country. Here they were, torn out of nowhere by force, with a total break between them and their past. They were like strangers stranded among other people in this country. They had no spiritual past, in the way that Western civilization has a past in mythology (particularly Greek mythology), in religious stories, in the history of heroes. This kind of heritage gives you some idea of the nature of your society—not your own identity, but the meaning or the nature of the culture in which you live. That is what *Roots* has done for the black people. It has created a mythology, and a very appealing one, an image of people in desperate circumstances who preserved their dignity, their spirit, and their individual morality.

I can well understand why both blacks and whites are enthusiastic about this presentation. But it is a shame, and perhaps a tragedy, that the man who created it gave it a different meaning. If his purpose was to discover his ancestors, I can't help wondering: what kind of slanted history did he give himself? If Kunta Kinte, the first man from whom he traces his lineage, was a heroic figure, what about the white man who raped Kizzy, the daughter? Alex Haley must include that white rapist among his ancestors. If he thinks that the heroism of Kizzy is, somehow, a noble reflection on his character, as her descendant, well, then the villainy of the rapist and of other people down the line are also a reflection on his character. Why do ethnics of this type always believe that if they can find a king or a hero in their past, it enhances them—but if they find a thug or a crook, well, it doesn't count?

The truth, of course, is that genealogy, race or tribe do not make or break your character. *You* do—and the credit or blame is exclusively yours.

If you have not seen the television film of *Roots*, I strongly recommend that you see it when it's shown again. It's really worth seeing. But draw your own conclusions about its meaning. [FHF 77]

You've praised Stirling Silliphant's screenplay for In the Heat of the Night. *Do you recommend anything else he's written?*

I read the original book *In the Heat of the Night*, and it was bad light fiction. Everything good about the movie—the serious touches—was added to it, which is why I like Silliphant very much. He's also written some of those big horror movies, one of which I saw the other night on TV, *The Towering Inferno*, which was very well done for what it is. He also wrote *The Poseidon Adventure*, which was horrible and boring. So he's somewhat irregular. *In the Heat of the Night* is his masterpiece. He's never equaled it. [OC 80]

I recently read Mary McCarthy's The Group. *Do you know her work?*

I've read half of one of her novels. I could not finish it. Incidentally, she is the lady I quoted, without naming, in "What Is Romanticism?"—she said the qualification of a writer is to be a back-fence gossip. Her collection of essays *The Humanitarian in the Bathtub* is fascinating in a morbid sense. If you want the exact opposite of Romanticism or Objectivism, read it (though she's not a worthy adversary). Her ideal writer is Tolstoy, and she admits that as much as she'd like to, she could never be as good, though she doesn't quite know why. [NFW 69]

Could you comment on the current status of literature?

No. I don't have a magnifying glass. [PO11 76]

Plot

> AR *defines plot as "a purposeful progression of logically connected events leading to the resolution of a climax" ("Basic Principles of Literature," in* The Romantic Manifesto). *She regards plot as the most important feature of fiction.*

How can one distinguish an inept plot, a mere story, and a modern "novel" with no story?

If the author ineptly leads a series of events to a certain resolution, only it didn't have to be resolved that way or it's resolved by coincidence, that's an inept plot.

It's a mere story when there is a certain progression of events that is not motivated by the goals or conflicts of the characters. This is an accidental progression of events. For instance, take any novel of Sinclair Lewis (who is the best American naturalist). He usually has interesting stories, which are not totally formless. They begin somewhere and end somewhere. But each is a progression of characters going through certain events and drawing certain conclusions, growing or deteriorating mentally. His characters don't determine the events or pursue particular goals. The events are determined more or less in part by their character, which is already established, and in part by social background and the accidents of those around them. The only Sinclair Lewis character who pursues particular goals is Arrowsmith, and he is the most inept of Lewis's characterizations. Even there, Lewis takes the story of a whole life and presents it in installments: First there is the relationship between Arrowsmith and his professor; then there are events in the various stages of his medical career; then he marries; then he goes on a mission to investigate some disease; then, by sheer chance, somebody breaks a bottle and his wife dies from an infection; Arrowsmith gets over it; he continues to struggle in a modest, plodding way. The meaning is always in the characterization, and the actions proceed from the characters as the author sees them. But they are not value-oriented. Values don't determine the course of their lives. It is the predominance of characterization over action that is the naturalist's distinguishing premise. The actions do not proceed one from the other, though there is a certain continuity. The author stops when he's convinced he has presented that character sufficiently for you to understand him. There is a story, but no plot.

As for books without stories, take any modern "novel"—a hodgepodge of events that begins nowhere and ends nowhere. When there is some progression of mood and incident, none of it connected to anything else—it only fills so many pages—then that's not even a story or a novel. In a naturalist story, there is some action. The characters do not merely sit and think and react. But when nothing happens (except mentally) then it's not a novel. Without events, it's not a novel. And when it becomes unintelligible (like today's "novels"), then it's not writing—it isn't even English. [NFW 69]

Does your short story "The Simplest Thing in the World" have a plot? If it doesn't, what's the difference between it and a plotless naturalistic or modern story? Since the story is uplifting, shouldn't it still be regarded as romantic rather than naturalistic?

It is certainly as plotless as it could be, because it is strictly the illustration of a psychological process. There's an internal conflict, but no action. Henry Dorn sits at his desk, struggles to write, and finally decides that he cannot. That's not an event, because it takes place in his mind. That's not a plot story.

"The Simplest Thing in the World" is not really romantic; but neither is it naturalism in the sense of a narrow concern with one character, such as a Babbitt or some other concrete statistical type. My character Henry Dorn stands for something wider; he is presented abstractly, not as typical of struggling authors. He's typical of a wider idea, which applies to all creative activity. In that sense, it's neither naturalistic nor romantic. It is merely a short story presenting a single psychological incident.

Compare "The Simplest Thing in the World" to the short stories of John O'Hara. He wrote many heartbreaking, malevolent universe stories, usually illustrating some one aspect of a character or a psychological process, or summing up a whole life in one incident. They are eloquent, and are sometimes cast naturalistically; they're certainly not romantic. They are purposeful psychological stories, and you could classify "The Simplest Thing in the World" that way.

The difference between "The Simplest Thing in the World" and a modern "novel" is that in the former there's a purpose and theme, and when it's presented, the story ends. You might be confused because you take modern writing as another *school* of writing. Keep in mind that modern writing is *not* literature—and I mean that literally—and there will be no confusion. But if you say my story has a certain purpose, whereas modern writing doesn't, you are defeating yourself, because every kind of writing—if it's *literature*—has a purpose. Naturalistic novels are still literature. Even horror stories are literature, at its lowest level. But below that, you are outside the medium.

With regard to "The Simplest Thing in the World" being uplifting, I thank you for the compliment; only now you are outside the field of esthetics. Literature (and art generally) is not to be defined by whether it's uplifting or depressing. That's a side issue that involves a reader's value premises. It's a philosophical, not a literary, issue. You might be uplifted by it because of your premises, whereas a deterministic collectivist would be depressed by it. I could write volumes on why Hugo uplifts me whereas Tolstoy does not; but that is not part of literary analysis. Never confuse a personal reaction of that kind with literary issues. All you could say literarily is: " 'The Simplest Thing in the World' presents ideas with which I agree, and it's carried out well enough for me to feel uplifted." But only the presentation is part of a literary consideration, not what the idea is nor how you personally react to it. [NFW 69]

Do the novels of Ian Fleming and Mickey Spillane have plots?

This might startle you given my admiration for Fleming, but he does not write plot stories. They are a series of actions and counter-

actions. They don't start with James Bond having to accomplish
something, but with Bond reacting to something. Some of his novels are better constructed (that is, have more unity) than others.
Moonraker is probably nearest to having a unified plot structure.
But most are simply a series of exciting events. They hold your interest mainly because you don't quite know what's going on. The
villain's purpose is usually mysterious. The suspense involves Bond
discovering who is doing certain evil deeds and for what purpose;
then the story ends. That is not plot progression. If Bond's assignment leads to a series of events—he goes somewhere, someone
tries to bomb his car, he gets hold of an underling who gives him
a mysterious hint and then dies, this leads him to another inquiry,
and so on—then there is a progression, but no plot.

Incidentally, many good detective stories have the same flaw
(which is not a technical flaw)—namely, that the villain initiates
the action. (An exception is my play *Think Twice*.) In a murder mystery, a detective acts only because somebody was murdered; then
he must take action to solve the mystery and avenge justice. I personally dislike stories in which the evil side is the motivating factor;
but that is predominant in literature today, because of the culture.
It's most plausible under an altruist morality, because if somebody
accepts altruism, he's unable to create conflicts among the good.

Mickey Spillane is a much cruder writer than Fleming, but his
stories always have plots, even if they are sometimes inept (when
the events are not logically necessary and when he introduces coincidence). But there's always a definite purpose. In his best stories, Mike Hammer has a *personal* interest in avenging the death of
a friend or fighting a particular criminal. Something personal is
always at stake, and through a series of events (more or less skillfully tied together), Hammer achieves his goal. [NFW 69]

Does the film High Noon *have a plot?*

No. It's a dramatization of the psychology of the marshal; but it
has no plot, because there's no conflict. The marshal must face
some bandits, and the townspeople aren't willing to help, so he
faces them alone and then leaves town. Where's the plot? The ac-

tion is centered around one incident—namely, the return of the bandits. So there's a central point around which the rest of the events revolve; but there is no *progression* of events. There's his clash with various townspeople, his reaction to them, his disappointment, and his lonely and bitter decision. At the end, he acts on his ideals, he wins and leaves, but he's not in conflict with anybody. The conflict is psychological: his psychology versus the psychology of the townspeople. It's not a conflict between him and the villain. [NFW 69]

Is it possible to write a plot story on a historical subject, where the ending is already known?

Yes. For example, Schiller's *Mary Stuart*. The audience won't be held in suspense if they know it's an accurate dramatization of a historical event, but then the issue is how the story is presented. The dramatic structure of the story can have the proper progression of a real plot story, even if the outcome is known and some of the suspense is lost. Schiller's *The Maid of Orleans* is jazzed up with the nonhistorical introduction of a romance, but you nevertheless know that Joan of Arc is doomed. Still, it's a very dramatic story. [NFW 69]

Determinism in literature

Determinism (which AR rejects) is the theory that man lacks free will— that every human idea and action is caused by antecedent factors beyond one's control.

You said [in the nonfiction-writing course] that you had originally planned to include in "What Is Romanticism?" something on the apparent paradox that naturalism is actually emotionally motivated via determinism. Could you expand on that?

The paradox I had in mind is this: If naturalists object so much to values and consequently to emotions, and they believe one must be factual and "realistic," why are they determinists? What element, psychologically, would prompt men to believe in determinism? Their emotions—the fact that they regard emotions as incomprehensible primaries, coming from nowhere and defeating rationality. *Determinists* are run by their emotions, not romanticists—who for over a century have been accused of emotionalism in contrast to the rationality of the naturalists. I decided this point is merely an objection to naturalism and so does not belong in an article in which I use naturalism only as a foil for defining romanticism. But it *would* make an interesting article on its own. [NFW 69]

Do determinists always present men as they see them?

If a writer believes that man is determined—that a man can't help being what he is—then in order to present his view of human nature, he must resort to the statistical method—that is, he must conclude that man is by nature what he sees the most. He will not find many admirable or heroic men that way. Statistically, in light of the philosophy the world holds, he'll find much more stupidity, depravity, and evil. At first, the naturalistic school presented serious problems and serious types of men of mixed quality (men who have some good and some evil in them, and who could not help being the way they are). But the blind alley of that school, the end of the road, is presenting nothing but unrealistic caricatures of depravity. I challenge anyone to find in real life the kind of characters William Faulkner or Erskine Caldwell write about. A couple of such creatures could perhaps survive to their twenty-first year or exist somewhere in the mountains of the South. The people they present are probably more exceptional than the ones I write about. What those writers do is take the most vicious people they've ever heard of, and exaggerate them, and this is presented as "such is life." Stories about dope fiends and drunkards and the dullest kind of depravity are supposedly justified on the grounds that such people exist. But (1) I challenge whether they do exist in the form in which they're presented, and (2) even if they do exist, what's the point of writing about them? The excuse those writers give is that this is their view of life, and these people are determined. In logic, they should say they couldn't help writing about depraved people any more than their characters could help being depraved. My response is that readers have free will and don't have to read that stuff. [FW 58]

> *Leonard Peikoff writes (in* Objectivism: The Philosophy of Ayn Rand*) that the "stolen concept" fallacy, first identified by Ayn Rand, "consists in using a higher-level concept while denying or ignoring its hierarchical roots, i.e., one or more of the earlier concepts on which it logically depends."*

Can naturalistic writers consistently present their characters as deterministic?

As a psychological experiment, try to read a naturalistic novel while constantly reminding yourself that the characters are robots—that whatever happens had to happen, that they couldn't help it. You will be bored within ten pages. If you keep reminding yourself of that premise, you can't go on, because there will be no sense in it. Naturalistic writers are guilty of the fallacy of the stolen concept: in order to function, they count on what they are denying.

Just as you would not read stories about puppets (and I don't mean puppets who are given human attributes) or stones or tree branches engaged in conflicts, so you could not write such a story beyond two sentences.

Observe that whenever animals are used as characters—in fables, fairy tales, or cartoons—they are given human attributes: voice, speech, choice, and the power to make decisions. Without these, you couldn't make a Mickey Mouse cartoon. So there is a basic contradiction in the whole approach of the naturalistic school. If man has no choice, one cannot write a story about men and there would be no point in reading a story about them. But if man does have choice, then it makes no sense to write a story or choose to read a story in which the sole meaning is that things happen because they happen.

No determinist can be a consistent determinist, particularly not if he's a writer. The naturalistic method notwithstanding, if someone were a determinist, there would be no point in writing anything because it wouldn't apply to the *next* person. For example, if you read what happens to Anna Karenina, you can't learn from it and discover whether this could happen to you, and if so, what you could do about it. So you cannot be a consistent determinist.

Never expect full consistency on an irrational premise. The free will premise of romanticism is found to some extent in all determinists. So when I divide writers into romanticists and naturalists, I don't mean that naturalists share none of the characteristics of romanticists. [FW 58]

Why do you think the heroes of ancient and Elizabethan plays are determined?

Because the concept of the tragic flaw is not the same as the concept of the tragic error. Tragic error or choice is something else. But in both classical and Elizabethan dramas, the hero possesses a tragic flaw that he could not help, and at no point is there any indication of why he acquired that flaw. Take King Lear. In the end, he decided he was wrong; but there's never any explanation as to why he got that wrong idea in the first place. He just had it. He simply possessed parental vanity (I think that's supposed to be his tragic flaw), it wrecked him, and he couldn't help it. The same is true of Oedipus. He is wrecked by fate; the gods made him marry his mother, and so on. He couldn't help it. All those tragedies are deterministic, and as such, morality does not apply to them. That's the basic conflict or contradiction in any deterministic drama. Aristotle did insist that the hero had to be noble and have great stature; but if you assume he is born with his flaws, he must also be born with his virtues and his stature, and thus none of it has any meaning.

As I've mentioned before, the fact that those plays are dramatic at all depends on the fact that the audience and the author cannot be consistently deterministic. You watch them and experience certain emotions only because you assume some choice is possible. And if the defeated hero still preserves some kind of nobility at the end, you give him some credit, on the premise that he has free will and that therefore *he* has maintained his spirit. But philosophically, those dramas are malevolent universe, because man is doomed by forces over which he has no control.

In contrast, an example of a proper, free will tragedy is *Cyrano de Bergerac*. The hero is frustrated both in his career as a poet and as a lover, and he does ultimately die. But he maintains his values—his benevolent universe—to the end. The justification for this tragedy is precisely the fact that nothing broke Cyrano's spirit, although the author put every kind of disaster in his way. We leave *Cyrano de Bergerac* crying, but uplifted. You wouldn't leave a classical or Shakespearean tragedy feeling uplifted. If you sit through them at all (which I don't like to), you leave depressed as hell, with the feeling that it was all pointless. [FW 58]

What's the difference between Gail Wynand's tragedy in **The Fountainhead** and that of Othello in Shakespeare's play?

The crucial question is: Is the character's weakness the result of a chosen premise, or is it innate and not subject to any choice? Othello is presented as jealous, but we're never told why he's jealous. What's very eloquent about Othello is that he could have checked on the facts so easily and discovered that Desdemona was innocent. But he never even tried. That's a dramatization of the difference between a tragic flaw and a tragic error. [FW 58]

Poetry

In "Basic Principles of Literature" (in The Romantic Manifesto*), AR writes: "A poem does not have to tell a story; its basic attributes are theme and style."*

Could you say something about your views on poetry?

Poetry is a combination of two arts: literature and music. Rhythm and rhyme, and the thought expressed, are the essence of poetry. [LP PO 12]

Who are your favorite poets?

Generally, I'm not an admirer of poetry, and find it impossible to discuss. My reaction is based solely on sense of life. I have few theories about it. My favorite poets are Alexander Blok, an untranslatable Russian whose sense of life is ghastly, but who is a magnificent poet, and Swinburne, who is also a magnificent poet with a malevolent sense of life. I like a few Rudyard Kipling poems very much, both in form and content. Strangely enough, I truly love "If." The moderns made a bromide out of it. I've seen it framed and sold in the five-and-ten. If a poem can survive that, it's great. "If" has helped me sometimes in depressed moments, and I hope it does the same for you. I also like "When Earth's Last Picture Is Painted," which is a magnificent poem qua poetry. [PO11 76]

Is narrative poetry—poetry that tells a story—a legitimate literary form?

Narrative poetry is a mixture that doesn't work well. A story should not be told in the form of a poem. The Russian Pushkin wrote a novel in verse, *Eugene Onegin*, which is a marvelous tour de force (though it's untranslatable). But the form in which it's written is inappropriate to the novel—and to the poetry. [NFW 69]

What is the Objectivist view of free verse?

That it's lower than free lunches. [PO11 76]

Miscellaneous

For those seeking a career as a writer in the present world, what studies or readings do you recommend in preparation? And do you foresee a greater prospect of success in writing political or other essays rather than novels?

First, I would recommend, above all, that you never take any classes in writing. You will not learn anything that way. Second, there can be no such thing as a rule establishing a greater likelihood of success in writing fiction or nonfiction. Your approach to these questions is all wrong. If you want to be a writer, ask yourself first of all what you want to say. That will determine in what form you will say it—whether it's properly fiction or nonfiction. The next question to ask yourself is: Why do I think that people will be interested in hearing this? Do I have something new to say? Is what I want to say important and, if so, why? Or am I just planning a rehash of what everybody has heard millions of times before? If you can answer these questions properly, you're on your way toward becoming a writer. These are the first steps.

Then you must develop your own understanding of what you regard as good writing or bad writing. You do it by identifying the quality of the books you read. Whenever you like something, ask yourself, if it's good—why? Whenever you don't like something, ask yourself, if it's bad—why? In this way you will acquire a set of principles of writing. But *you* have to be the author of that set. You have to understand it and it has to be rational—that is, you have to have reasons for the answers you give yourself and the principles you adopt. [FHF 77]

How do you distinguish between literature and popular writing?

Today, whether what you write is literature is determined by membership in the right literary clique, and by being so inarticulate that each person can read what he wants into your book. But let's omit the nonsense, and speak of serious literary distinctions.

The difference between literature and popular writing is the seriousness of approach. Literature has a serious, interesting theme, taking up philosophical, ethical, political, and psychological issues. Literature says something of a serious nature about human life. That's the best definition.

Popular literature is superficial: no serious ideas or themes; at best, good plots. Plots are an important element of literature, but even the plots in popular literature are not too original. Popular literature can offer you light entertainment without touching on serious themes. Today, however, popular literature is much better than "serious literature," from every aspect I mentioned. Popular literature, specifically detective stories, are much more serious and better written than what passes for serious literature. When I say "today's popular literature," however, I mean Agatha Christie and Dorothy Sayers—writers from the period between the two world wars. They made a high art out of popular literature. Incidentally, the detective story obviously needs the conviction of a rational universe, because it assumes that the detective must solve the case, and that justice will triumph. You couldn't ask for a better or more serious base; and no serious writers today—present company excepted—hold these ideas. [OC 80]

What do you think of science fiction?

It's a legitimate form of literature, but it's seldom good. Science fiction used to be original and sometimes interesting; today it's junk. I dislike it because it's too freewheeling. You can invent anything you wish and say that's the science of the future. They go too far that way. [OC 80]

Can a writer characterize the different sexes without having identified consciously the philosophical difference between men and women?

Yes. A writer doesn't need to identify consciously why a woman would want to be a hero worshipper and not president. [See "About a Woman President" (in *The Voice of Reason*).] As a rule, writers are not that philosophical. They hold their philosophies in sense-of-life terms and don't attempt to translate them into wider principles. As far as the psycho-epistemology of writing goes, it is unnecessary. Before you could arrive at a philosophical identification, you'd have to make numerous observations or the question wouldn't even make sense. You observe that there are psychological differences between men and women *before* you form a philosophical opinion on this issue.

A good writer holds in mind a sense-of-life conclusion about what's right for a man but not for a woman, and vice versa. He feels: A woman would not enter a room swearing (unless she were like Comrade Sonia), whereas a man might; swearing would have a different meaning depending on whether a man or a woman does it.

Incidentally, one way of telling the sex of a writer is in the attitude projected toward the opposite sex. Before I was known, I received fan letters for *The Fountainhead* addressed to "Mr. Rand" (you can't tell from the name "Ayn"). This pleased me, because the convention is that if a writer is logical, he must be a man. But I've always thought a perceptive reader could tell that my books were written by a woman. No man would write that way about men (nor about women). [NFW 69]

Since an artwork is created fundamentally for the artist's own purposes and enjoyment, is an artist justified in re-creating reality via a code of geometric symbols intelligible only to himself and those who possess the code?

No, not any more than a tea-leaf reader or an advocate of ESP or any other mystic is justified in what they do. Why would you want to create such a code? To deceive somebody. If you're dealing with reality and oriented toward reality, then even if you create something for your own enjoyment, you do it rationally—and that means by the code of symbols, of words, which are intelligible to you, primarily, and to anyone else. They must be intelligible to someone else to be valid and objective. If you want to devise your own geometric symbols, or your own language of "gloop and bloop," go right ahead, but don't talk about art. [PO11 76]

The Visual Arts and Music

subject - yes
style - no

Do the terms you apply to literature—for example, "realism," "naturalism," "romanticism"—apply to the visual arts as well? For example, Degas and Goya are often classified as realists, whereas I'd consider them naturalists.

The distinctions seem semi-plausible, but it's the same confusion I encountered in literature, where there have been no firm definitions. [She is referring to her derivation of the definitions of "romanticism" and "naturalism" in "What is Romanticism?"] I suspect it's chaos in painting as well. For instance, what is considered romanticism in painting, I'd call rank naturalism. So I wouldn't claim that the classifications I've defined for literature hold for the other realms of art. Someone would have to establish that.

All the arts suffer from a lack of valid and objective esthetics. There hasn't been any since Aristotle. Everything works by accidental observations on the part of various philosophers and commentators. People accept distinctions approximately and with no clear definitions. Let us lay the foundation for a different approach. [NFW 69]

Would you elaborate on Leonard Peikoff's statement [in "The Philosophy of Objectivism," lecture 11] that it would be anachronistic to classify Greek sculpture as Romantic art?

Romanticism is a nineteenth-century art movement. (It was defined then; the first Romantic novels appeared in late eighteenth and early nineteenth centuries.) It presupposed many philosophical ideas that were not available in Greek philosophy. Parts of Aristotle's esthetics provided the foundation for Romantic art, but that's not all there is to Romanticism, and it's completely inapplicable to Greece.

Romantic art is always stylized: the better the art, the clearer and more attractive and intelligent the stylization. Greek art is not stylized. It is beautiful naturalism. It presents a slightly exaggerated, idealized human form. But there is no deliberate or conscious choice of values. All it has in common with Romanticism is that it presents man at his best. They saw their gods in human form—as the best possible to man.

I don't like any ancient statues, except the *Venus de Milo*, and then technically, because she is so magnificently done. I saw her in person, and it's remarkable how the texture of the body is projected in the ancient, pitted marble. You feel you can touch the soft flesh. But that isn't enough for a sense-of-life approval. Ancient Greek statues of men are too "beefy" for my tastes. I specifically mention why in my description of Galt's body in the torture scene: they are not active men, modern men, Romantic men; Galt is. [PO11 76]

Who is your favorite sculptor?

I don't know his name. Whoever made the *Venus de Milo.* It's my favorite statue. Technically, Michelangelo is the greatest sculptor we know. Unfortunately, I don't like his sense of life. But artistically, certainly the greatest is Michelangelo. [FHF 71]

Can you have good art with a bad sense of life? For example, is Rembrandt's exquisitely rendered side of beef, which you mention in **The Romantic Manifesto,** *bad art because it's an unworthy subject, or is it good art presenting a bad sense of life?*

It's bad art, because he selected a bad subject. But it's bad art skillfully done. As for sense of life, you can't derive any from that painting, which is another reason it's bad art. It communicates nothing but the skill it took to present that beef realistically. Other Rembrandt paintings, however, have a *malevolent* sense of life. [PO11 76]

What do you think of the works of the artist Maxfield Parrish?

Trash. [FHF 77]

When I go to museums, I get very tired after looking at paintings for about a half hour. It isn't physical tiredness, because sitting down doesn't help. Do you know what causes this?

Yes. This is why you shouldn't go to a museum with the aim of carefully studying every painting. The reason is that in looking at different paintings, you are switching contexts—switching universes. The best method is first to get a general look at what's there, and then decide which paintings to study. [NFW 69]

What do you think of the work of Beethoven?

He is a great composer, but I can't stand him. Music expresses a sense of life—an emotional response to metaphysical issues. Beethoven is great because he makes his message so clear by means of music; but his message is malevolent universe: man's heroic fight against destiny, and man's defeat. That's the opposite of my sense of life. [FHF 81]

Which composers do you recommend today?

Buy yourself some classical records. I cannot listen to modern music. I can't hear it. It's anything but music. [FHF 81]

Beauty

What is beauty? Is beauty in the eye of the beholder, or is there a universal standard of beauty?

Beauty is a sense of harmony. Whether it's an image, a human face, a body, or a sunset, take the object that you call beautiful, as a unit, and ask yourself: What parts is it made up of, what are its constituent elements, and are they all harmonious? If they are, the result is beautiful. If there are contradictions or clashes, the result is marred or positively ugly.

For instance, the simplest example would be a human face. You know what features belong in a human face. Well, if the face is lop-sided, with a very indefinite jawline, very small eyes, beautiful mouth, and a long nose, you would have to say that's *not* a beautiful face. But if all these features are harmoniously integrated, if they all fit your view of the importance of those features on a human face, then that face is beautiful.

In this respect, a good example would be the beauty of different races of people. For instance, the black face, or an Oriental face, is built on a different standard, and therefore what would be beautiful on a white face will not be beautiful for them (or vice versa), because there is a certain racial standard of features by which you judge which features, which face, in *that* classification is harmonious or distorted.

That's in regard to human beauty. In regard to a sunset, for instance, or a landscape, you will regard it as beautiful if all the colors complement each other, or go well together, or are dramatic together. And you will call it ugly if it is a bad rainy afternoon, and the sky isn't exactly pink nor exactly gray, but sort of "modern."

Now since this is an *objective* definition of beauty, there of course can be universal standards of beauty—provided you define the terms of what objects you are going to classify as beautiful and what you take as the ideal harmonious relationship of the elements of that particular object. To say, "It's in the eye of the beholder"—that, of course, would be pure subjectivism, if taken literally. It isn't a matter of what you, for unknown reasons, decide to regard as beautiful. It is true, of course, that if there were no valuers, then nothing could be valued as beautiful or ugly, because values are created by the observing consciousness—but they are created by a standard based on reality. So here the issue is: values, including beauty, have to be judged as objective, not subjective or intrinsic. [PO11 76]

CONCLUSION: AYN RAND'S LIFE

AR was born in Russia in 1905, and left for America in 1926.

Could you comment on your education in Russia, with respect to how well it prepared you for your career as a writer?

Nothing in Russia or America prepared me. With regard to writing, I did it myself; that's why I don't believe in innate talent. You're not born a writer, and you need not wait for educational influences. You make yourself a writer.

The only credit I can give to my education is to a high school teacher (about three years before the end, when I was twelve or thirteen). It was a general language course—what here would be called English and there was called Russian. She made us read *Eugene Onegin* (a novel in verse by Pushkin), and gave us this assignment: Write a paper on what you think of the various characters, and indicate what in the novel made you come to those conclusions. It was the best lesson to teach us that if you judge the characters in a book, you must go by specific incidents, touches, or actions. The same applies to writing: If you want to communicate a character, put in the specific actions that will make your readers say: "It is this kind of character, because he did or said such-and-such." It was the best lesson in literary causality I ever had, and I've never forgotten it. I wrote all kinds of papers in high school, but that's what remained with me. It was excellent advice. Apart from that, I learned mainly from Victor Hugo. [OC 80]

What is your day-to-day attitude toward writing?

That I have no right to anything, except to run to my desk: No right to breathe, no right to live—that's my attitude. You stop only when you're ready to collapse. I imagine it's like being pregnant: there is something alive that demands priority over everything; you're under that pressure constantly. That's been my attitude, whether writing an article or *Atlas Shrugged*, which took thirteen years. [OC 80]

Why did you write Atlas Shrugged?

Because I liked the story. I always write primarily because I want to create the image of an ideal man in action. That was the goal of each of my novels. I don't write fiction primarily to spread my ideas. When that's my aim, I write nonfiction. Why then do I include philosophical ideas in my novels? To present an ideal man—or any man—one needs a (implicit or explicit) philosophical background. To make a statement about human life, one needs a philosophical frame of reference. I found that my conception of the ideal man—my ideas on ethics—contradicted most of what was written in philosophy. Of the existing philosophies—which are full of mystical contradictions—the only philosopher to whom I could acknowledge a debt was Aristotle. No philosophy corresponded to my ideas, so I had to define my own, in order to make my characters and my stories clear. [NC 69]

AR married Frank O'Connor in 1929, and they remained married until his death in 1979.

Of which of your achievements are you proudest?

I've never given it any thought. I don't measure my achievements that way. But on the spur of the moment, I'd say marrying Frank O'Connor. [FHF 72]

In view of the demands of a writing career, could you give any advice to the spouse of a writer, to show how harmony is possible?

How did you and your husband enjoy such a wonderful life together, in light of your writing priorities?

I can only refer you to Frank O'Connor, who unfortunately died recently. That was his accomplishment, not mine. He was overly conscientious in not disturbing me—letting me work late and keep odd hours—because he had such an interest in my writing. We were spiritual collaborators. I always told him I could not have written without him. He denied it; he thought I would have broken through. Perhaps the only tribute I can pay him with my readers is to say that I know it is impossible to hold a benevolent universe view consistently, as I had to hold it to write what I've written, when the world around us was getting worse and going in the direction of Ellsworth Toohey. I could not have written about John Galt if it weren't for the fact that I knew one person who did live up to my heroes and my view of life. He gave me the benevolent universe I wrote about. We were married over fifty years. [OC 80]

AR was sixty-four years old at the time she answered this question.

In the last twenty-five years, have you had any major change in your philosophical outlook?

I haven't changed my philosophical opinions—that is, my fundamental view of the nature of man, of existence, of human knowledge and of values—in the last sixty-four years. I've learned a great deal over the years, and frequently improved some formulations and details of my conclusions, but never the fundamentals. [FHF 69]

What is your purpose in life?

My purpose is to enjoy my life in a rational way: to use my mind to the greatest extent possible; to pursue, admire, and support human greatness; to make all my choices rationally; to expand my knowledge constantly. That's a pretty ambitious program, and I've achieved most of it. [FHF 69]

How do you face your own mortality?

I don't. I won't be here to know it when it happens. I'm concerned only with the time when I *am* here. Mortality, by definition, finishes me. So why worry about it? [FHF 73]

What do you think will happen when you die?

I assume I'll be buried. I don't believe in mysticism or life after death. This doesn't mean I believe man's mind is necessarily materialistic; but neither is it mystical. We know that we have a mind and a body, and that neither can exist without the other. Therefore, when I die, that will be the end of me. I don't think it will be the end of my philosophy. [FHF 69]

EDITOR'S POSTSCRIPT

As we celebrate the one hundredth anniversary of Ayn Rand's birth (February 2, 2005), the popularity of her novels and the influence of her philosophy of Objectivism continue to grow. Annual sales of her books have recently reached the half million mark; in total, over 22 million copies have been sold. More and more each year, Ayn Rand's ideas and writings appear in philosophy textbooks, in philosophy courses, and in papers delivered at philosophy conferences. The Ayn Rand Institute—founded in 1985 by Leonard Peikoff, Ayn Rand's associate for over thirty years, and her legal and intellectual heir—continues to flourish in its work of teaching her controversial and inspiring ideas to ever new generations of intellectuals.

INDEX